MEXICAN AMERICAN BASEBALL IN KANSAS CITY

Kansas Fast Pitch Softball at La Chicanada

Always *tiempo*
keeping tempo
on the pulse of America's pastime
reserving a Kodak moment
to catch a grin or
a glimpse of someone secretly
taking a snort
of sweet red wine
or Miller High Life
on sandlot baseball fields;
a place where young whippersnappers
hurled a softball
at 70 miles an hour
using verbal gymnastics
and poetic gesticulations
to dance and prance
and in some cases, find lifetime romance.
They were looking for that American dream
only to hear a loud scream
of "you're out."
Memories of *batos* from
other *comunidades*
Newton, Wichita, Hutchinson, Topeka, Emporia,
Kansas City, and Chanute
linger on. When La Raza was always ready
to throw hands at a bad call
made by an umpire
half blind with contempt
following a hook slide
into third base
followed by loud claps
for some *familias*
transformed into "Taps"
for others
after that ugly war
in Viet Nam.
Fast pitch softball
reminds me of stories
about heroes whose pictures
will never be seen
in history books. Accepting golden trophies
in front of *la comunidad*
con mucho orgullo
was all worth it.
There were always broken apparitions
a prophecy untold
revelation for some
reveille for others
while mothers
wiped away tears
caused by broken hearts
from sons who were
preparing for life's perils.
Softball at La Chicanada
a treasure chest full of memories
about kings of the *barrio* streets
with uptown beats.

—Ramón Del Castillo

Front Cover: The Stateline Locos were one of the men's fast pitch softball teams that competed regularly in the Mexican American Softball Association across a four-state region including Kansas, Missouri, Nebraska, and Iowa. The team took Woody Woodpecker (El Pájaro Loco) as their logo and mascot, and thus their name became Los Locos. (Courtesy of Tony Talavera Jr.)

Cover Background: Mexican American women formed several teams around Kansas City, including this c. 1940 club. Players include Irene Ivarra, Sarah Hernández, Mary Montes, Hope Ivarra, Vicky ?, Maggie ?, Vickie Gamino, Mota Fernández, and coach Carlos Montes. (Courtesy of Rose Montes Arroyo.)

Back Cover: This 1940s Azteca team played practice games against the legendary Negro League Kansas City Monarchs. The Azteca club drew players from several Mexican neighborhoods around Kansas City, including Argentine, Armourdale, the Bottoms, the Kansas side of the state line, and Kansas City, Missouri's, West Side. (Courtesy of Tony Taceña Jr.)

MEXICAN AMERICAN BASEBALL IN KANSAS CITY

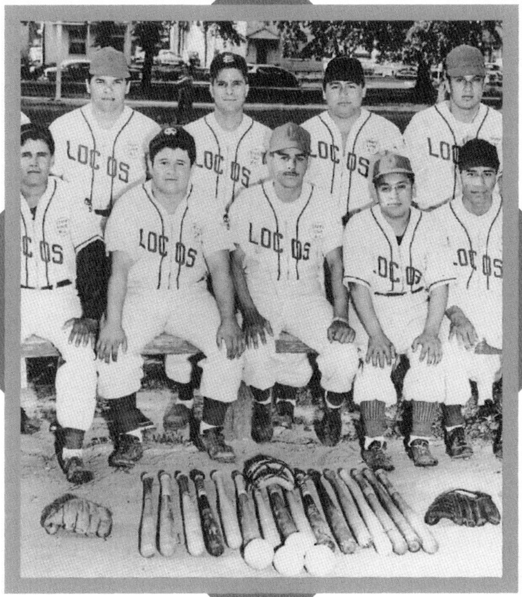

Richard A. Santillán, Gene T. Chávez,
Rod Martínez, Raymond Olais, and Ben Chappell
Foreword by Anna Marie Tutera

ARCADIA PUBLISHING

ISBN 978-1-4671-2875-9

Published by Arcadia Publishing
Charleston, South Carolina

Printed in the United States of America

Library of Congress Control Number: 2018939797

For all general information, please contact Arcadia Publishing:
Telephone 843-853-2070
Fax 843-853-0044
E-mail sales@arcadiapublishing.com
For customer service and orders:
Toll-Free 1-888-313-2665

Visit us on the Internet at www.arcadiapublishing.com

I dedicate this book to my miraculous wife Teresa—a blessing in my life since 1979 when I first met her and asked her to dance with me at La Rosa Café in East Los Angeles, not far from our second home, Dodger Stadium.

—*Richard*

I dedicate this book first to my loving family, including three adult children, nine grandchildren, and two great-grandchildren, with special thanks to my wife, Juanita, whose love of baseball inspired me to explore the subject. Thank you all for your patience with my many hours away from you. I also want to say gracias *to the many former and present players who shared their precious time, remarkable photographs, and wonderful memories with me.*

—Gene

In memory of my mother and father, Ramón and Valeria García Martínez, for their unconditional love, countless sacrifices, and complete devotion to their children, Rod, Robert, Richard, Christina, Michael, and Mona; we are eternally grateful.

—*Rod*

To the Newton's Mexican Railroad laborers and Ranchito descendants, who graciously welcomed me into their homes to document the rich history of an immensely proud community. A big abrazo *to Richard A. Santillán, who, over 25 years ago, inspired me to document Newton's Mexican American story after a Kansas University lecture on Midwest Mexican American history. And finally, countless* besos *to my wife, Patrice, who gave me never-ending guidance and untiring support.*

—*Ray*

To the Mexican American ballplayers of the Midwest, their families and friends, and all who work to keep their tradition alive.

—*Ben*

CONTENTS

FOREWORD

Kansas City has a deep, rich history and cultural heritage, and the stories of its people exemplify the city's vibrancy and unwavering spirit. At the Kansas City Museum—a museum of the city's local and regional history—we believe that telling these stories is critical to the city's preservation and growth and essential to building an inclusive, creative, and sustainable community. Today, museums and cultural institutions are places where we can engage in conversations, examine our perspectives, explore our collective memories, and share our stories. In doing so, we honor one another and reveal our common humanity.

In 2014, historian and curator Dr. Gene T. Chávez generously invited the Kansas City Museum to collaborate with him on a new exhibition to document and interpret the history and legacy of fast pitch softball players and leagues in Missouri and Kansas. As a result, in 2015, the museum and Dr. Chávez developed and presented Mexican American Fast Pitch Softball Leagues: Connecting Communities Across State Lines. This exhibition featured historical materials on loan, including photographs, uniforms, league documents, trophies, and memorabilia, as well as a documentary film based on oral histories of former players. Content explored how the early discrimination against and segregation of Mexican Americans in Kansas City led to the formation of fast pitch softball teams, which in turn ultimately engendered activism, community solidarity, and pride.

Programs and events created to coincide with the exhibition brought together historians, educators, former players, and the greater community to celebrate, learn, and explore future collaborations. After the exhibition, the museum became a partner in Latinos and Baseball: In the Barrios and the Big Leagues, a multiyear collecting initiative launched by the Smithsonian's National Museum of American History in Washington, DC, to identify artifacts for the collection of the Smithsonian and the Kansas City Museum that reflect the social and cultural influence of the game on Latino communities. Currently, the Kansas City Museum has artifacts on display at the National Museum of American History, elevating our local story into a national narrative. The Kansas City Museum continues to actively collect local historical artifacts and archival materials.

As the coauthors of this book continue to document, interpret, collect, and share the history of Mexican American baseball and fast pitch softball, the Kansas City Museum is proud to continue its involvement and is grateful for the opportunity to do so.

—Anna Marie Tutera
Director, Kansas City Museum

ACKNOWLEDGMENTS

The foundation of this project to publicize the rich history of Mexican American baseball and softball in Kansas City is the remarkable work of the Latino Baseball History Project at California State University, San Bernardino (CSUSB). Others who support this effort include the following at CSUSB's John M. Phau Library: Dean César Caballero and Sue Caballero, Jill Vassilakos-Long (head of archives and special collections), Ericka Saucedo, Amina Romero, Carrie Lowe, Manny Verón, Brandy Montoya, Hayley Parke, John Baumann, and Stacy Magtedanz.

The authors are indebted to dedicated individuals and groups, including the Kansas Humanities Council, El Centro Inc., Irene Salazar Caudillo, Guadalupe Centers Inc., Cris Medina, Manuel Hernández, Anna Marie Tutera of the Kansas City Museum, Denise Morrison, the Smithsonian's Latino Center, Eduardo Díaz, Margaret Porzio-Salazar, L. Stephen Velázquez, the Kansas City Museum staff, Los Sabios Mexican American players, Mexican American Softball Association of Kansas City, Chris González, Luís and Kari Madrigal, Paulie Hernández, Mario Escobar, Gilbert and Patricia Castro, Donna and Jaime García Sr., Tony Talavera Jr., Danny Salas, Frank Salas, Tony Ceceña Jr., Tony Quiroga, Anthony Oropeza, Louis Oropeza, Danny García, Anthony Scott Gómez, John Tórrez Jr., Paul Briones Jr. and his West Side Women's Softball Leagues, Manuel Jaso, the Mexican American Fast Pitch Softball Tournament, Dave and Christina Martínez Trujillo, Joyce Warshaw, Pat Stevens, Melissa McCoy, Ernestor De La Rosa, Ruth Ann Waldron, Johnetta Holmes-Hebrlee, Chris and David Rodríguez, Linda Espinoza, Mardie and Nate Cornejo, Advera Remigio, Andy Ramírez, Fred Medina, the Dodge City Kansas Heritage Center, Kansas Historical Society, Nebraska State Historical Society, the Frank Palma Collection, Frank Martínez Sr. and Delores "Dee Dee" Martínez, Agatha Alba de Ramírez, Al Martínez, and the former players and their families who have so generously shared their treasured photographs, memorabilia, and time to make this book an accurate reflection of the game of baseball in its many forms. Also thanks to Bill Soto-Castellanos, the Mitla Café, Irene García, Joe and John Tostado, Carlos Salazar, Jerry García, Sandra Uribe, the Medina family, Reynaldo Santa Cruz, Norma Gallego, Christine Marín, Bobby Lovato, Bobby Durán, Art Velarde, Beatrice Salazar, Gabriel and Jody López, Tito García, the *Greeley Tribute*, Alvin García, Robert Durán, the Guerra family, Isabel Ramírez, Margaret Villanueva Lambert, the Mexican American Historical Society of the Midlands, Tony Solíz, Hank Carrillo, the Southeast Historical Society, Michael D. Innis-Jiménez, José Inez Santa Cruz, Florencio Perea, Ray Lozano, John Fraire, Frank Jacinto, and Francis Nuno.

We recognize again our in-house editor, Elisa Grajeda-Urmston, for her noteworthy professional work, and our sincere admiration and gratefulness to our technical consultant Monse Segura. Finally, the Latino Baseball History Project extends its deepest feelings of appreciation to Arcadia Publishing, Jim Kempert, and our marvelous longtime editor and *amigo* Jeff Ruetsche.

INTRODUCTION

The story of baseball and fast pitch softball leagues among the Mexican American communities of the Midwest goes back at least 80 years. During the first four decades, blatant anti-Mexican sentiments prevailed, which led to discrimination and segregation in most public accommodations, including baseball parks and teams. In 1927, Saturnino Alvarado, a Mexican immigrant living in the Argentine district of Kansas City, Kansas, challenged the local school board's policy against admitting Mexican American students. With the assistance of the Mexican consulate and the US Department of State, he forced the school board to admit his children and other Mexican American children to Argentine High School.

This event and countless others are landmarks in the history of Mexican American civil rights, moments when people of Mexican descent claimed their right to belong in the United States and rejected the second-class status implied by social barriers such as segregation. They did so by forming organizations and seeking legal means to challenge their marginalization.

Around the same time, in the middle of the country, Mexican American people made other moves as well. In 1946, railroad track workers in Newton, Kansas, like many across the country at the time, enjoyed the fast-paced game of softball, which was a major source of entertainment in the small town. They organized a tournament for other Mexican teams in the area. That tournament occurred annually for the next 70 years and still continues today, serving as a gathering point and reunion for family and friends, many of whom tell stories of epic extra-innings pitching battles, of great ballplayers who went from the softball field to the majors, or at least almost had their chance, and of teams navigating the segregated hotel and restaurant industries on the road to another town's tournament.

The rising Mexican American generation of the 1940s sought social progress through activism. They also created organizations and new traditions and framed their particular history by playing ball. Society was obsessed with baseball, and Mexican Americans embraced a chance to play the sport that was at the center of the American mainstream at the time. Playing hardball or softball for their towns, churches, or workplaces, they claimed space between the foul lines. Yet sport offers drama with an open script. Who would win the confrontation on the field, and how they would do it, unlike many matters in a segregated society, was never scripted. By claiming a chance to compete, people of Mexican descent sought an opportunity to test themselves in ways otherwise denied them. These are some of those people and some of their stories.

1

Mexican American Baseball in Kansas City

Kansas City has long been the seat of the region. Rogers and Hammerstein declared in their well-known musical *Oklahoma* that everything is up to date in Kansas City.

Kansas City, Missouri, was founded in 1838 and beat out Westport to become the predominant city west of St. Louis. The Kansas City metroplex, with a population of nearly 2.5 million, includes 15 counties and straddles the border of Kansas and Missouri. Starting in the 1540s, the Spanish explored the area but did not settle. In the early 1800s, French fur trappers were licensed by Spain to trade with indigenous tribes. At the confluence of the Missouri and Kansas Rivers, Kansas City became strategic in the development of the Santa Fe, Oregon, and California Trails. The Santa Fe and California Trails evolved into two-way thoroughfares with the Spanish-speaking Southwest.

The large exodus of Mexicans from their homeland due to the Mexican Revolution brought workers to the United States between 1910 and 1930. Many settled in the Midwest, bolstering the labor force in the agriculture, railroad, meat packing, hospitality, garment, and steel industries. Kansas City became an economic and cultural hub of the region for Mexican immigrants.

Kansas City has long been a baseball town. The Kansas City Cowboys (American Association) started in 1886. The Kansas City Blues (American Association) started in 1888 in Kansas City, Missouri, and played through the 1954 season. The Blues signed the first Mexican-born major-league player, Baldomero "Melo" Almada, in 1934. The Philadelphia Athletics became the Kansas City Athletics in 1955. Today, the two-time World Series champion (1985 and 2015) Kansas City Royals boast many Latino players. The Kansas City T-Bones moved from Duluth, Minnesota, to Kansas City, Kansas, in 2003 and play in the American Association of Independent Professional Baseball. Kansas City was home to the Monarchs, the mainstay of the Negro Leagues, which now has its hall of fame and museum in Kansas City, Missouri.

Amateur teams were organized in both Kansas and Missouri. From the 1920s through the 1960s, many Mexican players were forced to play on segregated teams due to both covert and overt racism. Mexican-only teams served to bring Mexican Americans together for fair competition, camaraderie, a sense of ethnic identity, and community involvement throughout the region. This chapter features some of the early teams and players who, despite the challenges of oppressive discrimination, grueling hard work, family responsibilities, and dedication to their religious obligations, found precious time to play the game they loved and respected.

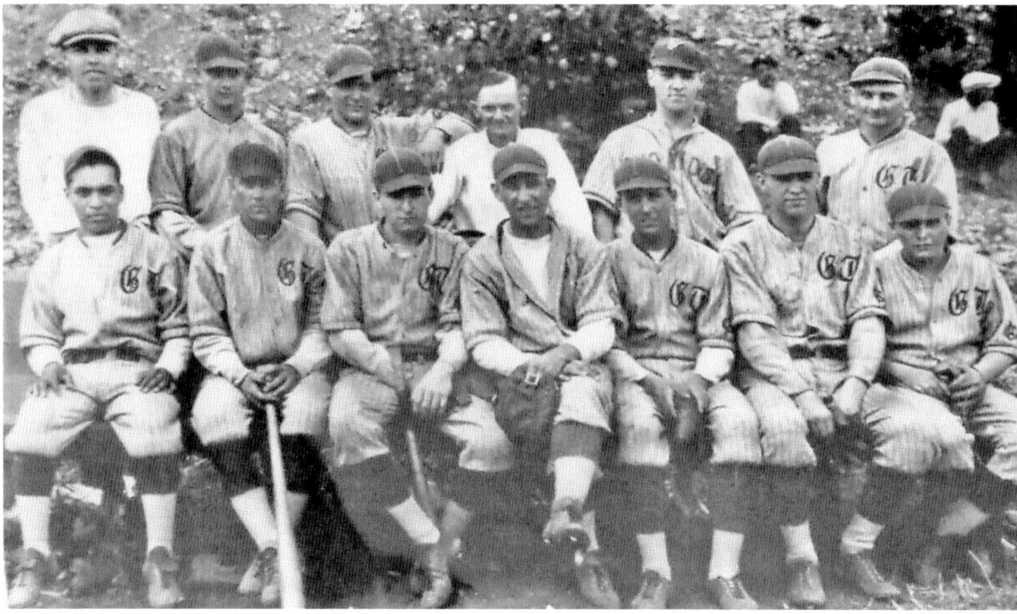

The 1926 Gamma Tau baseball club was one of many industrial-league teams that scouted Mexican immigrant players. The Mexican players on this team are not known, but they are thought to have eventually started their own team, Los Aztecas of Kansas City. Many company teams were open to Mexican players, who sometimes experienced racial slurs, insults, and discrimination in public accommodations. That maltreatment led Mexican players to form their own teams and later their own leagues. Those teams often competed against African American and Native American teams. (Courtesy of Frank Salas.)

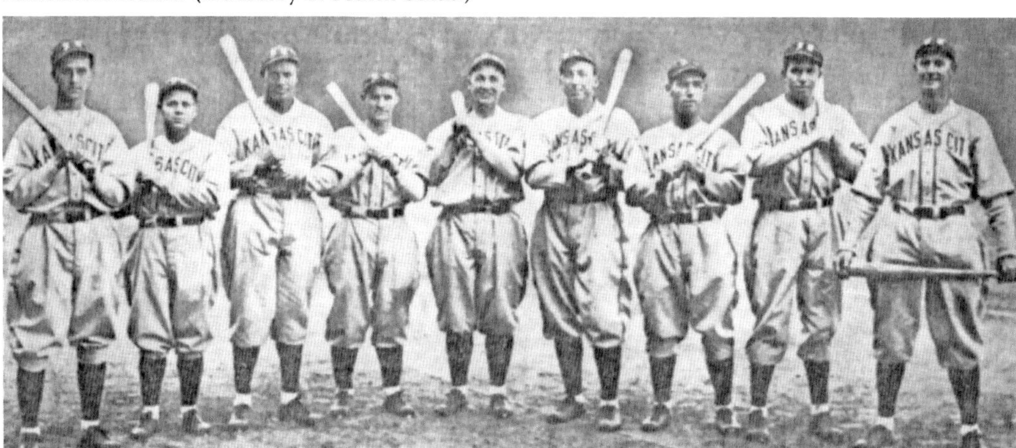

Baldemero "Melo" Almada (second from right) was an exception to the racial barrier when he played for the Kansas City Blues, which became a farm club of the Pittsburgh Pirates and was later affiliated with the New York Yankees. Because of his skills, the Boston Red Sox recruited him in 1933, making him the first Mexican-born player in the major leagues. He went on to bat .284 in 646 games with the Sox, Senators, Browns, and Brooklyn Dodgers across seven seasons. (Courtesy of Eduardo B. Almada T.)

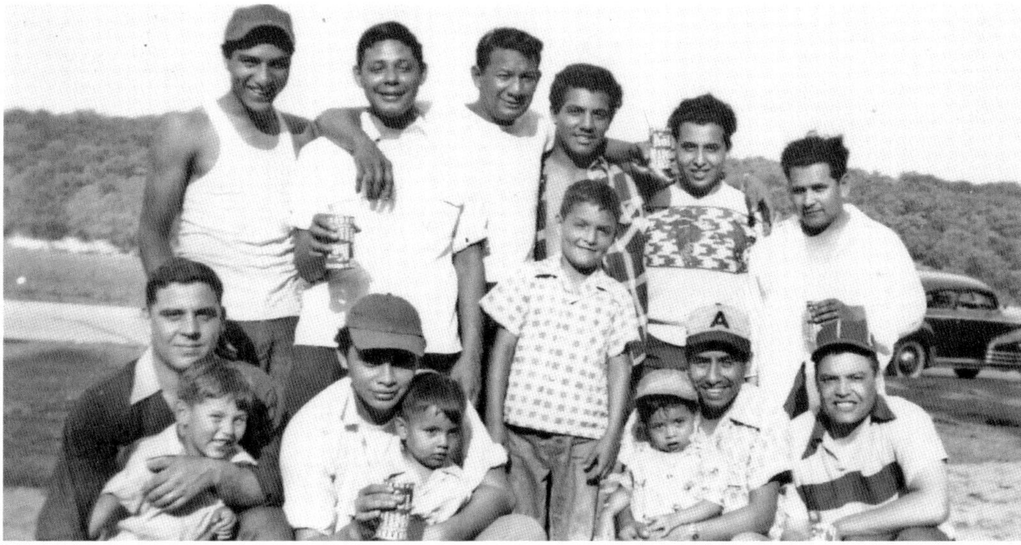

This photograph was taken in the late 1940s at an informal setting like a picnic in a Kansas City park. Such outings were often attended by immigrant extended families and friends. Baseball teams were formed from such gatherings. From left to right are (first row) Manuel Mejía with son René, David Quirarte with son Davy, unidentified, Tony Ceceña Sr. with son Richard, and Chuck Lombrano; (second row) Jesse Salas, Daniel Villegas, Paul Hernández Sr., Tony Ceceña Jr., Margarito Romero, and unidentified. (Courtesy of Modesta Campos.)

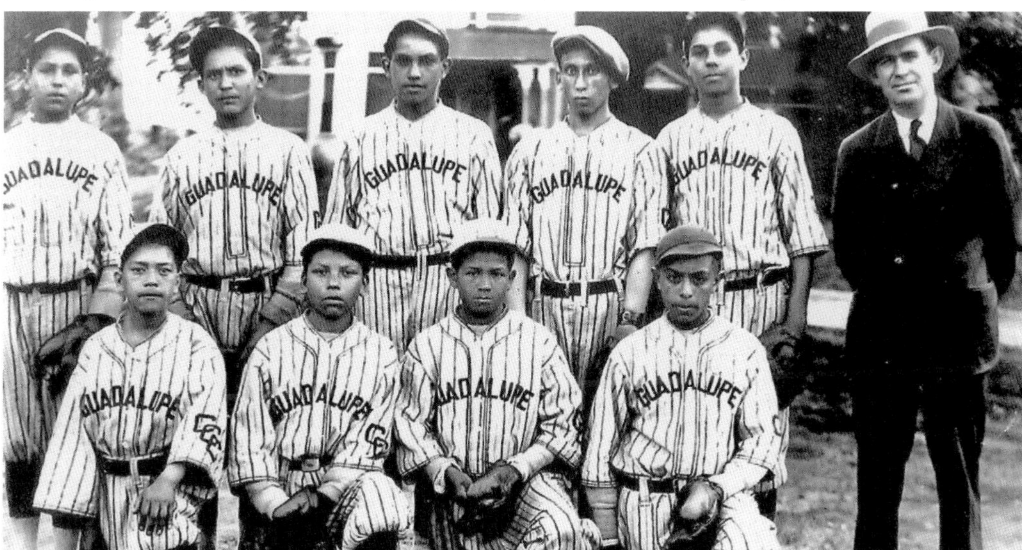

When Mexican immigrants arrived to work in Kansas City, most of them faced racial and language barriers. There were virtually no Spanish-speaking institutions such as churches, markets, or schools. Their first parish, Our Lady of Guadalupe, opened in 1914 with Fr. José Muñez as the first priest. A Catholic school by the same name soon opened its doors to Mexican immigrant children, such as these ballplayers in 1926, including Ralph Hernández (second row, far left), and Cuco García (second row, third from left). (Courtesy of Guadalupe Centers Inc.)

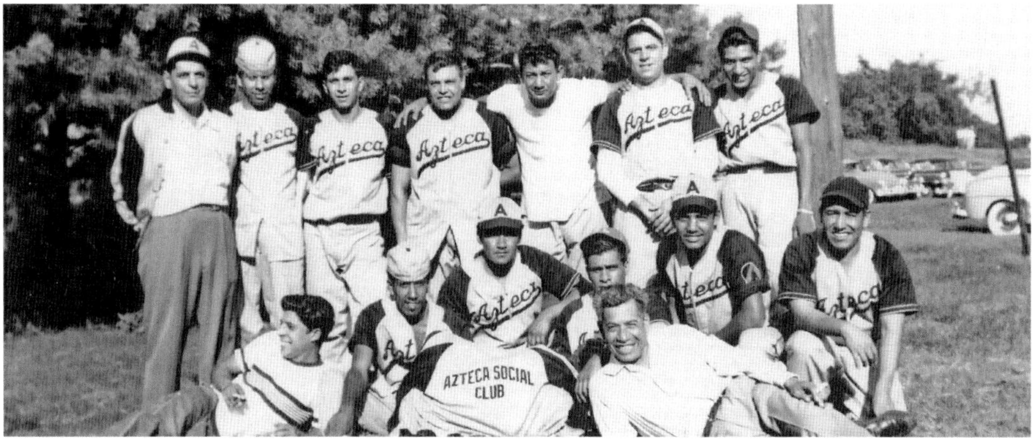

Azteca Social Club is pictured in the early 1940s. The club evolved into a team that competed across the region and beyond, sometimes playing against the Kansas City Monarchs and Native American and Italian American teams. This photograph is believed to have been taken in Topeka, Kansas, at a Mexican American baseball league tournament. From left to right are (first row) unidentified, Nabe Villa, Silvestre Ayala, Carlos Montes, Tony Ceceña Sr., Tony Ceceña Jr., and Fred Sauceda; (second row) Lupe Molina, Richard Ceceña, John Compos, Chuck Lombrano, Paul Hernández Sr., Manuel Mejía, and Jesse Salas. (Courtesy of Modesta Campos.)

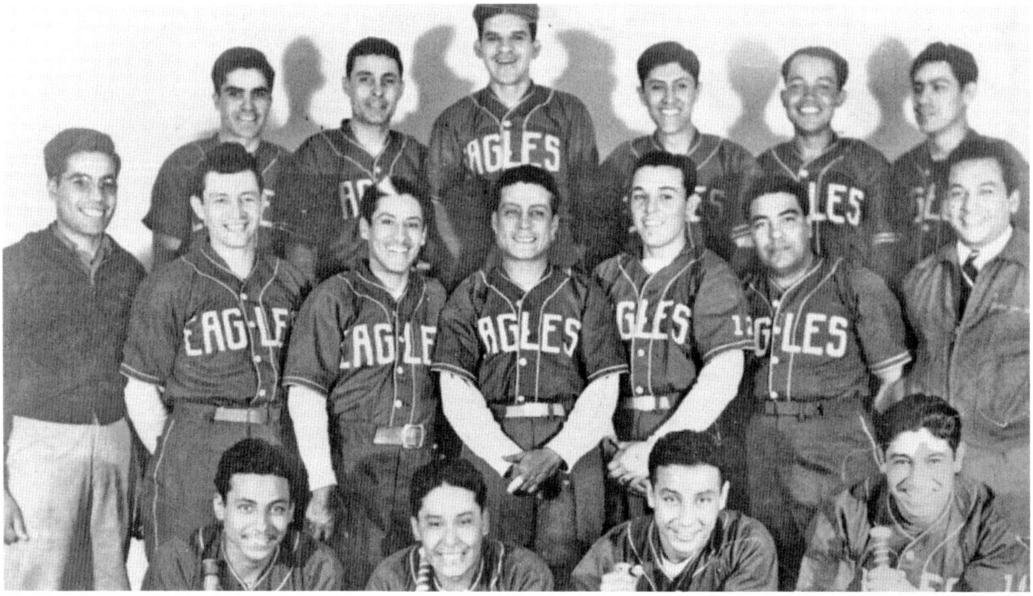

The Argentine Eagles Vets Club developed from Mexican immigrant families who played on local industrial teams like the Railways Ice Company team before World War II. After the war, men's fast pitch softball swept the nation. These veterans are, from left to right, (first row) Andy Medellín, Stanley Castañeda, Froylan Hernández, and Fred Sauceda; (second row) Bobby Valverde, Lupe Rodríguez, Paul Sauceda, Jerry Hernández, Jesse Castro, Joe Marrón, and John Joe Salazar; (third row) Tony Jamie, Manuel Pérez, John Méndez, Vince Sauceda, Juan Pacheco, and Paul Contreras. (Courtesy of Fidel Sauceda Jr.)

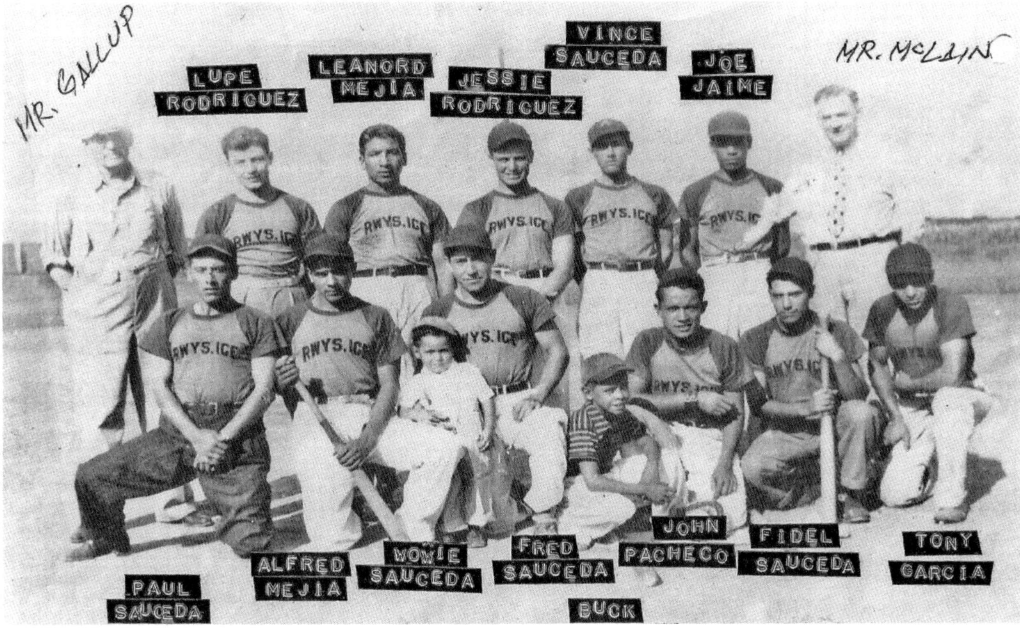

Like many other employers of the era, the Railways Ice Company chose its best players to compete against other teams in the industrial leagues. This 1940 team included, from left to right, (first row) Paul Sauceda, Alfred Mejía, Fidel Sauceda Jr., Fred Sauceda, Buck Madrigal, John Pacheco, Fidel Sauceda Sr., and Tony García; (second row) ? Gallup, Lupe Rodríguez, Leonard Mejía, Jesse Rodríguez, Vince Sauceda, Joe Jaime, and ? McLain. (Courtesy of Vince Sauceda.)

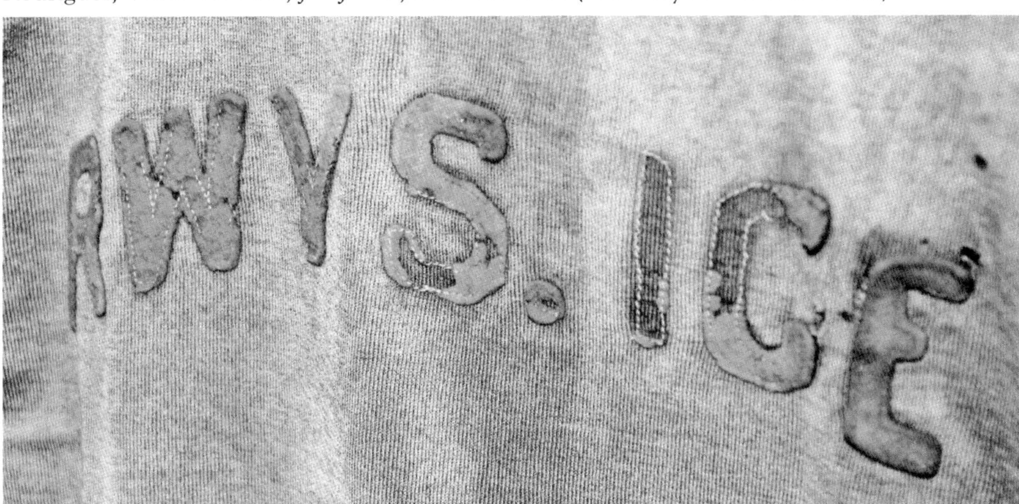

This Railways Ice Company jersey belonged to Vince Sauceda, who started playing baseball with his brothers and uncles at an early age. His father, Fidel Sauceda Sr., helped his sons build their own ball field, where they invited neighborhood kids to come and play. Fidel Sr. often fashioned bats out of thick branches off their trees. After playing for Railways Ice Company, Vince was one of the founding members of the Argentine Eagles. He passed away on October 30, 2017, at the age of 95, still remembering his playing days. (Donated to the Kansas City Museum by Vince Sauceda.)

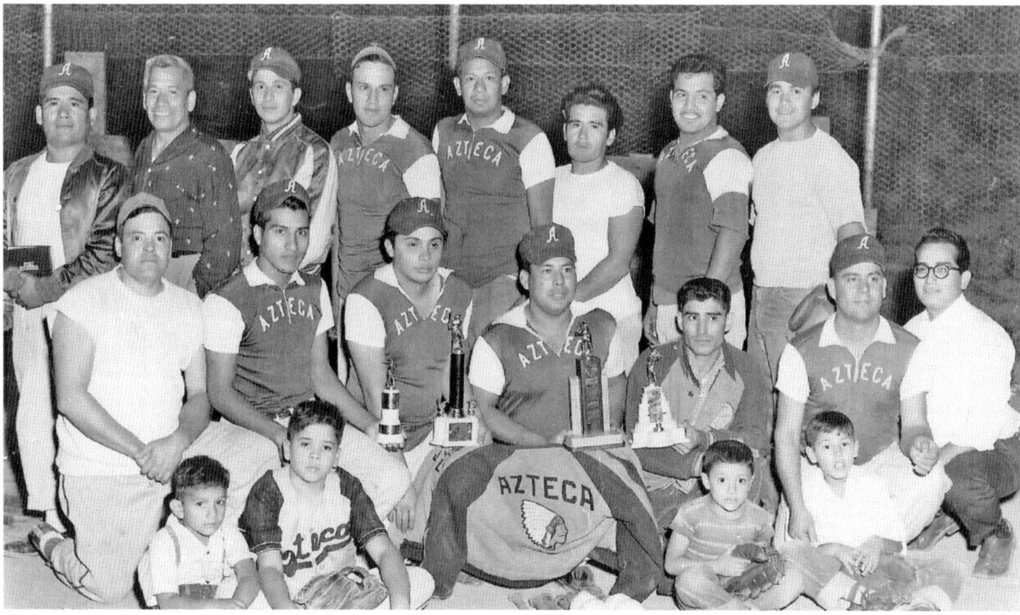

This mid-1950s Kansas City Azteca photograph represents three generations of Mexican Americans. From left to right are (first row) Eddie Hernández, son of Paul Hernández Sr.; ? Rodriguez; ? Ávila, Tony Ávila's son; and René Mejía, Manuel Mejía's son; (second row) Chuck Lombrano; Jesse Salas; David Quirarte; Manuel Guerra; Tony Ávila; Manuel Mejía; and ? Ávila, Tony's brother; (third row) Bernie Ayala; Tony Ceceña Sr.; John Compos; Bernie Porras; Paul Hernández Sr.; Silvestre Ayala; Tony Ceceña Jr.; and Mickey Cisneros. (Courtesy of Tony Ceceña Jr.)

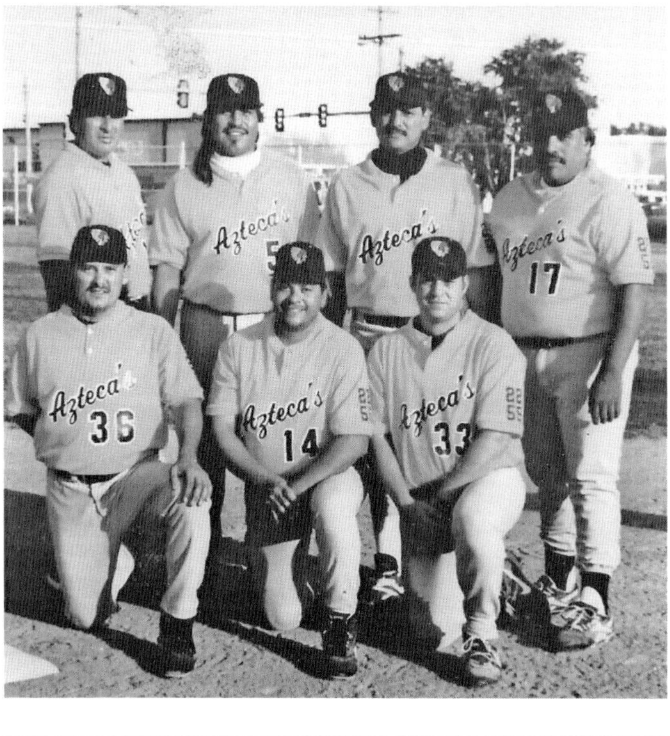

The Azteca softball team developed from the Azteca baseball teams. When the veterans came back, men's fast pitch softball was sweeping the nation. Many of the Azteca vets took up the game. Later, their children and grandchildren joined. The Azteca fast pitch softball team lasted until 2005, according to Danny Salas, son of Jesse Salas. These Azteca players are, from left to right, (first row) Mike Ceceña, Harry Medellín, and Steve Roach; (second row) Ron Porras, Chris González, John Amayo, and Dan Salas. (Courtesy of Danny Salas.)

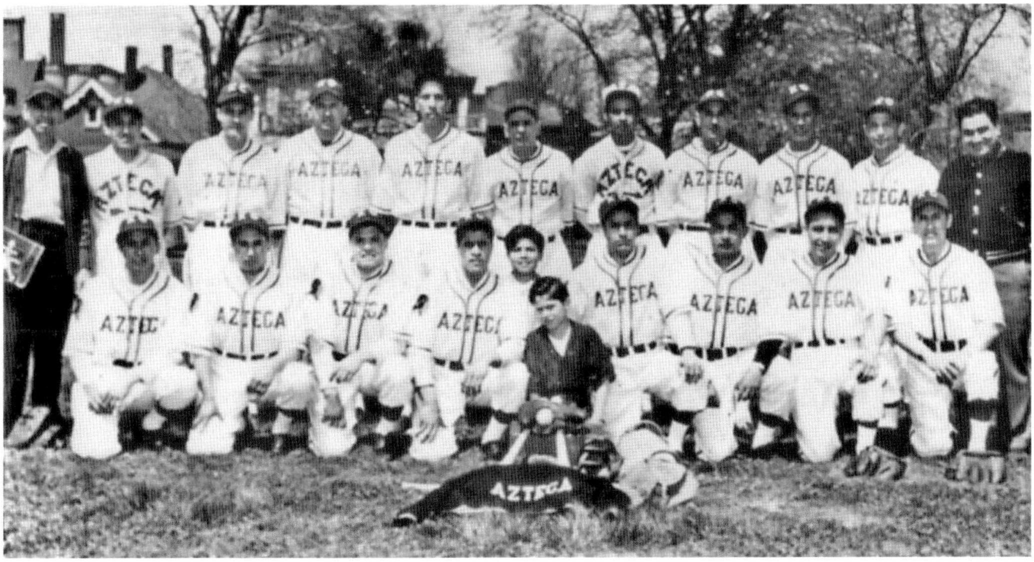

This 1940s Azteca team played hardball, drawing players from Mexican immigrant families in several areas of Kansas City: Armourdale, the Bottoms, and Kansas City, Missouri's, West Side. From left to right are (first row) John Campos, Frank Solís, Chuck Lombrano, Carlos Móntez, two unidentified, Louie Barboza, Vince Sauceda, and two unidentified; (second row) Tony Ceceña Sr., three unidentified, Joe Moráles, two unidentified, Manuel Zuñiga, Simón Montoya, unidentified, and Danny Ontivéros. (Courtesy of Tony Ceceña Jr.)

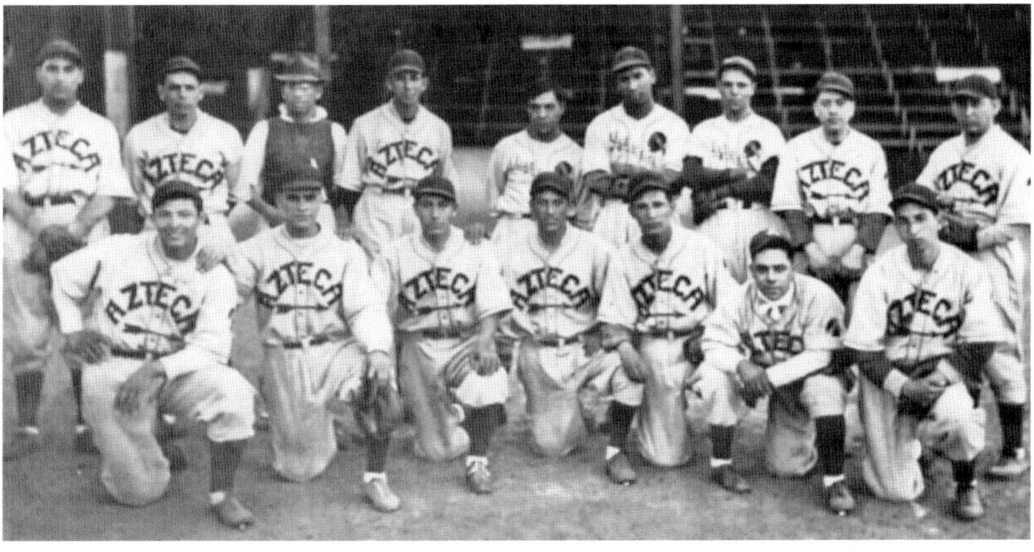

Los Aztecas were known as one of the best teams in the area and were considered the premier team among the Mexican American community. Old-timers still say that a person had to be good to play with the Azteca team, so it is likely that these players were. From left to right are (first row) Manuel Zuñiga, Lupe Molina, Tony Ceceña Sr., two unidentified, Mosi Fernández, and Carlos Móntez; (second row) Lupe Rodríguez, Lefty Móntez, unidentified, Apolonio Sauceda, Paul Sauceda, unidentified, Louie Barboza, unidentified, and Lalo Nieto. (Courtesy of Tony Ceceña Jr.)

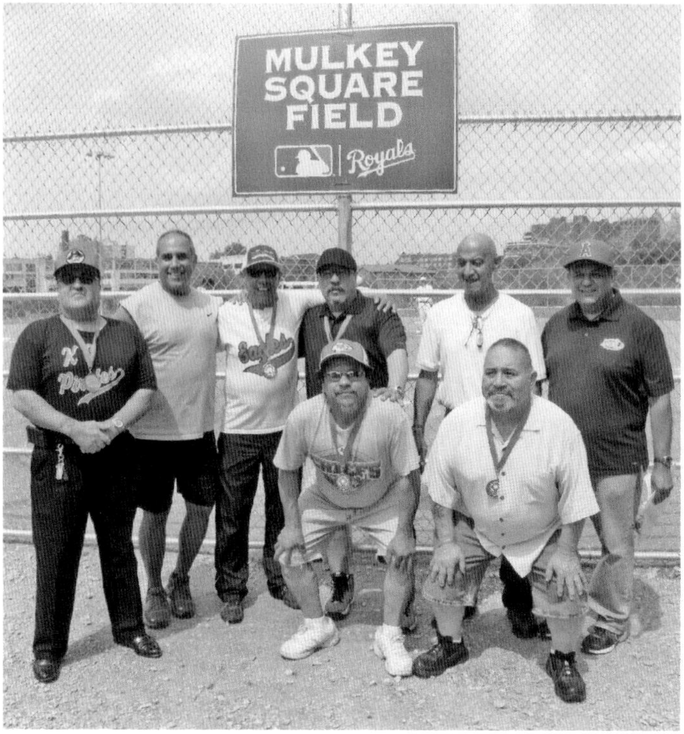

Mulkey Field, on a bluff overlooking downtown, has served as the home field for Guadalupe Centers Inc.'s baseball programs for many years. Ahead of the MLB All-Star Game in Kansas City in 2012, Major League Baseball donated $250,000 to Guadalupe Centers Inc. to renovate the field. Here, the Kansas City Angels' annual hall of fame recipients are recognized. From left to right are (first row) Gilbert Tinoco and unidentified; (second row) Jesse González, Sylvester Bustamante, Chris Ramos, Cándido Chávez, Paul Hernández Jr., and Cris Medina. (Courtesy of Guadalupe Centers Inc.)

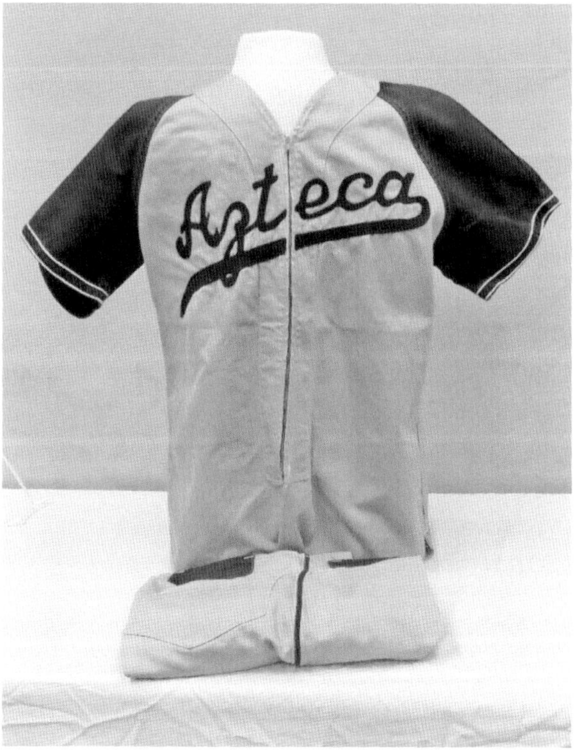

Steve Reyes wore this jersey playing for the Azteca men's fast pitch softball team in the early 1950s. The Reyes family lived in Armourdale, Kansas City, Kansas, when they and other families were displaced by the devastating Kansas River flood on July 13, 1951. Many families barely escaped with the clothes on their backs when the flood hit. The fact that Steve's uniform survived the flood is a miracle, says his longtime friend Frank Salas. (Courtesy of the Kansas City Museum.)

Paul "Paulie" Hernández Jr., pictured here, is the son of Paul "Waxie" Hernández Sr. Waxie started his baseball career with the Guadalupe Center youth team in 1936, and played and coached baseball and fast pitch softball for over 40 years. He was still coaching when he fell ill and died in 1992. He passed on his love of baseball to his children and grandchildren. Paulie became one of the most outstanding fast pitch softball players in the Kansas City region. (Courtesy of Sidonia Moreno.)

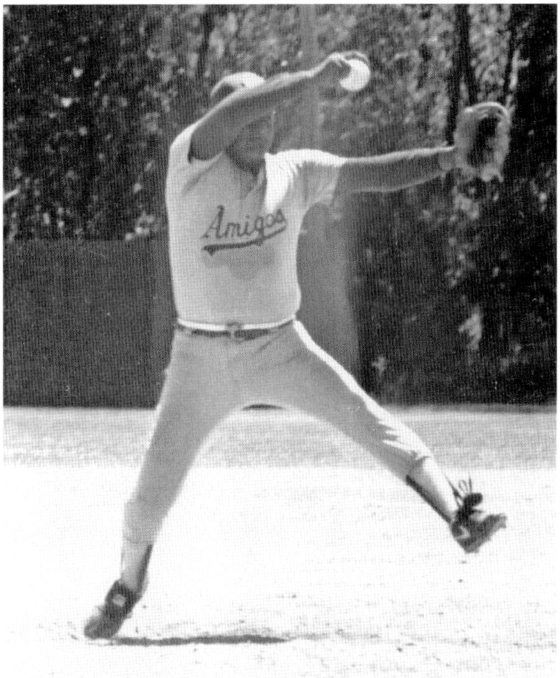

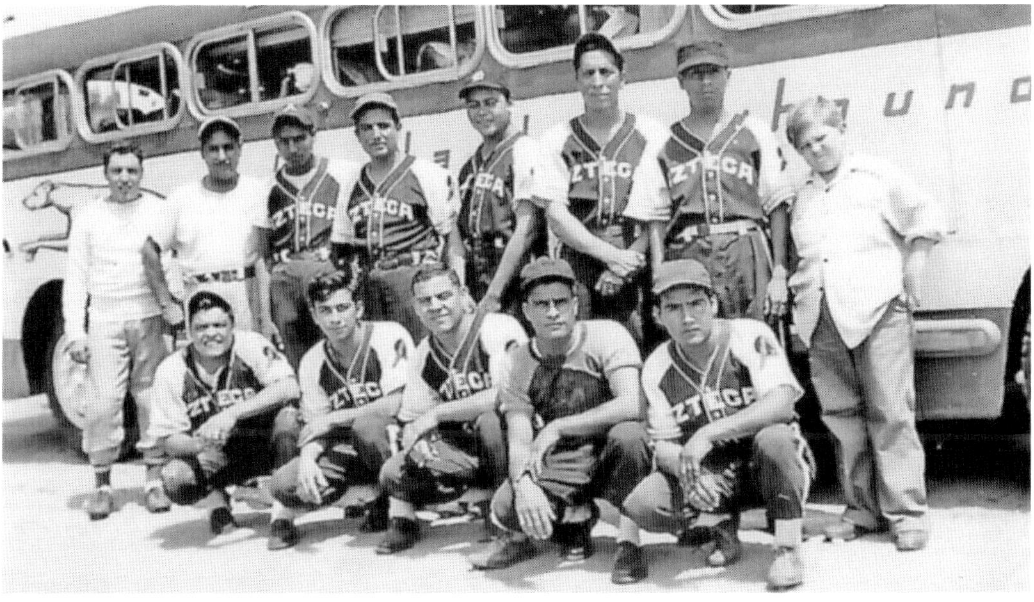

This 1950s Azteca fast pitch softball team traveled to Omaha, Nebraska, for a regional tournament. During the heyday of Mexican American fast pitch softball, summers were filled with team practice, neighborhood games, and fiesta-like double-elimination weekend tournaments. There were Mexican food booths, and of course, dances on Saturday nights. Representing the Aztecas are, from left to right, (first row) Chuck Lombrano, John Campos, Manuel Mejía, Carlos Móntez, and Sylvester Ayala; (second row) unidentified, Manuel Zuñiga, Jesse Salas, Merle Cisneros, Joe Morales, Tony Ceceña Sr., and two unidentified. (Courtesy of Tony Ceceña Jr.)

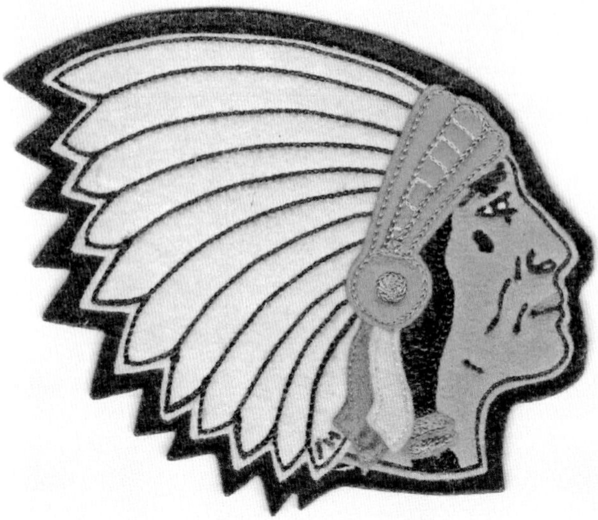

John Campos played for many years with the Aztecas and eventually managed the team. His widow, Modesta Campos, donated this Kansas City Azteca logo to the Kansas City Museum. Modesta tells how John wanted to update the team's uniforms, and after an extensive search for the perfect logo, he found a drawing that he liked. He had a uniform company make this patch, which was placed on the team's jerseys, caps, and warmup jackets. (Courtesy of the Kansas City Museum.)

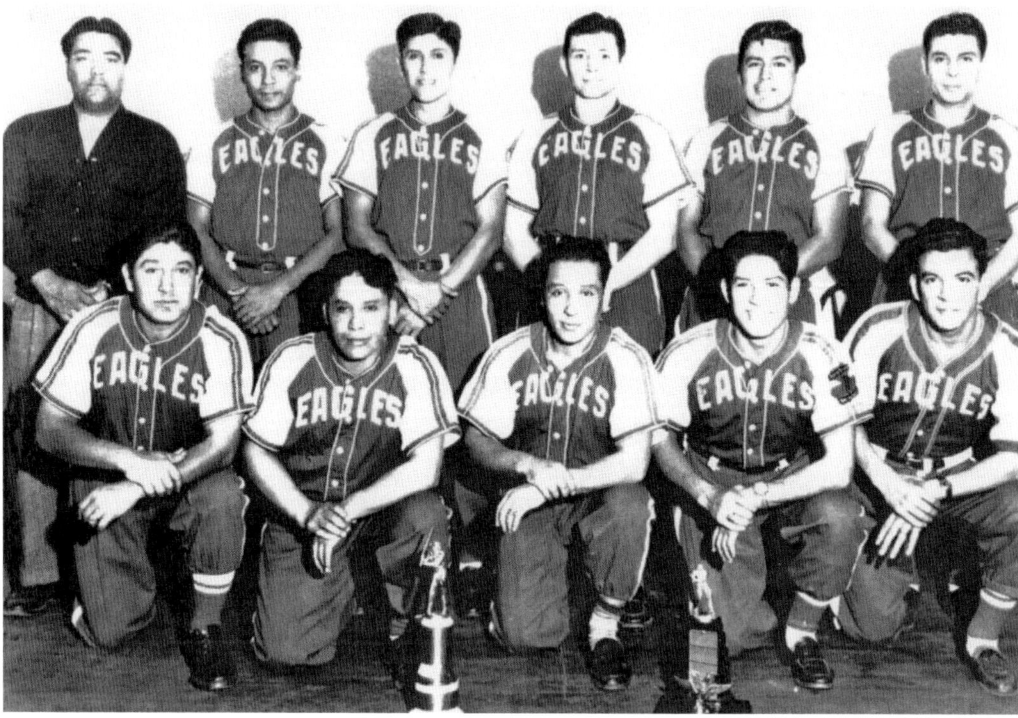

Mexican American veterans in the Argentine district of Kansas City, Kansas, formed the Eagles Vets Club in 1948. They came together around fast pitch softball, but their involvement expanded beyond the ball field. Many of these players were signatories to the charter for American Legion Post 213, commonly known as the "Eagles Nest." From left to right are (first row) Fred Sauceda, Stanley Casteñeda, Froylan Hernández, Apolonio Sauceda, and William Salazar; (second row) Joe Marrón, Andy Medellín, Vince Sauceda, Lupe Rodríguez, Fred Contreras, and Manuel Pérez. (Courtesy of Fidel Sauceda Jr.)

These trophies are from the Sauceda family, representing the many years that they played baseball, fast pitch softball, and basketball since the 1920s. Many baseball and fast pitch softball players engaged in other sports, including basketball, soccer, and bowling. The most recent trophy here is from 1988, when Fidel Sauceda Jr. led the Argentine Eagles to win the North American Fastpitch Association's (NAFA) National Fast Pitch Softball Class B Tournament in Las Cruces, New Mexico. (Courtesy of Fidel and Rick Sauceda.)

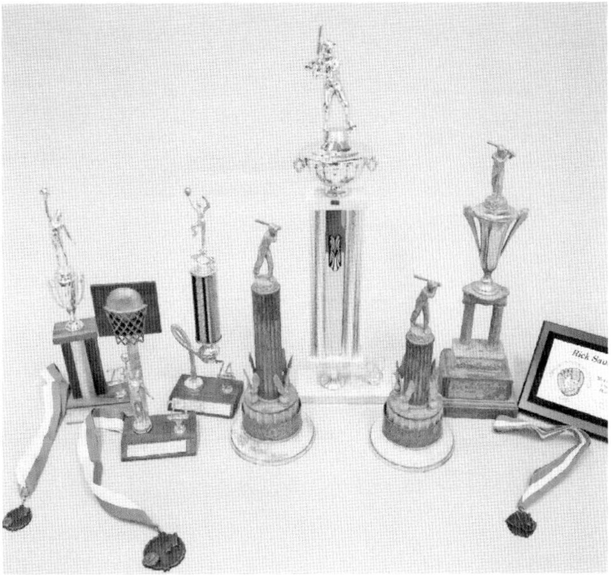

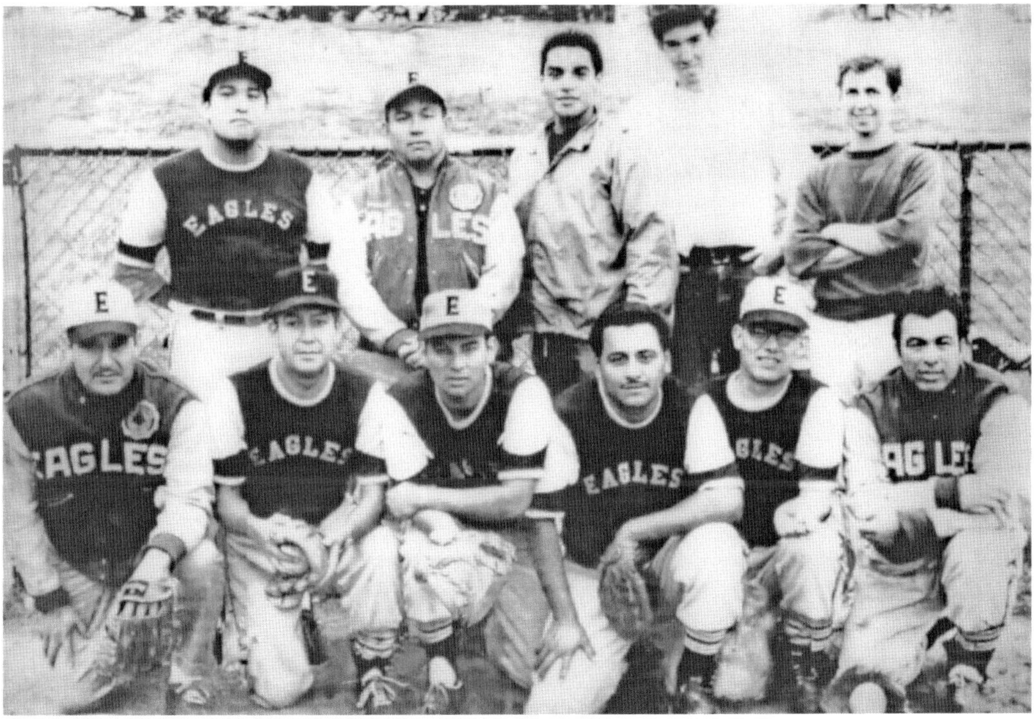

The 1966 Argentine Eagles brought many Midwest tournament trophies back to the Eagles Nest, American Legion Post 213. Post commander Fidel "Wowie" Hernández Jr. (second row, far left) was especially active in promoting the team. Besides regular fast pitch softball throughout the spring and summer months, Post 213 helped with community projects and events, hosted holiday family parties, and raised funds for the needy year-round. (Courtesy of Patricia Castro.)

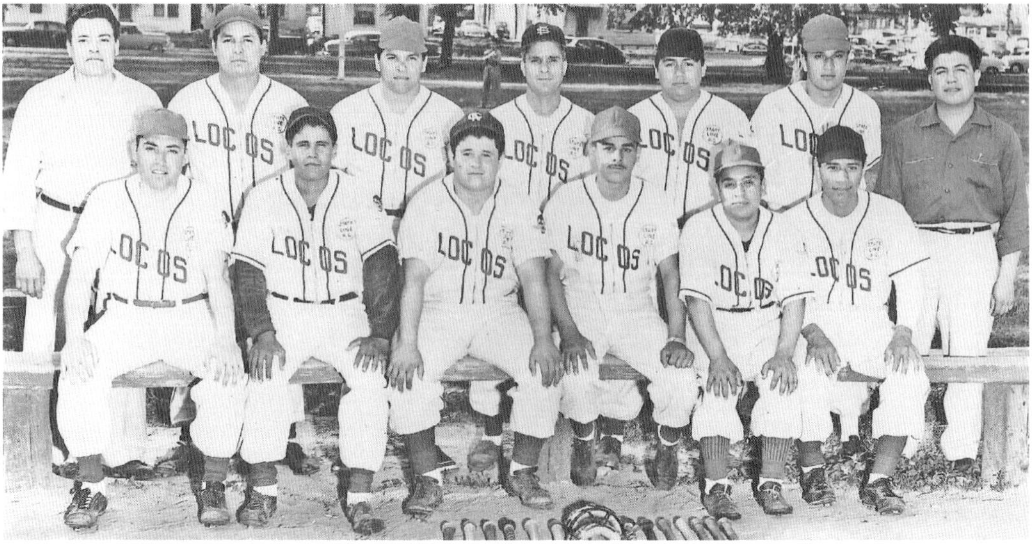

The Stateline Locos competed regularly in the Mexican American Softball Association across a four-state region including Kansas, Missouri, Nebraska, and Iowa. The team continues today with regular league play and tournaments. These 1950 Locos include, from left to right, (first row) Joe Solís, Tony Talavera, Joe Segura, unidentified, Gilbert Rodríguez, and Frank Salas; (second row) Chuck Lombrano, two unidentified, Carlos Móntez, George Pérez, Bernie Porras, and unidentified. (Courtesy of Tony Talavera Jr.)

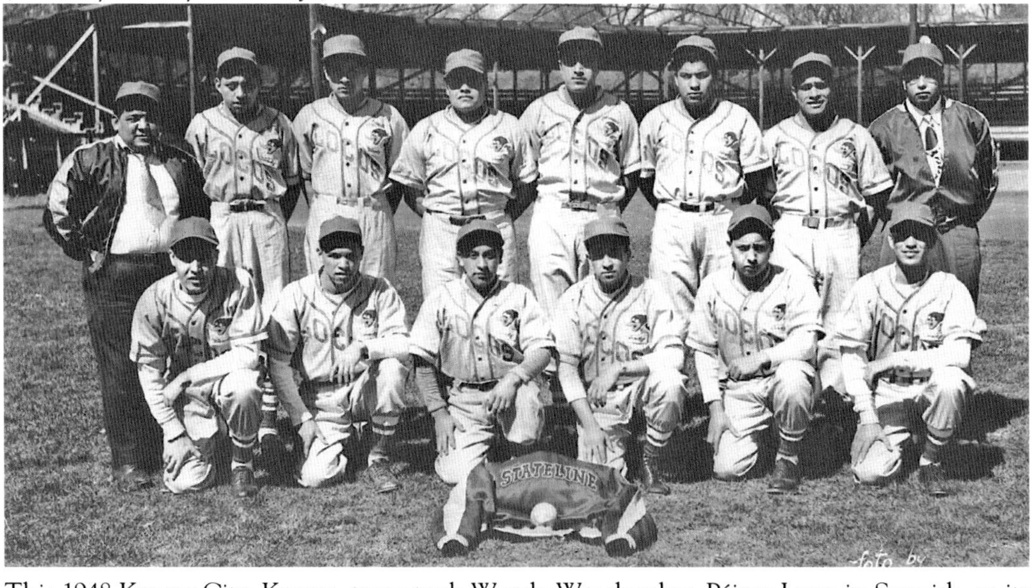

This 1948 Kansas City, Kansas, team took Woody Woodpecker, Pájaro Loco in Spanish, as its logo and mascot. When they took to the field, people would say, "*aquí vienen los muchachos del Pájaro Loco.*" Their name became the Stateline Locos. From left to right are (first row) Robert Lombrano, unidentified, John Dúran, Fred Lombrano, Pete Rodíguez, and Joe Segura; (second row) Nieves Valdez, Richard Ríos, David Segura, Chuck Lombrano, Tony Segura, unidentified, Carlos Móntez, and Félix Ortego. (Courtesy of Tony Talavera Jr.)

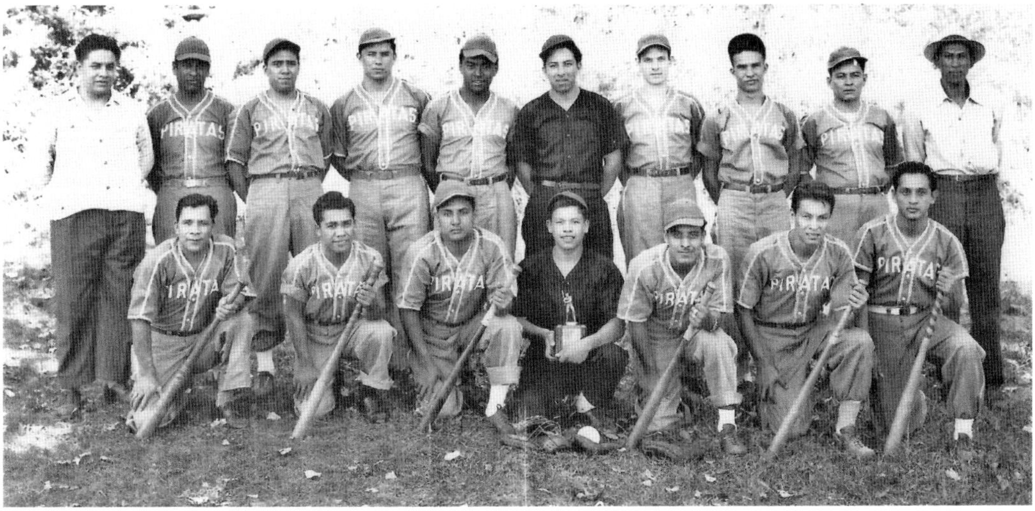

Many Mexican immigrant families settled in the Northeast Sheffield barrio of Kansas City, Missouri, finding work at the Armco Steel plant. Very few Protestant churches sponsored Mexican baseball teams, but Blue Valley Baptist Church was one. From left to right are (first row) Joe Caudillo, Tony Velázquez, Margarito Martínez, Bennie Velásquez, Bart Rodríguez, Patrick Gutíerrez, and Lupe Espinosa; (second row) Paul Santillán, Nickolas Olvera, Tony Móntez, Ignacio Santillán, Frank Velásquez, Eddie Slater, Bobby Davis, Pete Campos, John Móntez, and unidentified. (Courtesy of the Michael Martínez family.)

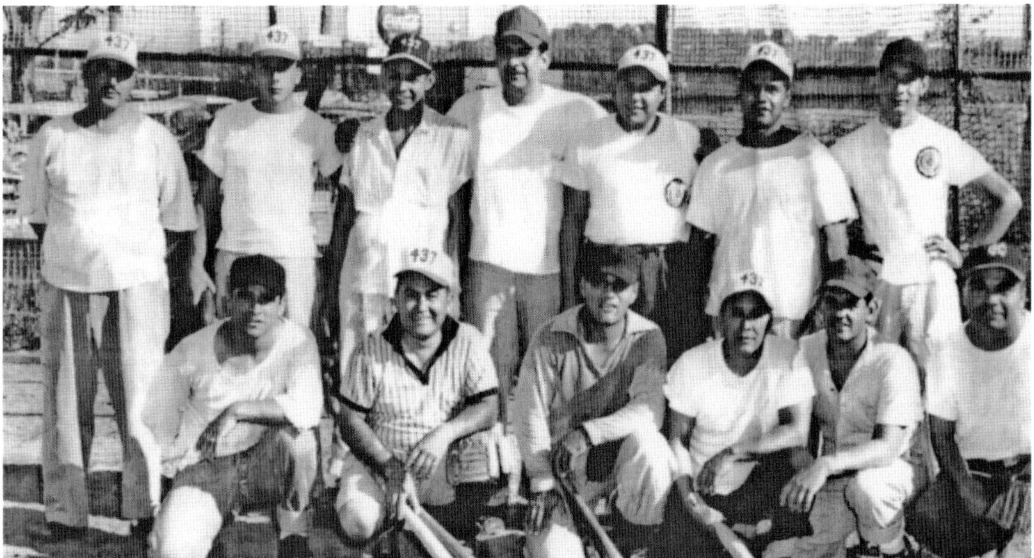

The Ralph Sifuentes American Legion Post No. 437, in Kansas City, Missouri's, West Side, was named after the first soldier to die in World War II from the Guadalupe Parish. Post 437 frequently played against American Legion Post 213. While the two posts were across the state line from each other, family, religious, and cultural ties brought them together frequently to enjoy camaraderie in competition. This 1950s photograph shows Post 437's fast pitch softball team. (Courtesy of Patricia Castro.)

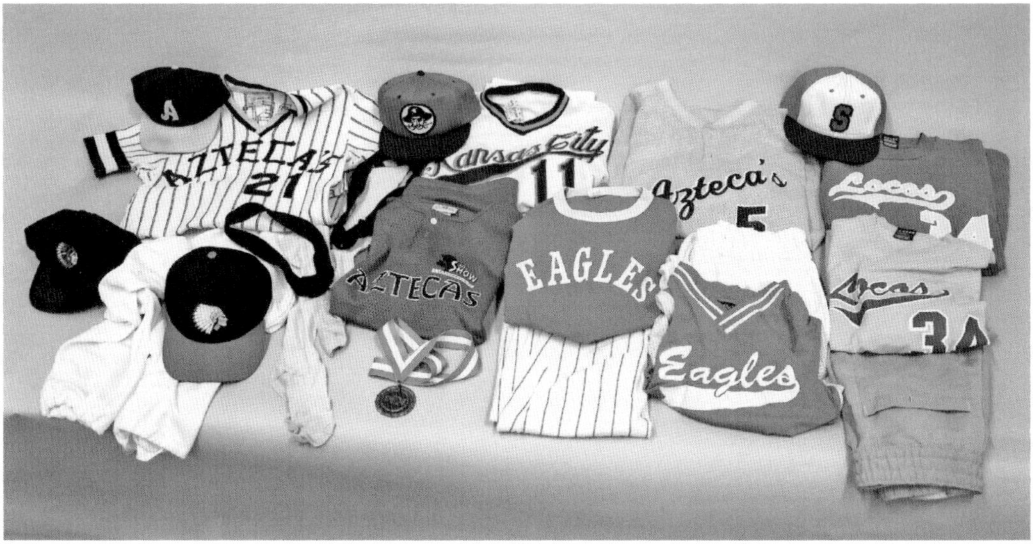

These artifacts represent only some of the many Mexican American men's fast pitch softball teams that existed in the region. Kansas City, Missouri's, Northeast and West Side and the neighborhoods of Argentine, Amourdale, and Rosedale in Kansas City, Kansas, all had teams. Some lasted for decades, while others persisted for just a few years. The games were well attended and provided a sense of community solidarity and camaraderie. (Courtesy of Chris González.)

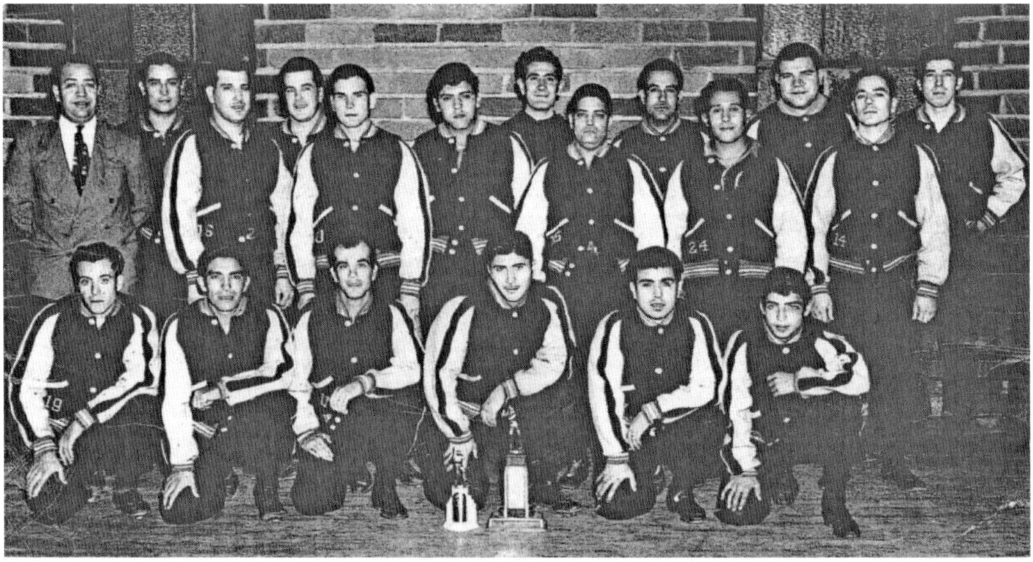

Mexican American communities beyond the Kansas City metropolitan area also supported fast pitch softball teams. Members of this 1948 Guadalupe Church team in the Kansas state capital of Topeka include, from left to right, (first row) Babe Muñoz, David Méndez, Abel Alcalá, John Serna, Cristy Serna, and Alfonzo Padilla; (second row) Nate Moráles, Raymond Aguirre, Raymond Alcalá, Jesse Alcalá, Benny Rodríguez, Tony Flórez, and Joe Méndez; (third row) Joe Oliva, Lawrence Serna, Fr. Francisco De La Vega, Joe Rodríguez, Manuel Arredondo, and John Alonzo. Some of these players became well known throughout the Midwest. (Courtesy of John Tórrez Jr.)

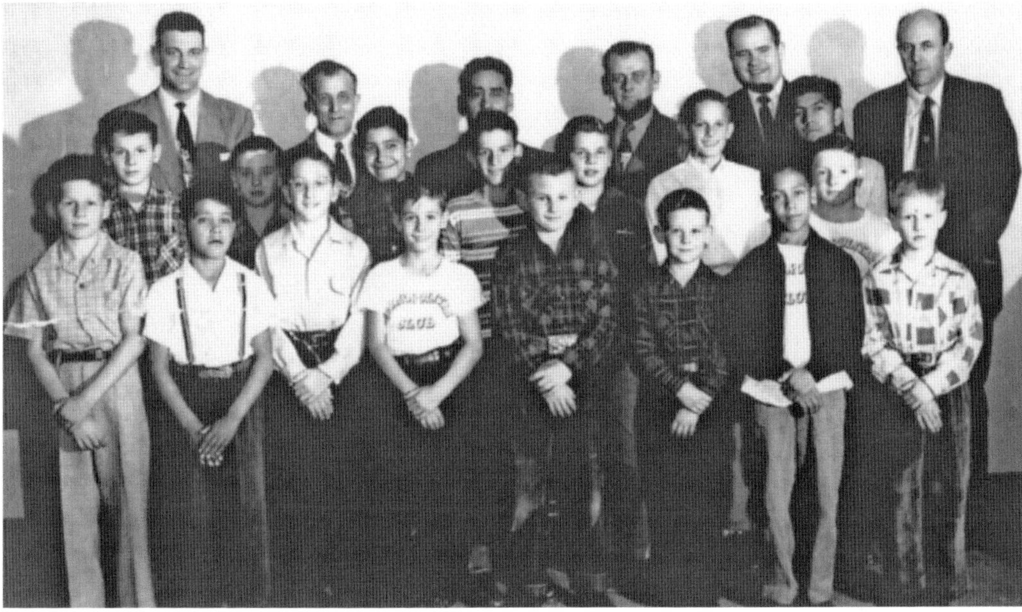

John P. Tórrez Sr. (third row, third from left) was one of the coaches for the Topeka Cosmopolitan Club Baseball League in the late 1950s. His sons include Mike Tórrez (first row, second from left) and John Tórrez Jr. (second row, third from left). John Jr. became a fast pitch softball pitcher and youth coach, and his younger brother Mike made major league history. (Courtesy of John Tórrez Jr.)

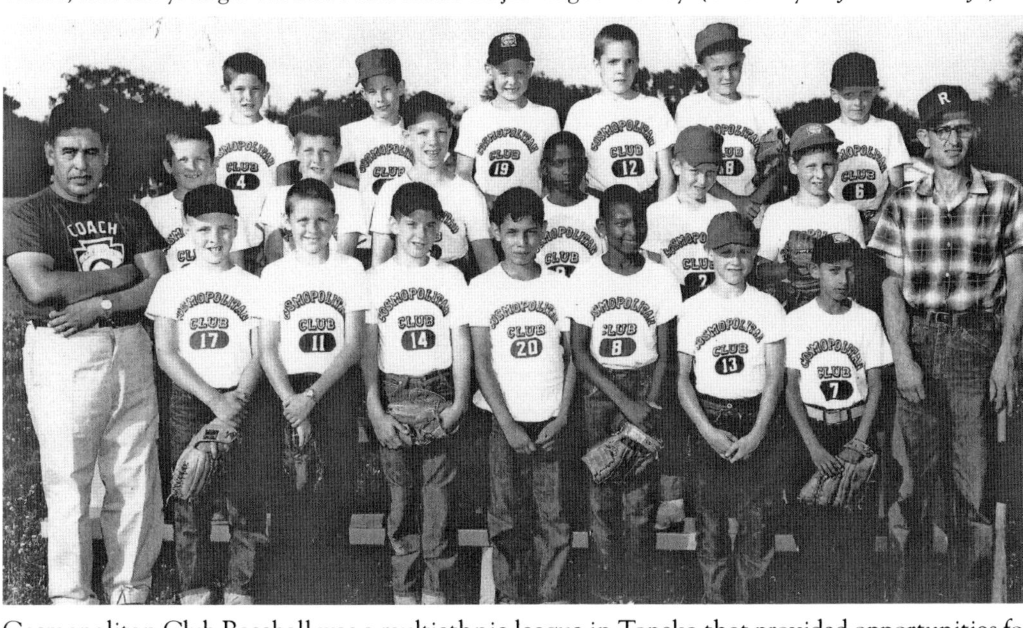

Cosmopolitan Club Baseball was a multiethnic league in Topeka that provided opportunities for youth to compete. John P. Tórrez Sr. (far left) coached this team in 1962 with his son Richard (No. 20) as a player. An annual tournament crowned a single city champion each year. The Tórrez family was very much engaged in helping Topeka's youth get involved with baseball and fast pitch softball. (Courtesy of John Tórrez Jr.)

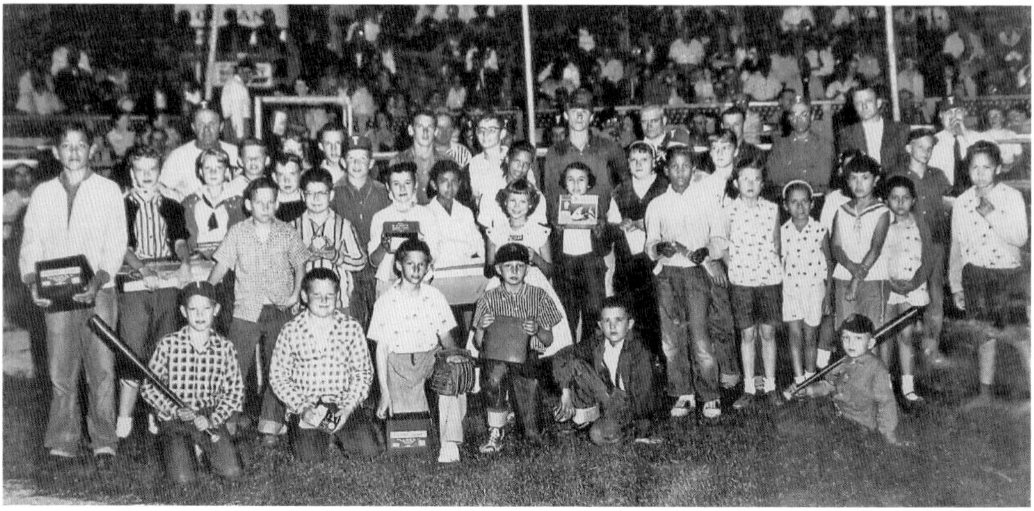

This photograph of a young Mike Tórrez (second row, holding a plaque) portends a great professional pitching career. The Topeka Reds, a minor-league team affiliated with the Cincinnati Reds, held a throwing contest in Owls Ballpark in Topeka that Mike won. He says that he went from throwing potatoes when he worked picking them with his family to throwing baseballs. He was recruited by the St. Louis Cardinals during his senior year of high school. (Courtesy of Mike Tórrez.)

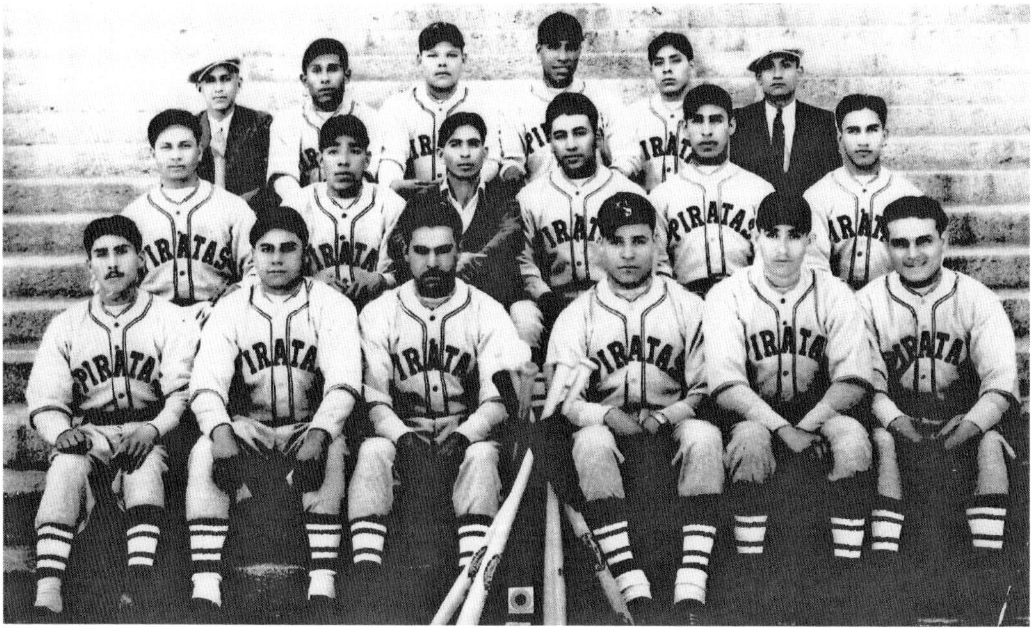

The Topeka Piratas competed against Negro League teams and American Indian teams, since they were mostly segregated from Anglo teams in Topeka. This 1930s team includes, from left to right, (first row) Jerome Serna, Roy Tinoco, Cruz Durán, Louie Alejos, John Gómez, and Manuel Cruz; (second row) Tom López, Perfecto Tórrez, Esperion Ramírez, John Pérez, John P. Tórrez Sr., and Pilar Soza; (third row) Philemon Gutíerrez, Lawrence Serna, Elario Hernández, James Adame, Frank Muñoz, and ? Tinoco. (Courtesy of John Tórrez Jr.)

2

Second Generation Takes the Field

Midwest Mexican workers established residences around meatpacking plants, railroad yards, and steel mills. In Kansas City, Omaha, and Chicago, they worked in the slaughterhouses and meatpacking plants for Wilson, Swift, Cudahy, and Armour. They raised their families in the Argentine and Armourdale barrios in Kansas City, Kansas. Others settled on the West Side or in the Sheffield neighborhood of Kansas City, Missouri. Families seeking work also lived around the Kansas City region, including Topeka, Emporia, Chanute, Omaha, Des Moines, and the Quad Cities of Iowa and Illinois. These families permanently settled in areas where employers provided rudimentary housing. Some families later rented and built homes in neighborhoods near their jobs, maintaining a strong sense of ethnic identity and pride.

The children of these immigrants followed their fathers, uncles, and later, their mothers and aunts onto the "fields of dreams." Both young men and women played in organized leagues throughout the region. Women's teams in Kansas and the Midwest exemplified women's struggle for gender and sports equality in competitive softball. Since remnants of discrimination existed even after World War II, Mexican American baseball and fast pitch softball leagues provided these communities the opportunity to rally around their favorite pastimes, baseball and softball, building a strong awareness of ethnic pride and unity for this second generation. Scholars of Mexican American history often refer to this second generation as the "GI Generation" for their immense and significant wartime contributions on the battlefield and the home front during World War II.

Apolonio "Loney" Sauceda shares the story how vets challenged discrimination in 1947. Mexican American veterans were denied membership in local American Legion Post No. 111. The vets immediately left the building and decided to form their own post. In August 1948, John Joe Salazar was installed as the first Argentine Eagles American Legion Post 213 commander. Post 111 is long gone, but Post 213 is still going strong today. Popularly known as the Eagles Nest, it has sponsored baseball and softball teams for years and has a recently renovated field on which it hosts a tournament.

Most Americans think of baseball as "America's Game." But "America's game was our game too," asserts former player Enrique A. Chaurand Jr. in a short film on Mexican Americans playing baseball and softball in the Kansas City metropolitan area. The film was produced by Guadalupe Centers Inc. of Kansas City and was shown at the 2012 MLB All-Star Game in Kansas City.

This chapter explores the teams established by the offspring of the first Mexican generation in greater Kansas City. Most of these teams moved from baseball to fast pitch softball. They were culturally inspired by their immigrant elders to pass on the rich tradition of ball to future generations.

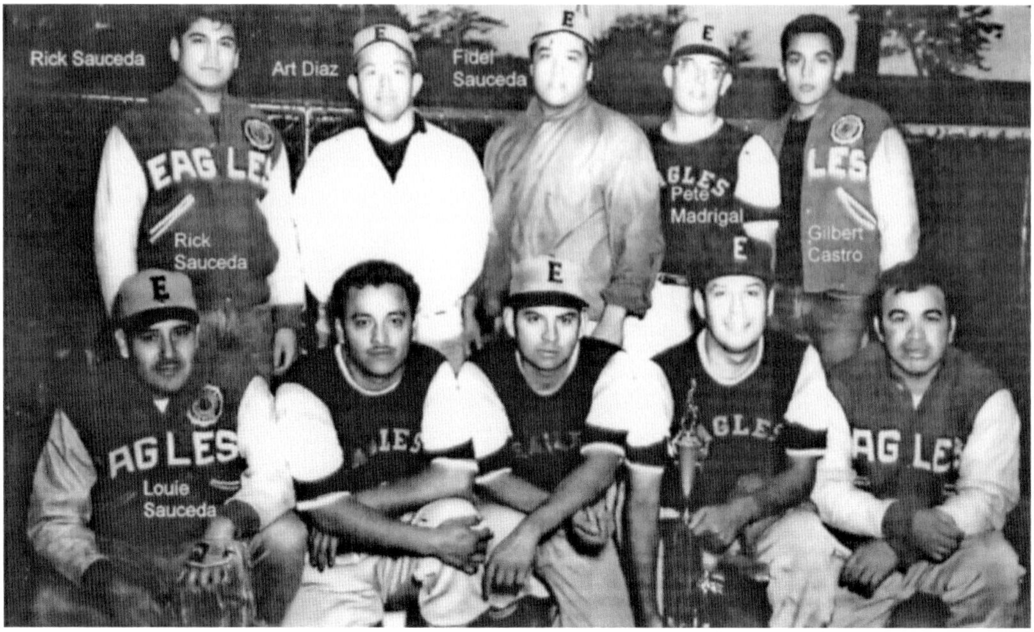

By the mid-1960s, the Argentine Eagles were comprised of second generation Mexican American fast pitch softball players. Discrimination in public accommodations was decreasing, and players were in their glory days. From left to right are (first row) Louie Sauceda, Cruz Hernández, John Sánchez, Apolonio Sauceda, and Genio Hernández; (second row) Richard Sauceda, Art Diaz, Fidel "Wowie" Sauceda Jr., Pete Madrigal, and Gilbert Castro. (Courtesy of Gilbert Castro.)

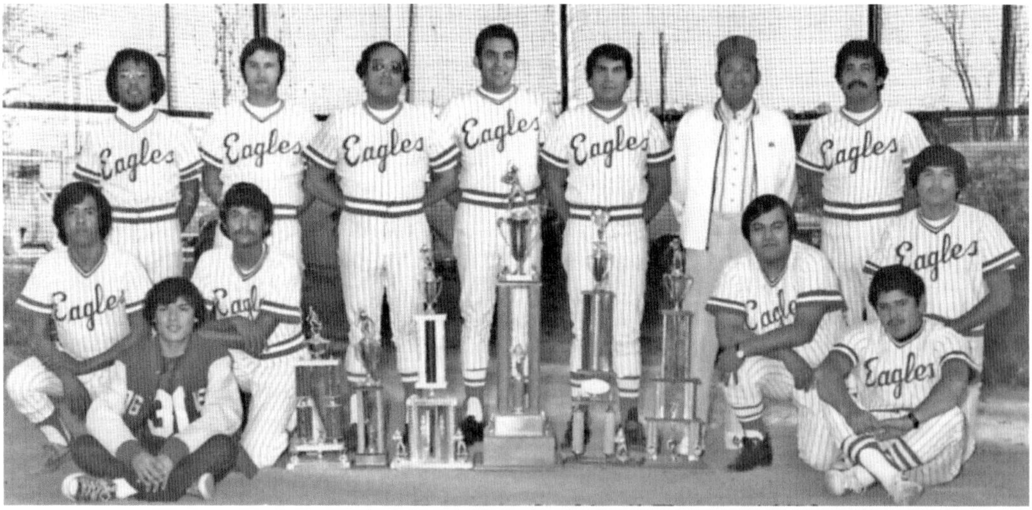

The 1972 Argentine Eagles are pictured at their home field at the American Legion Post 213. The post is located in what was called "Little Mexico" in the bottom land and flood-prone area of Kansas City. From left to right are (first row) Chris Rosas, Chuck Salazar, Mike Medellín, Junior Ortega, Greg Quiroga, and Ralph Sauceda; (second row) Tony Salazar, Larry Hernández, Fidel "Wowie" Sauceda Jr., Gilbert Castro, Richard Sauceda, Milo Hernández, and Sal Cervantes. (Courtesy of Patricia Castro.)

By the time Mexican Americans in South Omaha moved from a storefront church to the new Our Lady of Guadalupe parish church, some had already played for 15 years on the parish baseball team. This second-generation multiethnic team represents players pursuing community competition within Omaha as well as better access to the American experience. Traveling across state lines to play with other Mexican American teams brought players better awareness of organizations like the League of United Latin American Citizens and the American GI Forum. (Courtesy José F. García.)

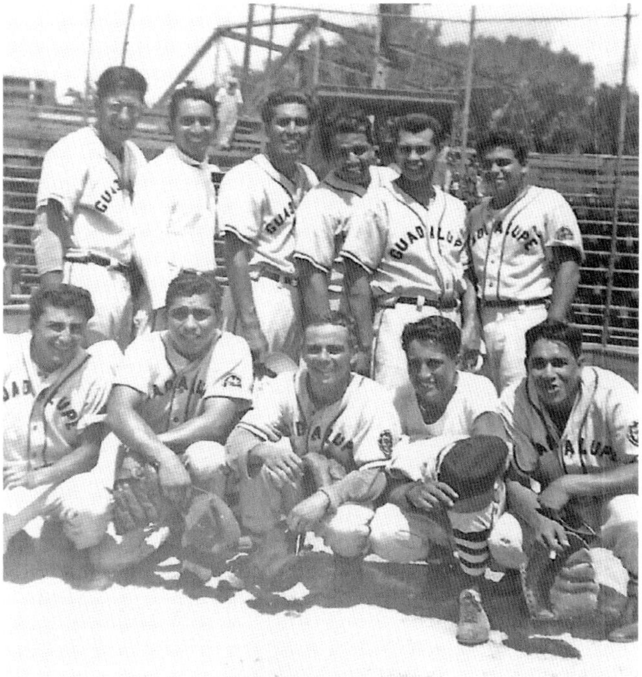

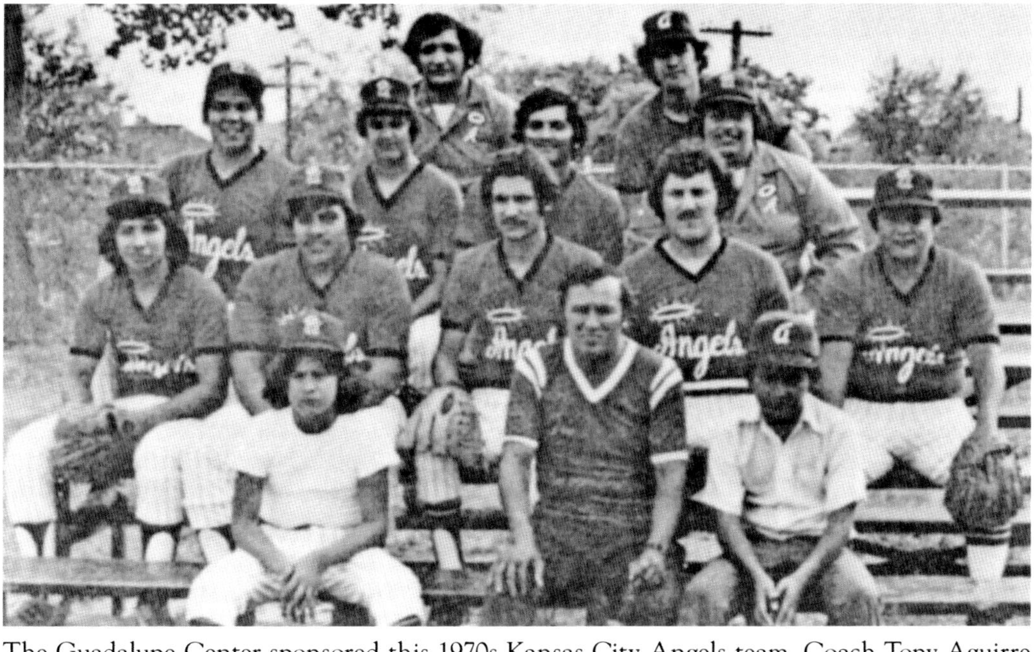

The Guadalupe Center sponsored this 1970s Kansas City Angels team. Coach Tony Aguirre (first row, center) started coaching for the center in 1946 at the age of 17, and served as the sports director for 60 years. From left to right are (first row) Mike Tinoco; (second row) Mike Rivera, Dan Salas, Eddie Muñoz, Ralph Paredes, and Don Álvarez; (third row) John García, Cris Medina, Fred Muñoz, and Ignacio García Jr.; (fourth row) John Muñoz and Albert Valdivia. (Courtesy of the Guadalupe Center Inc.)

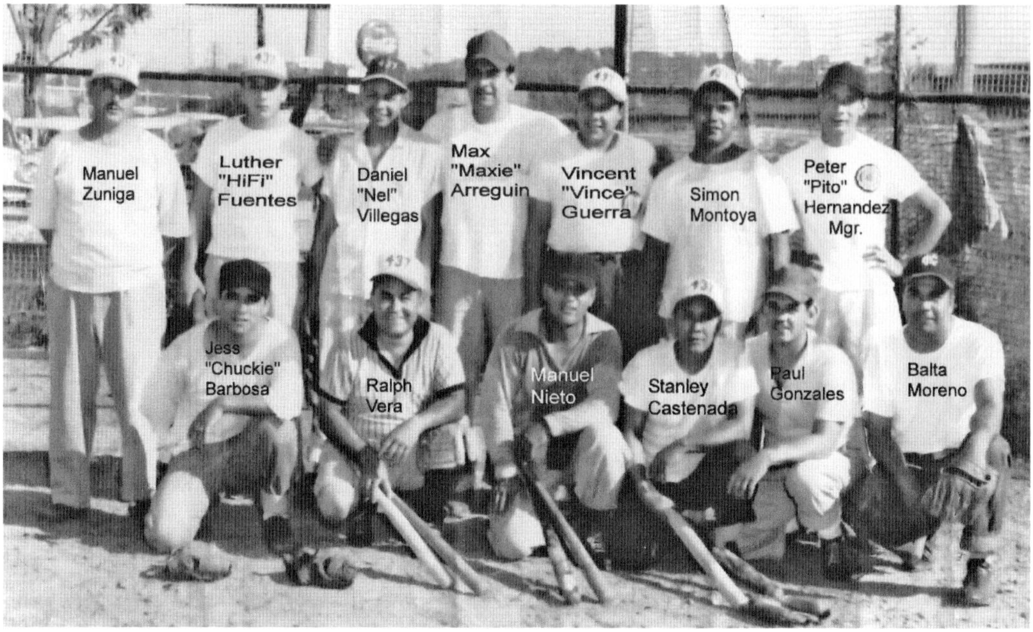

The Ralph Sifuentes American Legion Post No. 437, in the heart of Kansas City, Missouri's, West Side barrio, fielded men's fast pitch softball teams, especially in old-timers games. The vets shown here in 1957 at the Eagles Nest field are baseball and fast pitch players who loved their games. The Sifuentes post folded by the 1980s, but the memories of the post and its players linger in the minds of those who enjoyed playing with and against their teams. (Courtesy of Patricia Castro.)

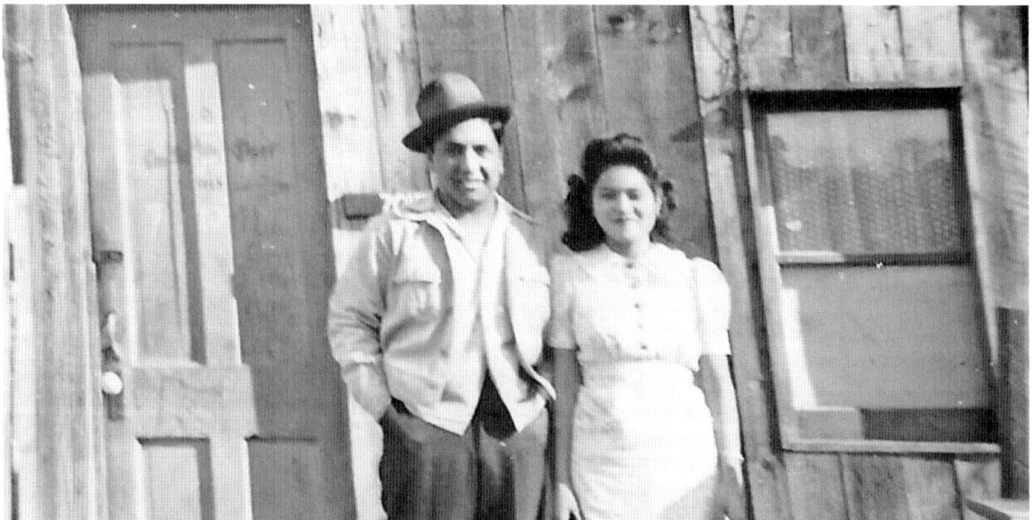

Margarito "Mousee" Martínez and his wife, Katiee Martínez, were the offspring of Mexican immigrants who settled in Kansas City, Missouri's, Northeast in the late 1930s or early 1940s. Margarito was a World War II veteran who loved baseball and was instrumental in organizing teams in his community. Their children stayed in Kansas City, Missouri, and raised Margarito and Katiee's grandchildren there. (Courtesy of the Michael Martínez family.)

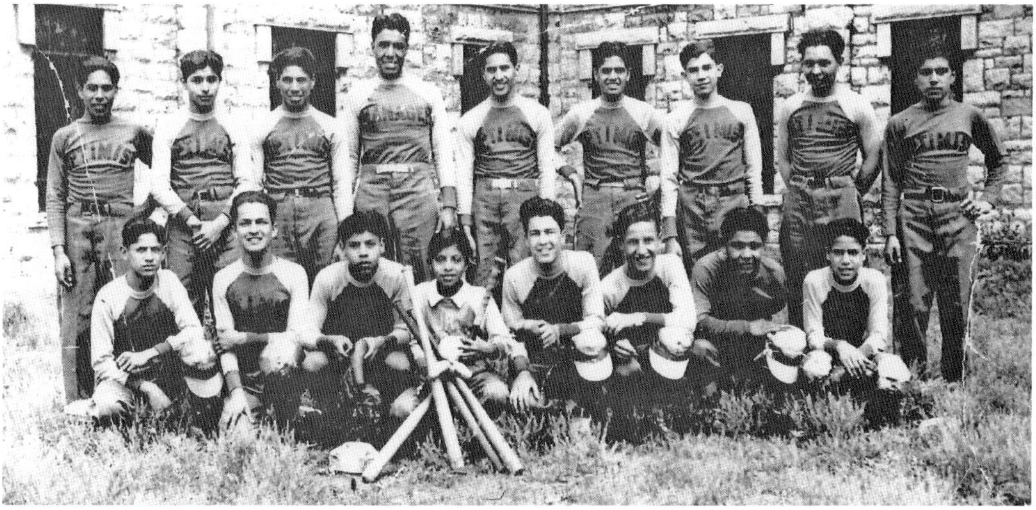

The Optimist Club of Topeka sponsored a Mexican American baseball team in the early 1930s. The mission of Optimist International is to bring out the best in youth through community volunteers. The Optimist Club of Topeka helped Mexican immigrant families adjust to living in the United States by getting the youth involved in baseball and softball. The organization still operates baseball programs in Topeka. Many of the young players shown here moved on to form the Piratas team in the Mexican American community. (Courtesy of John Tórrez Jr.)

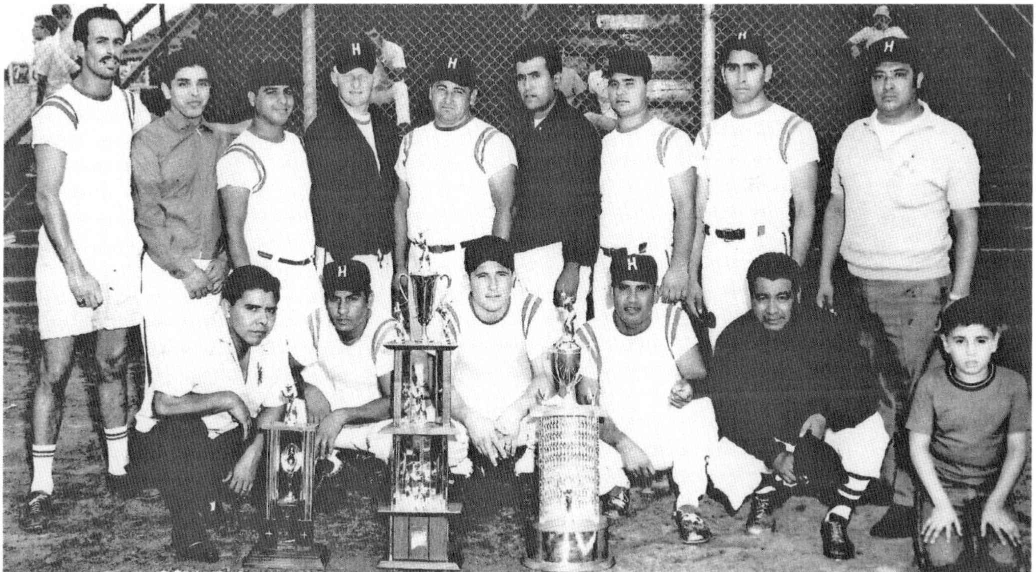

In the late 1960s and early 1970s, the top Mexican American fast pitch team in Topeka was Harold's Prize Package. Other great softball teams that came along—Livingston's Fashions, American GI Forum, and Cousin's Tavern—all based their success on great pitchers. Pete "Blanco" Gómez, Joe "Rocket" Rocha, Manuel Arredondo, Joe Hernández, and John "Johnny Boy" Tórrez Jr. were some of the greatest. Other Topeka families that produced outstanding players were Barranco, Escobar, Muñoz, Proctor, Zarazura, and Zuñiga, just to name a few. (Courtesy of John Tórrez Jr.)

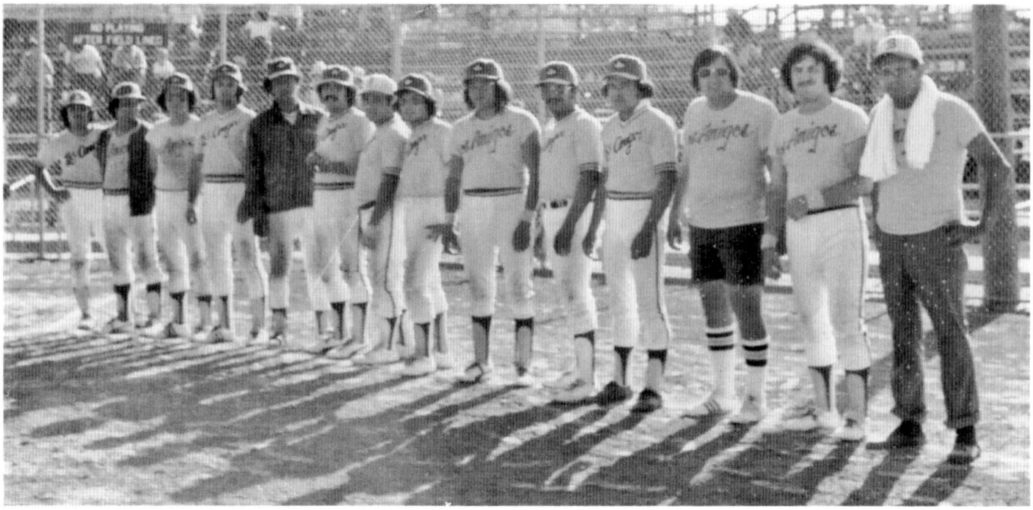

In 1972, the Kansas City Amigos competed in the Oldtimers Tournament in Austin, Texas. After that tournament, they traveled to San Antonio and Houston for two other tournaments. Three Hernández brothers played on the team coached by their father, Paul "Waxie" Hernández Sr. From left to right are Tony Salazar, Manuel Hernández, Larry Hernández, Paul Hernández Jr., Sal Cervantes, Tom Ramírez, unidentified, Albert Franco, Phil Gutíerrez, Richard Moreno, Ralph Villegas, Ralph Paredes, unidentified, and Paul Hernández Sr.. (Courtesy of Paul Hernández Jr.)

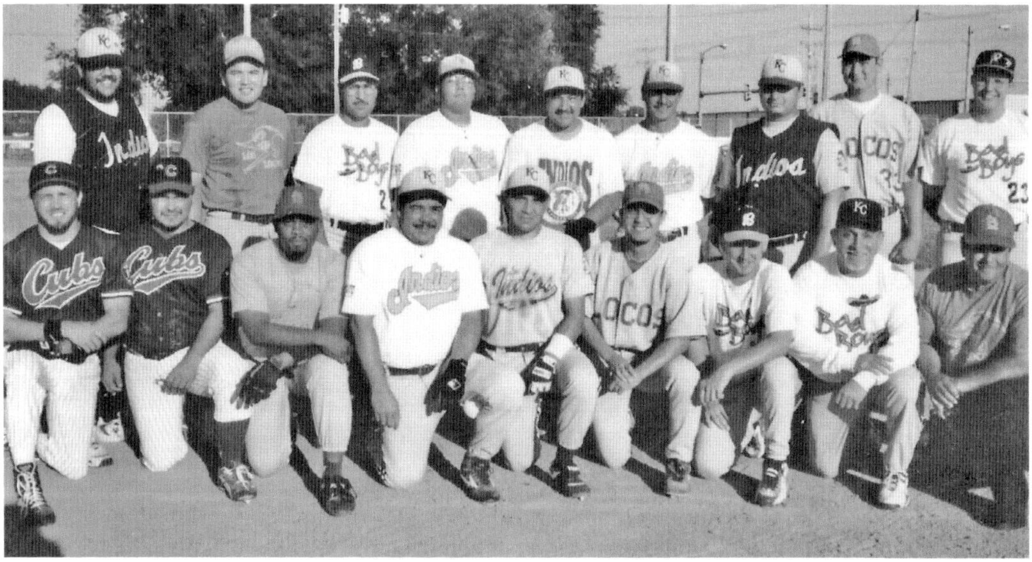

This all-star fast pitch team includes, from left to right, (first row) Terry ?, Dave Carr, unidentified, Victor García, unidentified, Tony Oropeza Jr., Richie Lándiz, Ralph Pacheco, and Tony Talavera Jr.; (second row) Arturo García Jr., unidentified, Tony García, Louis Oropeza, Danny García, Lon Ramírez, Albert García, Luke Folscroft, and ? García. The setting is Shawnee Park, a field located in the heart of Armourdale, one of the Mexican American barrios in Kansas City, Kansas, and a battleground for many of the Mexican American fast pitch softball games and tournaments. (Courtesy of Tony Talavera Jr.)

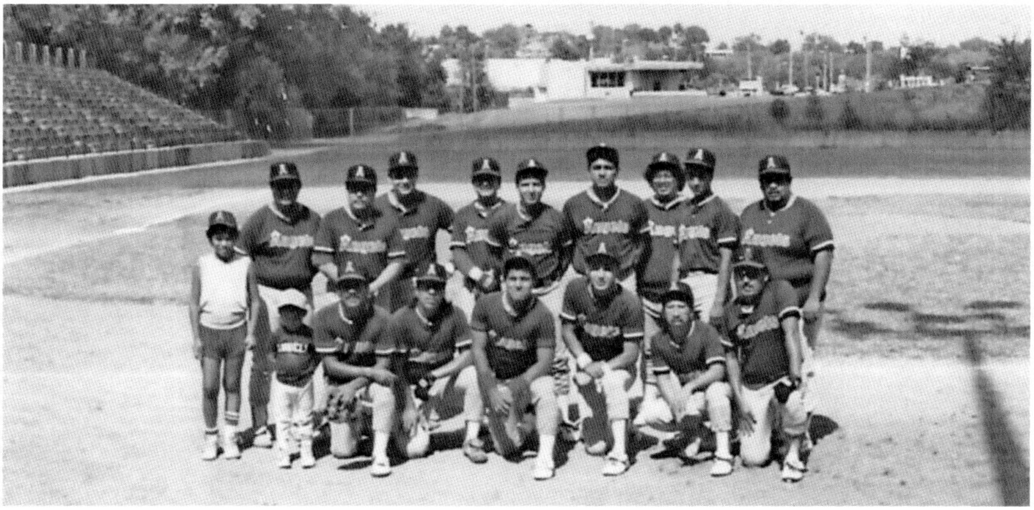

The Kansas City Angels drew players from the Mexican American community, mostly from the West Side. This team from the 1980s includes, from left to right, (first row) unidentified, Tony Rodríguez, Candido Chávez, Tomás Melgoza, Larry Bustamante, John Fierro, and A.J. Montes; (second row) unidentified, Cris Medina, Art Ruíz, Danny Rojas, Arthur Díaz, Beto López, David Ward, John García, Francisco García, and Ignacio García. The team is still active today with new players, the friends and family of former members. (Courtesy of Guadalupe Centers Inc.)

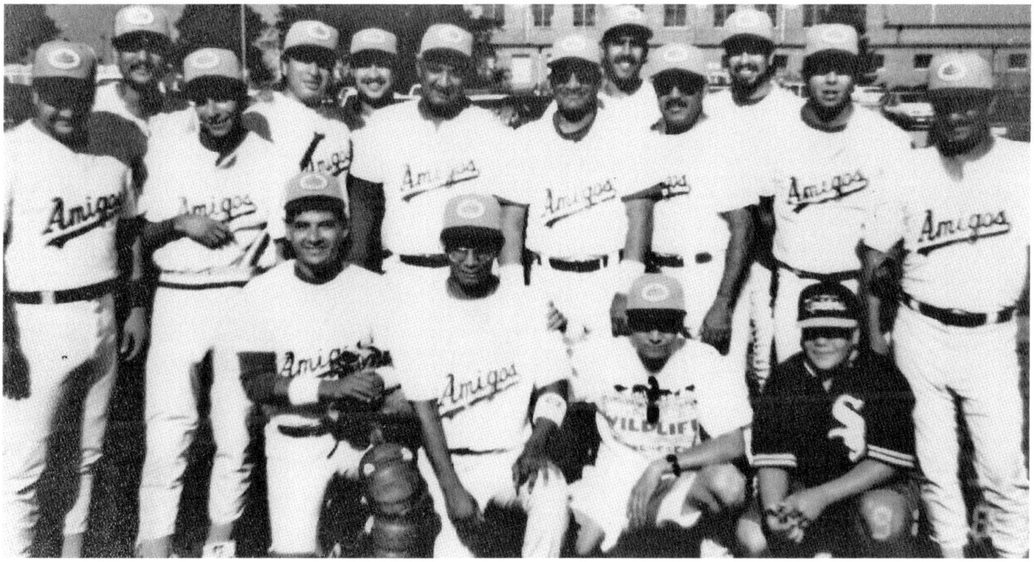

The 1991 Kansas City Amigos were the first Mexican American team to win the Amateur Softball Association 4-State Midwest Tournament in Fargo, North Dakota. The Amigos were formed by Cris Medina and his friends from Kansas City, Missouri's, West Side barrio. From left to right are (first row) Art Ruíz, Patrick Hernández, unidentified, and Demetri García; (second row) Jim Reyes, Brian Padilla, Paul Hernández Jr., Eddie Hernández, Mario Escobar, Jude De Villa, and Manuel Hernández; (third row) Bill Músquiz, Ron Porras, Herb La Fuente, Sylvester Bustamante Jr., and Richard Ceceña Jr. (Courtesy of Cris Medina.)

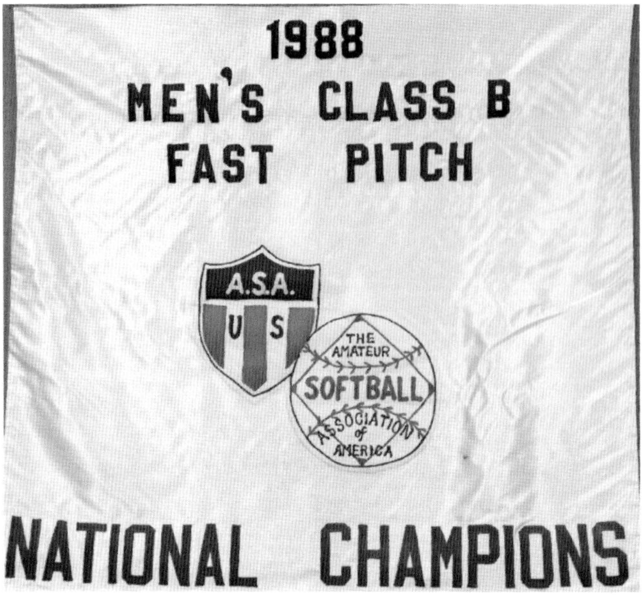

The ASA, based in Oklahoma City, was founded in 1933 and is the strongest softball organization in the country. The growth and development of the association led the US Olympic Committee to name the ASA the national governing body of softball pursuant to the Amateur Sports Act of 1978. The ASA regulates competition to insure fairness. The Argentine Eagles brought home the 1988 national championship banner to American Legion Post 213. (Courtesy of Fidel Sauceda Jr.)

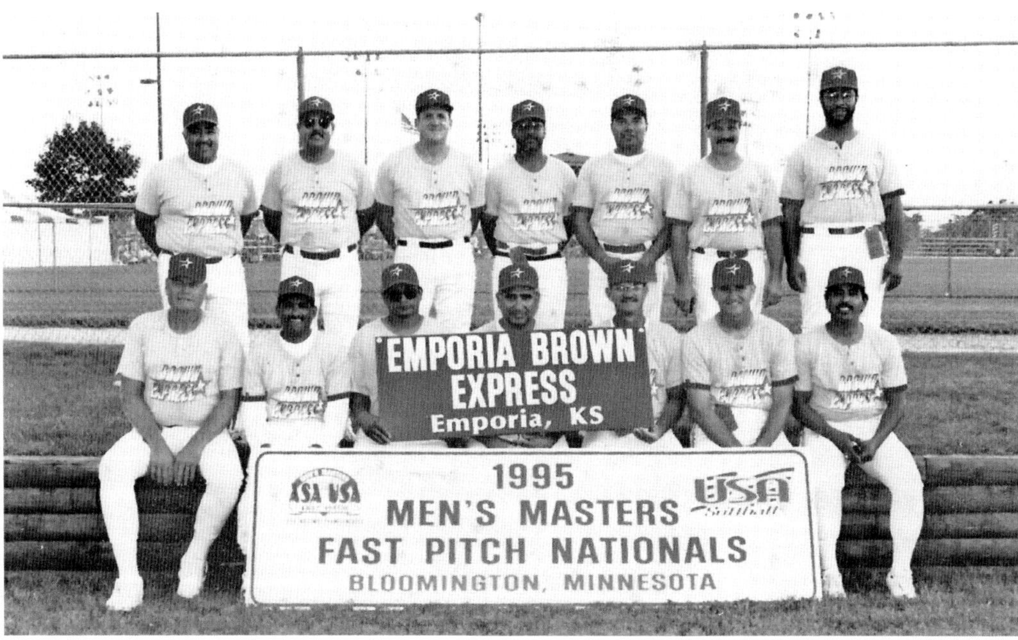

In 1995, the Emporia Brown Express, playing for Emporia, Kansas, won the ASA Fast Pitch National Tournament in Bloomington, Minnesota. The team, which included Mexican American players from Newton and Topeka, was made up of, from left to right, (first row) Irwin Fink, Steve Jaso, Richard Toledo, John Tórrez Jr., Danny Workman, Gary Zinn, and Greg Escobar; (second row) Richard Escobar, Mario Escobar, Doug Stroth, Larry Lindsey, Javier Marrón, Tom Lindblad, and Butch Brown. In addition to their skills on the field, players were recruited to the Brown Express through work and family connections. (Courtesy of John Tórrez Jr.)

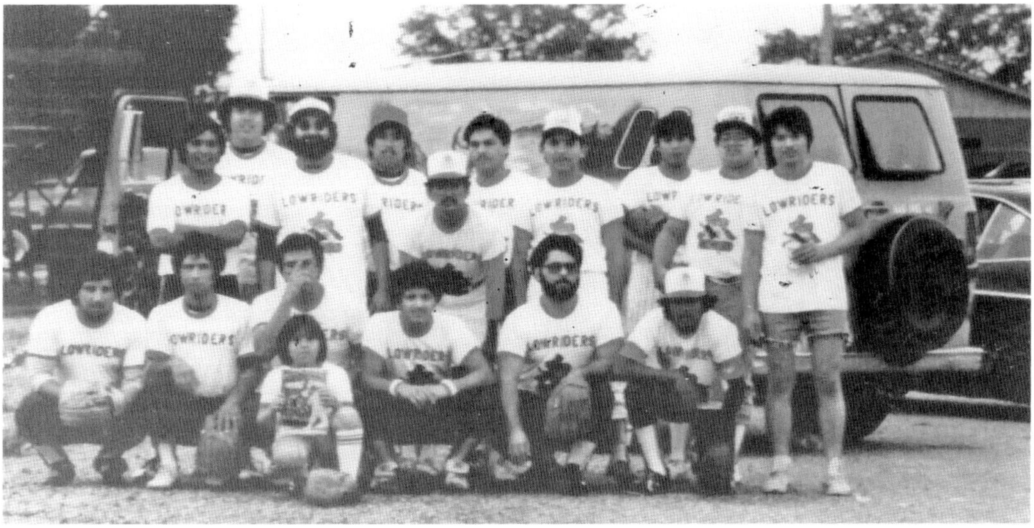

This 1983 photograph shows a group of young men from Wichita who called their team the Low Riders. Not much is known about them, but their name reflects the time in which the Chicano movement was still underway among Mexican American youth in Midwestern cities. According to Kansas University professor Ben Chappell, the lowrider cars and culture were a way for them to lay claim to streets in their towns and cities. This group apparently laid claim to the ball fields in their area. (Courtesy of Patrick Martínez.)

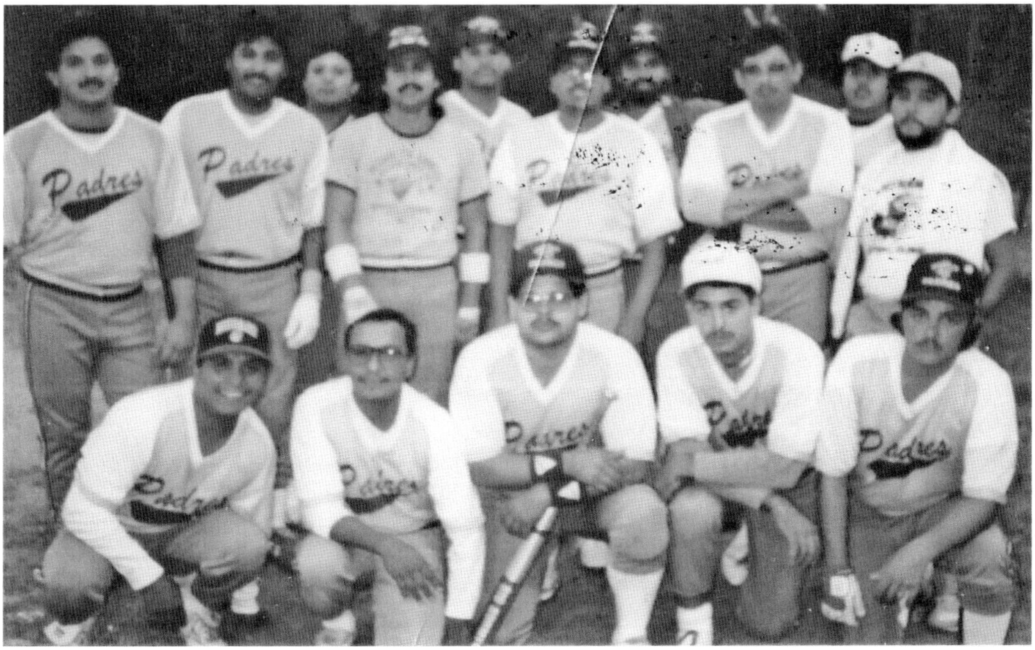

The Wichita Padres, seen here in the mid-1980s, are, from left to right, (first row) Don Díaz, Ronald Darzell Díaz, Bubba Martínez, T. Burns, and Kevin Ketcher; (second row) R. Chávez, Eddie Díaz, J.D. Díaz, Mike Galván, B. Sánchez, Rudy García, and G. Ontiberos; (third row) Gator Palacioz, Chris Gerrero, and Mido Robles. (Courtesy of Patrick Martínez.)

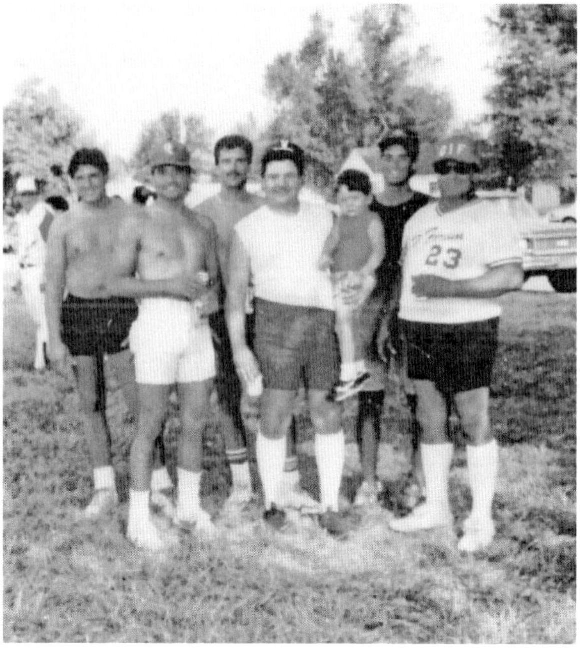

Pete "Blanco" Gómez's family pauses between rounds of tournament play in 1985. From the 1960s through the 1980s, Pete Gómez (first row, far right) was considered one of the best fast pitch softball pitchers in the Midwest. Besides pitching for Topeka clubs, he was often called upon to pitch for other clubs across the region. He was a dedicated family man who often took his children with him during the summer months. As his sons got older, they often played right along with him. Here he is playing for the Topeka GI Forum team. (Courtesy of Anthony Scott Gómez.)

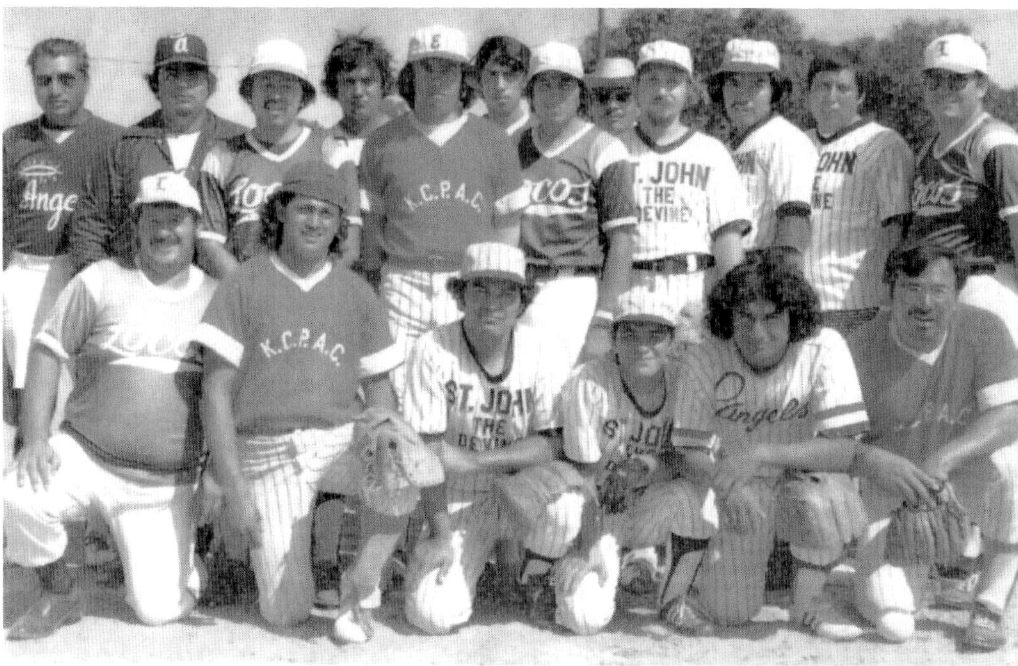

In one of the all-star games of the 1970s, opposing teams had an opportunity to select their best players and play with, instead of against, one another. At one of the annual games are, from left to right, (first row) Joe Segura, Mike Tinoco, Tony Oropeza, Steve Galván, Mike Hernández, and Regino Hernández; (second row) Jesse Salas, Ignacio García, unidentified, Chris Ramos, Joe Hurtado, Froylan Pacheco, Javier Marrón, Tony Villegas, and Manuel Ortíz; (third row) Cris Medina, Mike García, and George Pérez. (Courtesy of Guadalupe Centers Inc.)

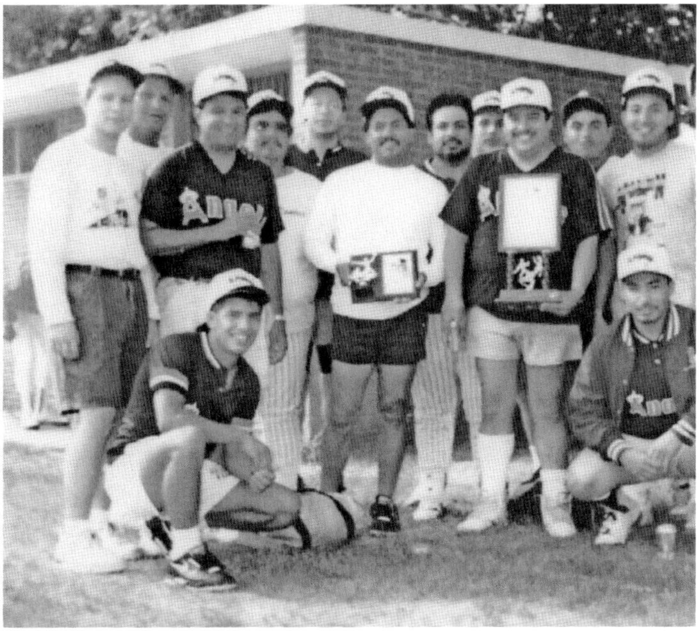

Kansas City, Missouri's, late 1980s Angels team poses at Penn Valley Park, where the "Waxie" Hernández fields are located. From left to right are (first row) Hugo Melgoza and Jesse García; (second row) Enrique Chaurand Jr., Cris Medina, Tony Rodríguez, Mike Arroyo, and Larry Móntez; (third row) Paul Hernández Jr., John García, Larry Bustamante, Ignacio García, Danny Rojas, Eddie Díaz, and Sylvester Bustamante. (Courtesy of Guadalupe Centers Inc.)

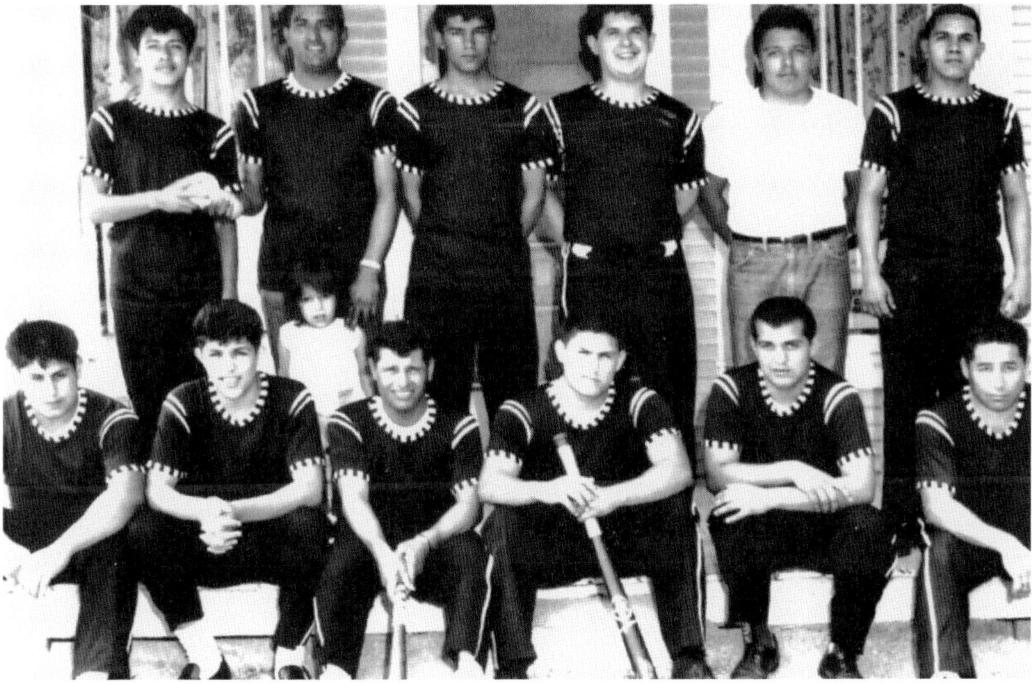

The 1966 Chanute, Kansas, GI Forum fast pitch team was outstanding. From left to right are (first row) Lucio De La Torre, Tony De La Torre, Ray Bonilla, Román De La Torre, Lupe Ponce, Joe Godínez, and Pattie Ponce; (second row) Albert Godínez, Joe Ponce, Frank Bonilla, Harley Ponce, Billie Joe González, and David Savala. Tony De La Torre and Joe and Harley Ponce have been inducted into the Kansas City Angels Hall of Fame at the Guadalupe Center in Missouri and the Newton, Kansas, Hall of Fame. (Courtesy of Gene T. Chávez.)

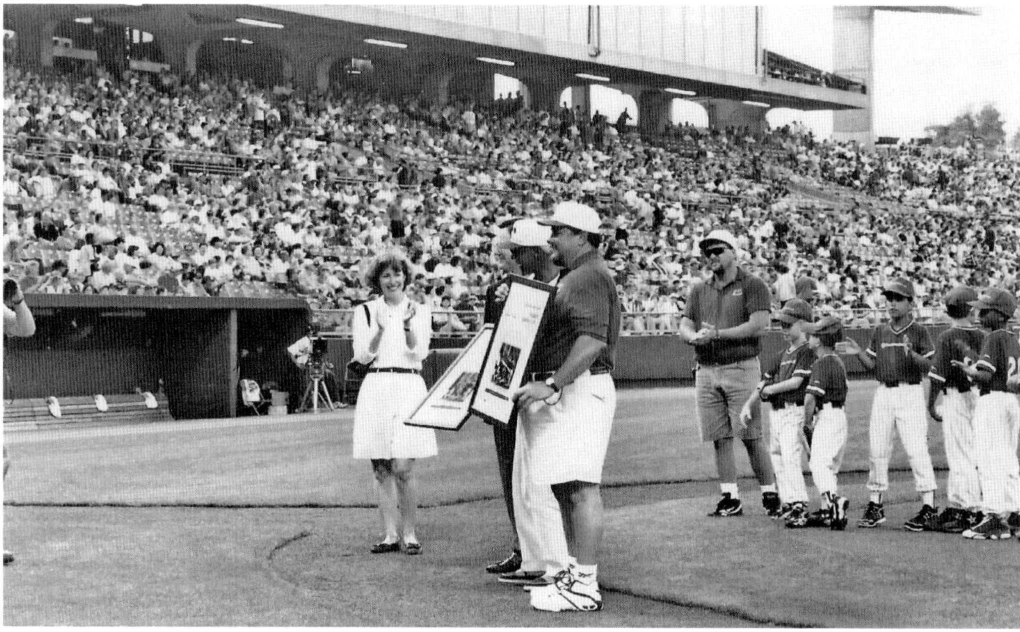

In 1998, the Kansas City Bandits, a youth team from the Argentine district coached by Anthony Scott Gómez, was honored at the Kansas City Royals' Kauffman Stadium. The team won a number of local and national baseball tournaments and was selected by Southwestern Bell to be honored along with Buck O'Neal of the American Negro Leagues. O'Neal was a first baseman and later the manager of the Kansas City Monarchs. (Courtesy of Anthony Scott Gómez.)

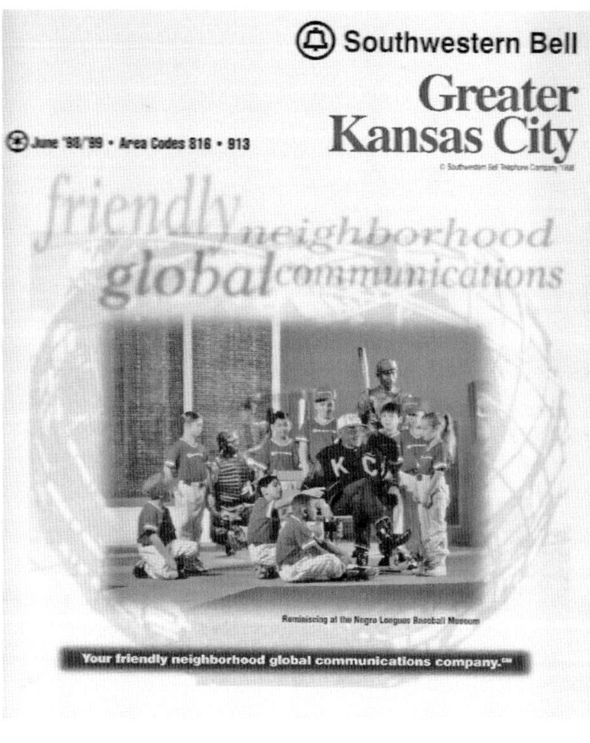

In 1998, Anthony Scott Gómez was honored by having his team, the Kansas City Bandits, featured on the cover of the Southwestern Bell Greater Kansas City White Pages. Players shown with the famous former Negro Leagues player Buck O'Neal are, from left to right, (first row) Josh Gutíerrez Joséph Santoyo, Marc Wilson, Buck O'Neal, unidentified, and Brian Gómez; (second row) Ben Marsh, C.S. Alvarado, unidentified, and Drew Martin. (Courtesy of Anthony Scott Gómez.)

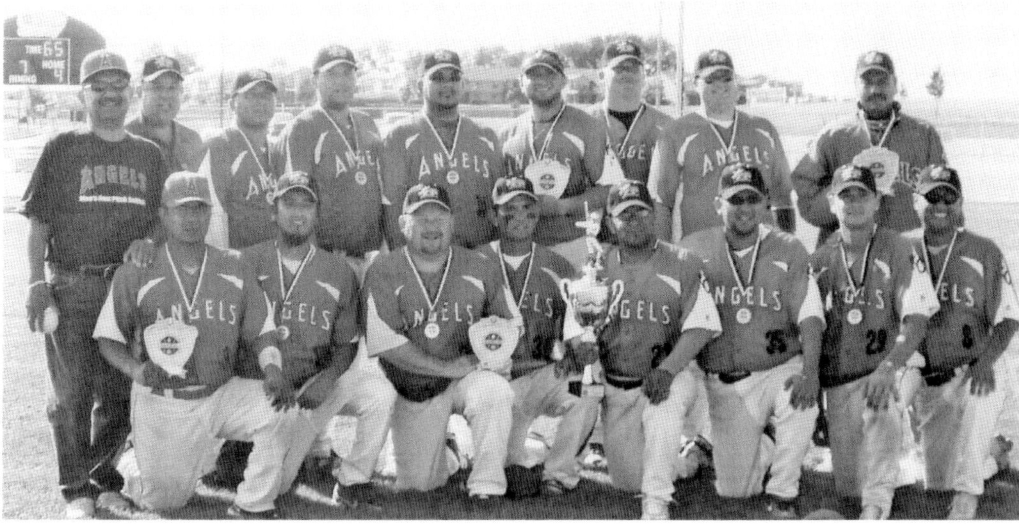

NAFA annually hosts the largest men's fast pitch tournament in the world. The Kansas City Angels won the NAFA 2009 World Series Championship in Sioux Falls, South Dakota. From left to right are (first row) Pat Hernández, Ralph Sánchez, Joe Quinn, Eddie Díaz Jr., Brian Hernández, Anquilino Villegas, Cris Medina Jr., and Anthony Villegas; (second row) Manuel Hernández, Cris Medina Sr., Bubba Hernández, Steve Roach, Frank Oropeza Jr., Fernando Esquivel, Joe Monslow, Chad Miller, and Miguel Barrón. (Courtesy of Cris Medina.)

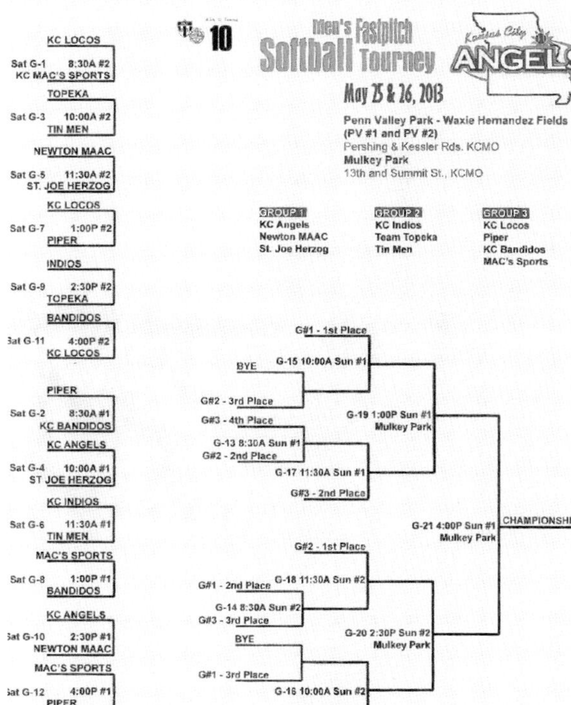

The Kansas City Angels had a long tradition of holding an annual tournament during the Memorial Day weekend. In this double-elimination tournament bracket from 2013, each team played twice before proceeding to the winners' bracket. The teams in the tournament came from Newton, Topeka, Piper, and Kansas City, Kansas, and from St. Joséph and Kansas City, Missouri. Tournament games are played on fields in the Mexican American barrios. Over the years, a tournament dance has typically been held on Saturday nights. (Courtesy of Guadalupe Centers Inc.)

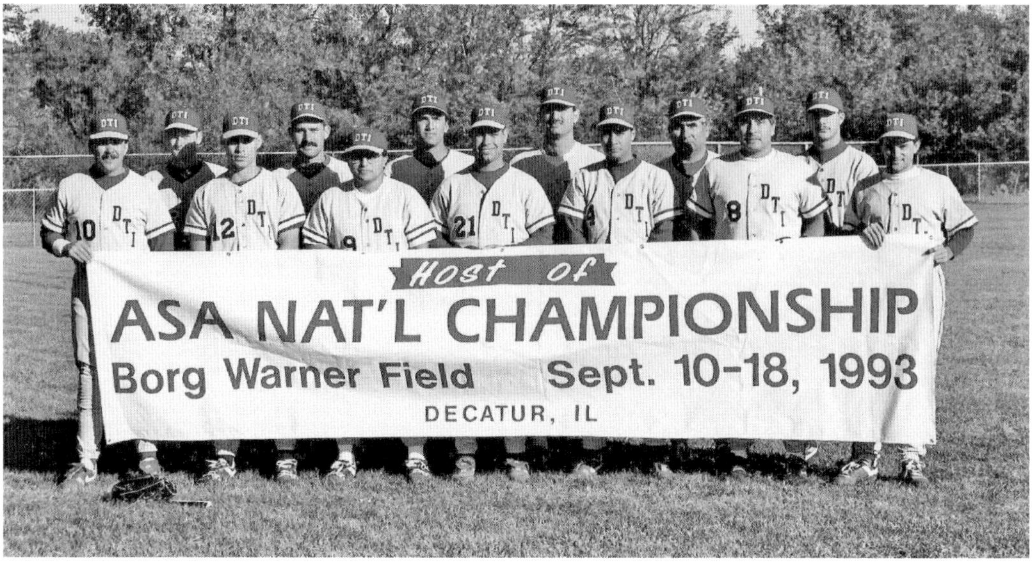

Men's fast pitch softball is governed by the American Softball Association, which holds national tournaments each year. The Topeka DTI team worked its way to the nationals in Decatur, Illinois. From left to right are (first row) Jimmy Davis, Tony Buckley, Al Barranco, Troy Procter, Angelo Zuñiga, Juan Barranco, and Greg Dew; (second row), unidentified, Tony Procter, Bill Roman, John Procter, John Tórrez Jr., and unidentified. (Courtesy of John Tórrez Jr.)

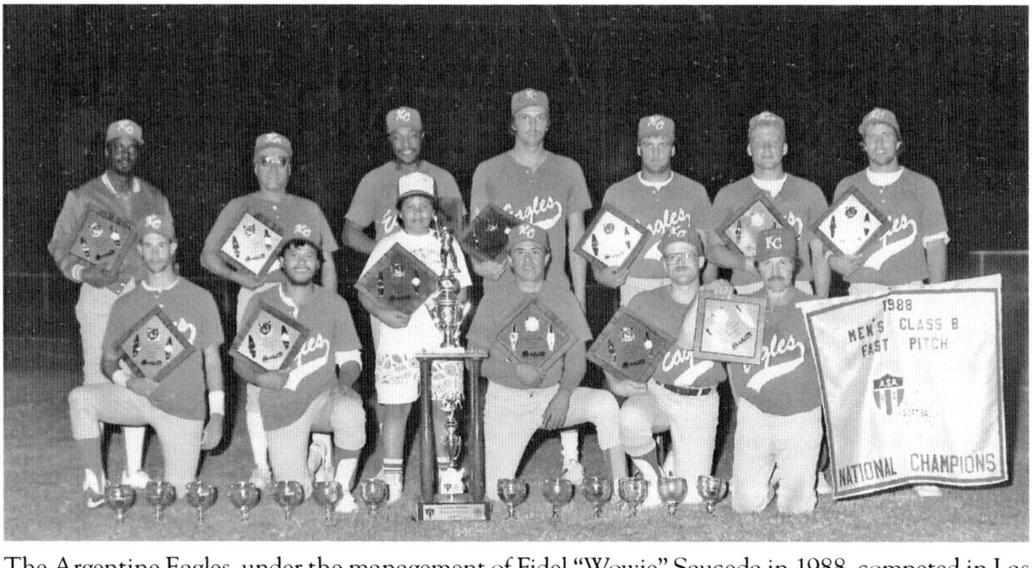

The Argentine Eagles, under the management of Fidel "Wowie" Sauceda in 1988, competed in Las Cruces, New Mexico, at the ASA Men's Class B Fast Pitch Softball Championship Tournament. Top regional finishers from this classification were invited to advance to the Class B ASA/USA National Championship Tournament. From left to right are (first row) Harry Medellín, Chris Ramos Jr., Chris Ramos Sr., Joe Carlsen, and Tom Lindblad; (second row) Ray Marshall, Fidel Sauceda Jr., Vernon Coats, Herman Kump, Mike McCall, Billy Callahan, Dave Smith, and Kelly Hammonds. (Courtesy of Fidel Sauceda Jr.)

Along with the Kansas City Angels Memorial Day tournament, the Angels held their Mexican American Softball Hall of Fame induction ceremony in 2013 in Kansas City. In the flyer shown here, the inductee and their team are listed. Fast pitch softball players from the Kansas City region consider it a great honor to be inducted into the hall of fame. In addition to the Kansas City Mexican American Hall of Fame, the Newton Annual Fast Pitch Softball Tournament Hall of Fame induction is also highly coveted. (Courtesy of Guadalupe Centers Inc.)

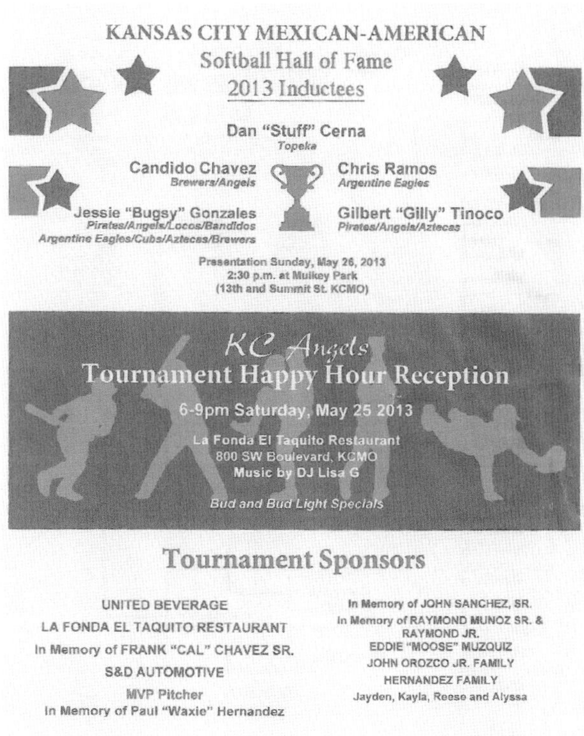

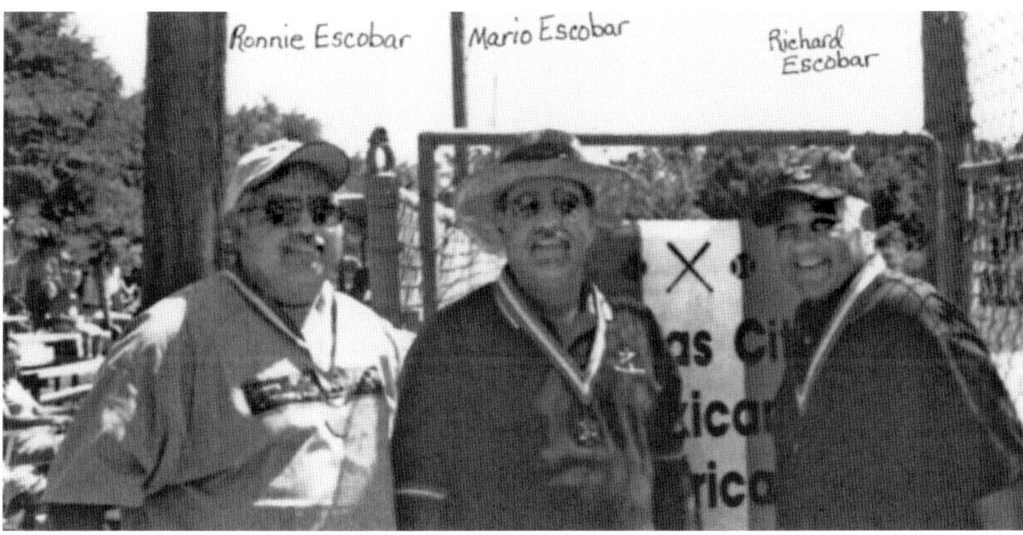

The Escobar brothers were inducted into the Kansas City Mexican American Softball Hall of Fame in 2001 and 2002. Their father, Vincent "Bernie" Escobar (not shown), had been inducted long before his sons. Ronnie, Mario, and Richard grew up in Topeka, where their father worked for the Santa Fe Railroad. The brothers come from a baseball and softball fast pitch family. They were extensively involved in Mexican American leagues in both Kansas and Missouri. Because of their extraordinary skills on the diamond, their father and all three brothers were also inducted in the Newton Mexican American Athletic Hall of Fame. (Courtesy of the Escobar family.)

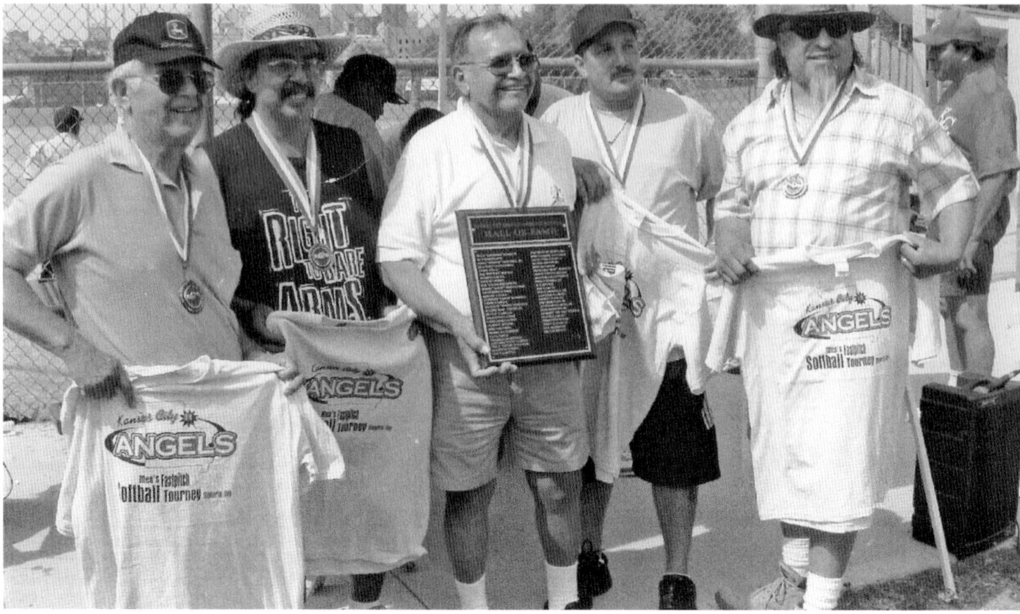

In May 2006, the Kansas City Mexican American Softball Hall of Fame recognized the following fast pitch softball players, from left to right: Harley Ponce, John García, unidentified, Steve García, and Chris González. The photograph was taken at the "Waxie" Hernández Fields on the grounds of Penn Valley Park in Kansas City, Missouri. These players all grew up in the Mexican American men's fast pitch leagues, and Chris González was a distinguished player with many teams during his career. (Courtesy of Chris González.)

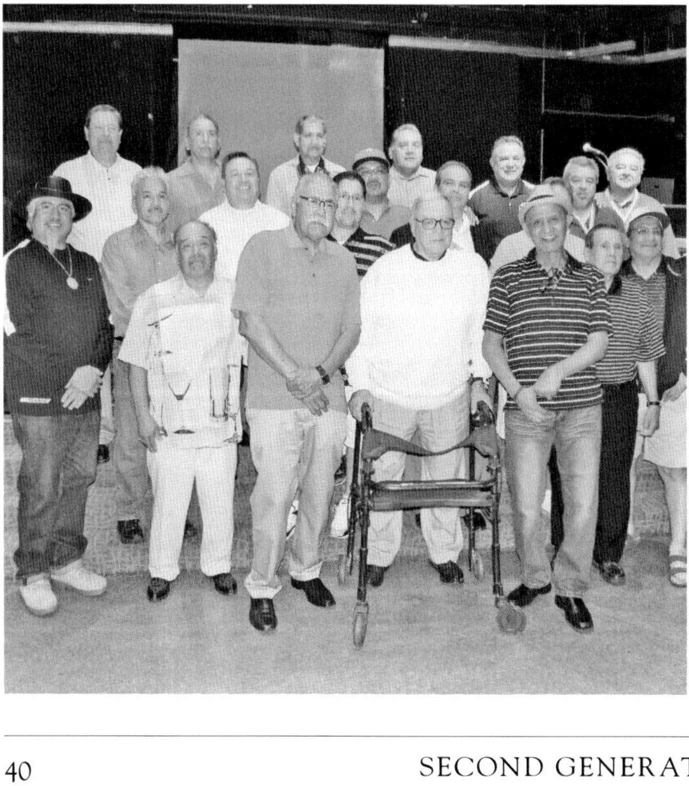

This photograph was taken at the 2016 Kansas City Mexican American Softball Hall of Fame reunion. From left to right are (first row) Larry García, Paul Vega, Pete Gómez, Paul Hernández Jr., Tony Talavera Jr., and Eddie Hernández; (second row) Chris González, Art Díaz Jr., Gil Solís Sr., Steve García, Manuel Hernández, Eddie Aguirre, Jim Reyes, and Mike Arroyo; (third row) Anthony Scott Gómez, Eddie Muñoz, Rick Sauceda, Gilbert Castro, Cris Medina, and Félix Arroyo. (Courtesy of Guadalupe Centers Inc.)

3

Third Generation Takes the Field

Persuading kids today to turn off their electronic devices and commit to baseball and softball practice is a major challenge. Finding young players willing to spend time honing their pitching, catching, and throwing skills is darned hard. Keeping the games alive and relevant among new generations of Mexican American players has been difficult given all the social distractions offered young people in the 21st century.

Nevertheless, while it is true that Mexican American baseball and fast pitch softball games may never return to the grandeur of prior generations, there are many concerted efforts in the Kansas City region to faithfully recruit young people to participate in the game. For example, Guadalupe Centers Inc., (GCI) of Kansas City, Missouri, is in its 99th year helping Mexican immigrants and Mexican Americans adjust to living in the United States while maintaining their cultural values, customs, and sense of ethnic identity. GCI has continuously sponsored youth baseball and fast pitch softball teams along with other sports. Its staff recognizes that baseball and softball teach boys and girls lifelong skills and life lessons that will enhance their futures.

American Legion Post 213 fielded the Argentine Eagles for over 40 years. Many Argentine Eagles players' children have followed in their footsteps. The Sauceda family has consistently provided generations of outstanding players to team rosters. When the Eagles folded in the 1990s, many of the players moved to other Mexican American teams. The Eagles Nest Field has recently been renovated for the primary purpose of attracting young people to this amazing game.

According to Cris Medina, the founding teams of the Mexican American Softball Association (MASA) of Kansas City were Los Aztecas, Los Amigos, Los Indios, Stateline Locos, Kansas City Pirates, and St. John the Divine of the Argentine district. These and other Mexican American teams practiced on ball fields in their barrios. They held annual tournaments and traveled to participate in tournaments against other Mexican American teams in cities across Kansas, Missouri, Nebraska, and Iowa.

The history of Mexican American baseball in Topeka, an hour west of Kansas City, is closely connected to that of Kansas City. Because of the Santa Fe Railroad, Mexican American ball players were sometimes transferred to the Argentine district repair center. The Tórrez, Gómez, and Escobar families were Santa Fe employees from Topeka who frequently played for and against Kansas City teams.

This chapter highlights the most recent generation of Mexican American baseball and softball teams and players and how they too are contributing to the extraordinary legacy of ball in the Kansas City region.

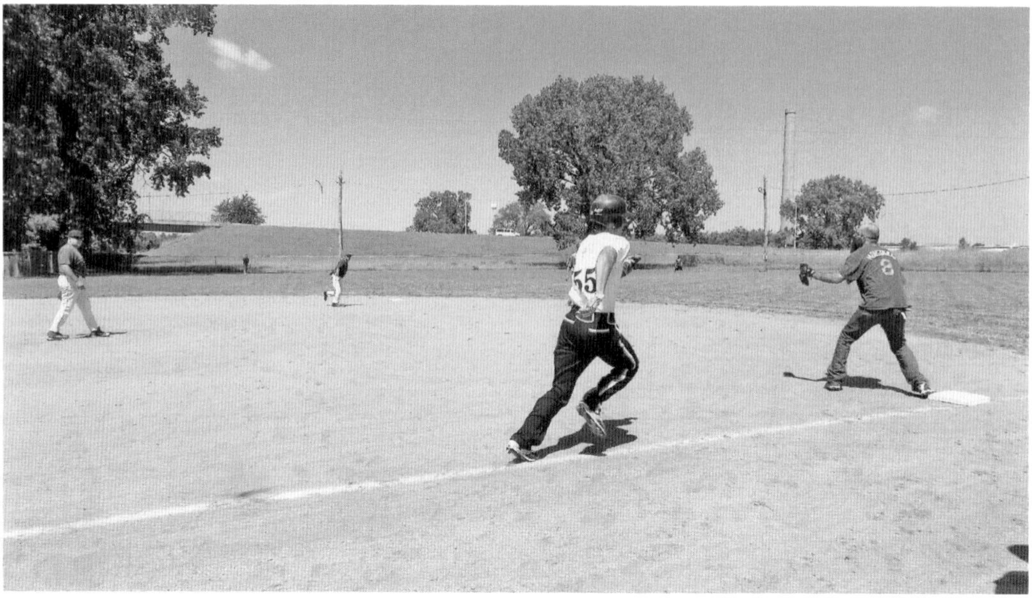

American Legion Post 213 was the home of the Argentine Eagles Vets Club men's fast pitch softball until the team folded in the 1990s. Over the last several decades, the field fell into considerable disrepair. It was the vision of Chris González to restore the field and open it once again to MASA league play, have youth practice, and host annual tournaments. With the assistance of his brother Erick González and Kari and Luís Madrigal, post commander funding was obtained to bring the field back to regular use. (Courtesy of Gene T. Chávez.)

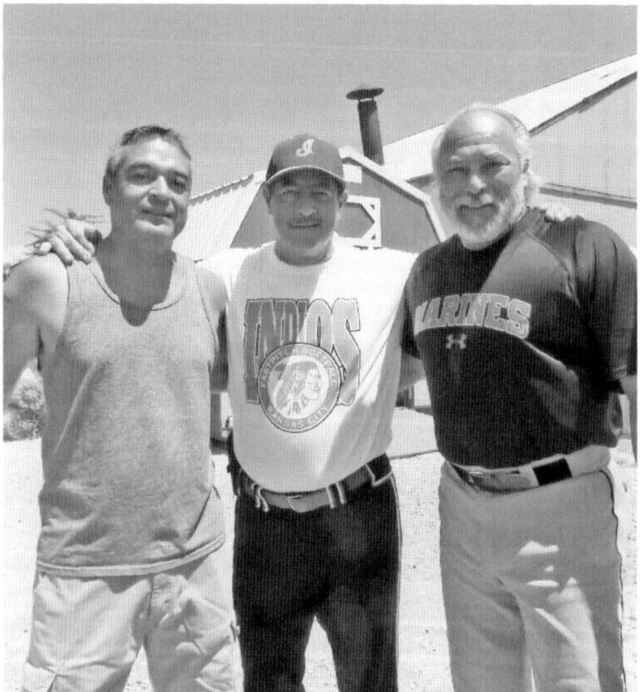

The Eagles Nest MASA League resumed play in the summer of 2017. These former players enjoying an afternoon of ball at the Nest are, from left to right, Mike Quiroga, Lou Ramírez, and Ray Foster. Mike Quiroga grew up at the Eagles Nest learning to play ball from his father, Tony Quiroga, and his uncles, who played for the Argentine Eagles starting in the 1940s. Mike's grandfather Melquíades Quiroga, a Mexican immigrant, played for Los Híeros of the Railways Ice Company. Melquíades's three sons, Peter, Tony, and Gregory, all played for the Argentine Eagles. (Courtesy of Gene T. Chávez.)

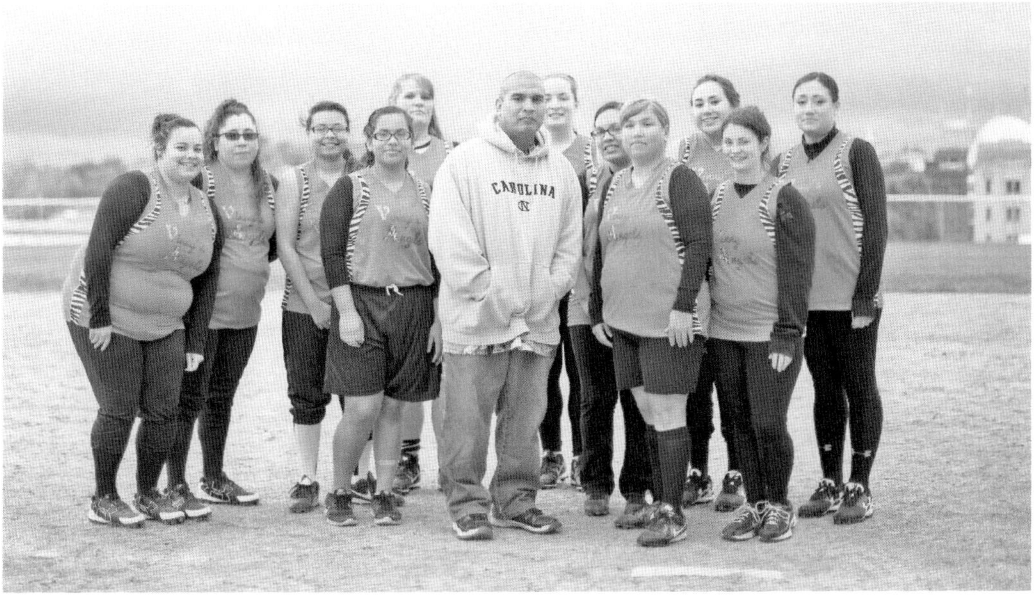

The women's softball team Vinny's Angels is pictured with Paul Briones Jr., a nephew of the late Anthony "Tony" J. Aguirre. Tony invested over 60 years in the West Side of Kansas City after starting his coaching career at 17 for Guadalupe Center Inc. Paul Briones Jr. was taken under Tony's wing and was nurtured in the game of baseball. Tony's influence led Briones to follow in his uncle's footsteps and develop the vibrant West Side Latina Softball League. (Courtesy of Deborah and Paul Briones Jr.)

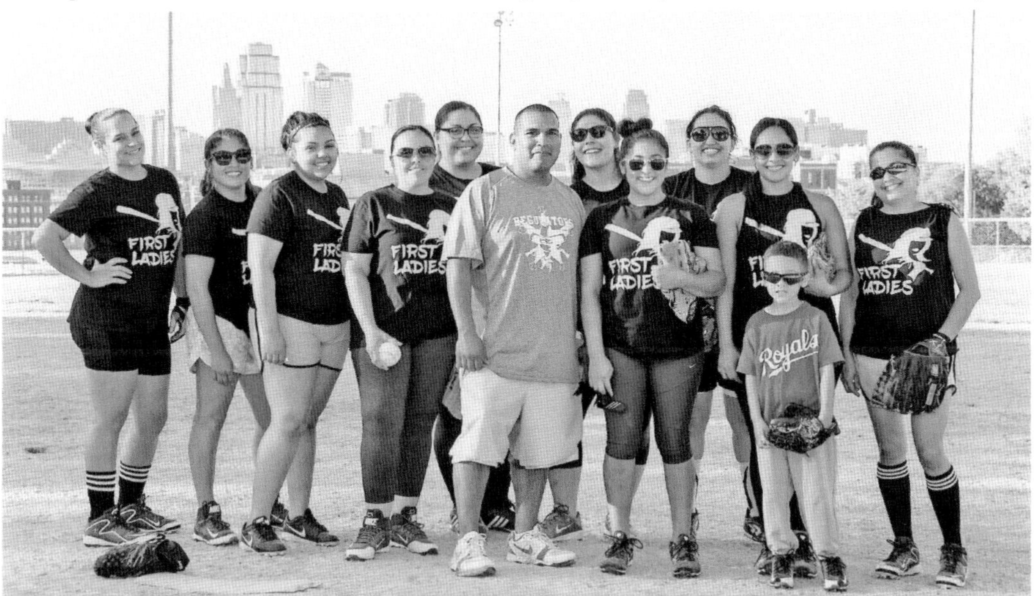

The First Ladies of the West Side Latina Softball League are, from left to right, (first row) Melonie Rojas, Jessica Gutíerrez, Marissa Alaviz, Sabrina Harris, Paul Briones Jr., Kristin Tinoco, Lauren Ríos, Tino Eredig, and Jeanette Hernández; (second row) Alicia ?, Kayla Ortega, and Catlyn Smith. (Courtesy of Deborah and Paul Briones. Jr)

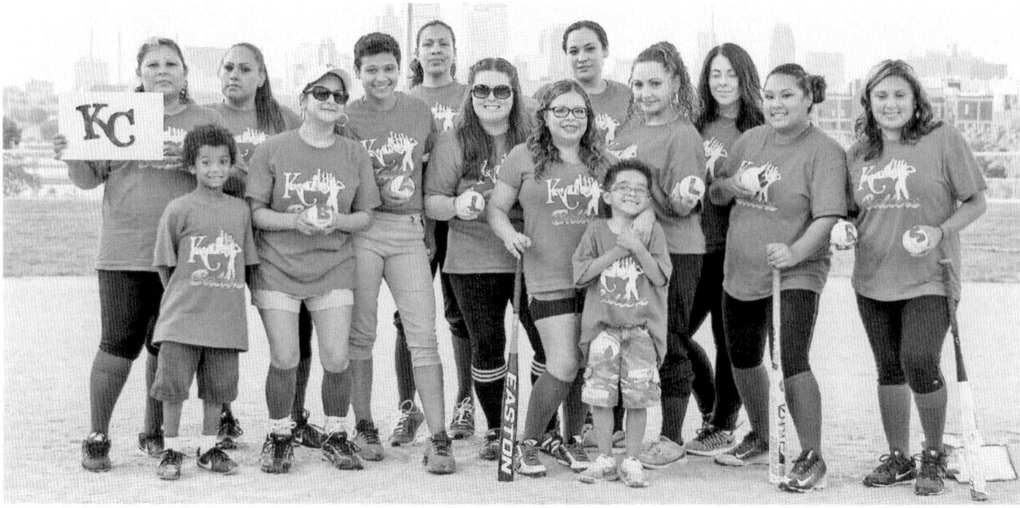

The Kansas City Ballers, a proud team in the West Side Latina Softball League, enjoy a day at the Paul "Waxie" Hernández Fields in Penn Valley Park. Downtown Kansas City provides a beautiful background. From left to right are (first row) unidentified, Irene Aguilera, Jessica Prado, Rachel Bell, Chela Millán, unidentified, Anna García, Karla Rodríguez, and Eina Rodríguez; (second row) Silvia Mora, Perla Longoria, Rachel Tyler, Ángel Harjo, and Emily Pérez. Regular league play and tournaments draw hundreds of family members and other supporters to the park throughout the summer. (Courtesy of Deborah and Paul Briones Jr.)

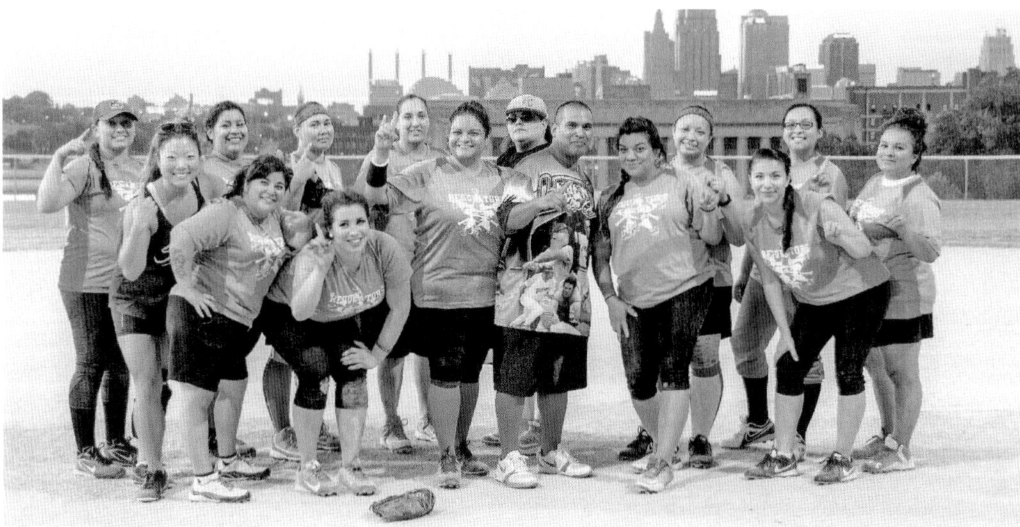

The Regulators, coached by Deborah Briones, are a mainstay of the league. From left to right are (first row) Teresa Boldridge, Rhiannon Mendez, Melissa Oropeza, Paul Briones Jr. (manager), Deborah Briones, and Sandra De Peralta; (second row) Alicia Marcille, Hyeyin Rwon, Angie Tinoco, Jennifer Amayo, Yolanda Ramírez, Rosemarie Peola Washington, Ángel Cervantes, and Sidonia Hernández Moreno. The team, despite managing family, school, and careers, holds together because of its love for the community and its long tradition of baseball and softball. (Courtesy of Deborah and Paul Briones Jr.)

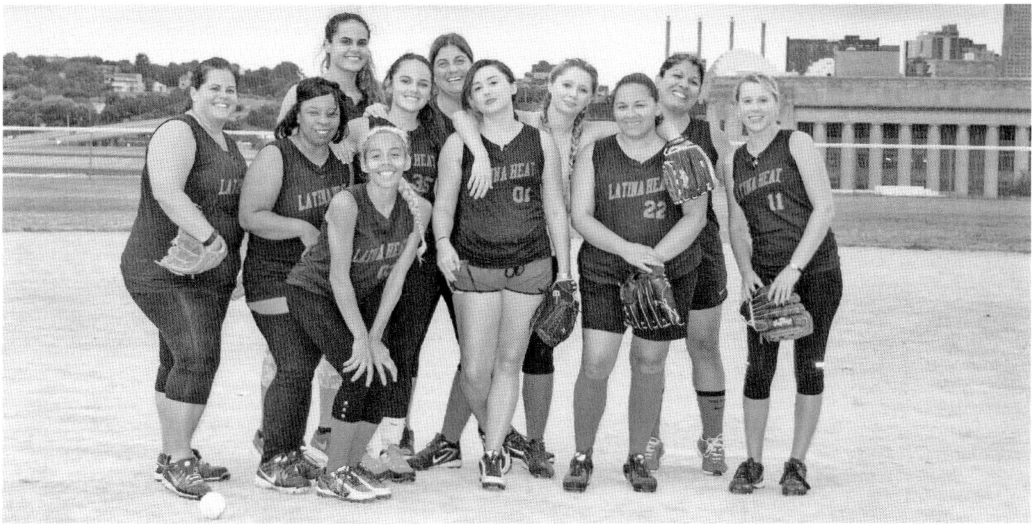

The Latina Heat of the West Side Latina Softball League is shown at the Paul "Waxie" Hernández Fields. In the background at left are the hills of the famed West Side Barrio. Many Mexican American baseball and softball teams over the last century originated from this neighborhood. From left to right are (first row) Jackie Guerra, Angela Vargas, Tina Witherspoon, Maddie Nesselhuf, Candace Moreno, and coach Angela González; (second row), Makinzie Nesslhuf, Terri Collins, Brandi Gutíerrez, Tammie Márquez, and Lizzie Esparza. (Courtesy of Deborah and Paul Briones Jr.)

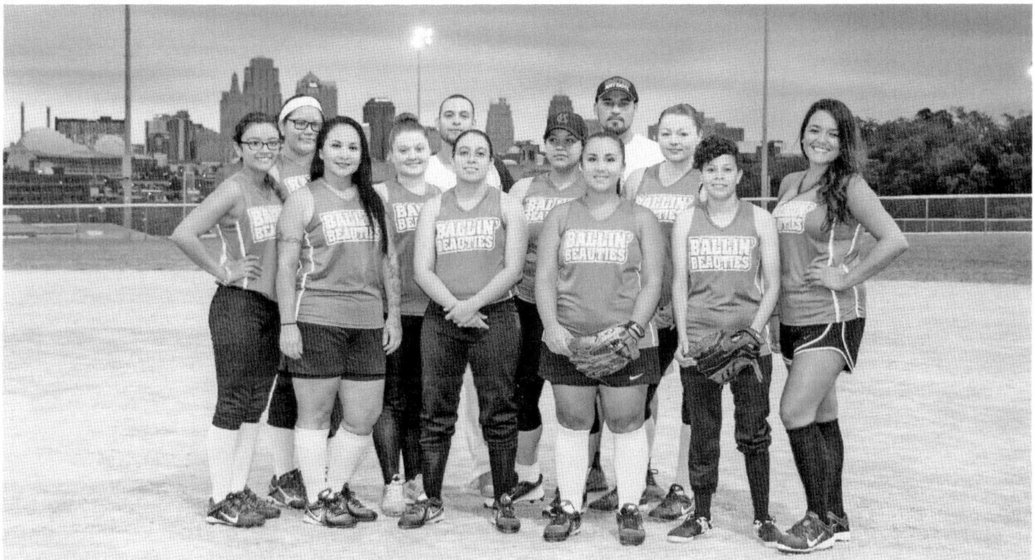

The Ballin' Beauties of the West Side Latina Softball League play throughout the summer. With their games usually scheduled on the weekends, the ball fields take on a fiesta atmosphere, and many families and friends gather to enjoy the competition. From left to right are (first row) Mariah Sánchez, coach Jacquie Gallo, Gabriella González, Stefanie Lockhart, Marissa González, and Amanda Ruíz; (second row) Kristiana Delgado, Taylor Duffy, Ariana White, Ricardo González, David García, and Destiny Busby. (Courtesy of Deborah and Paul Briones Jr.)

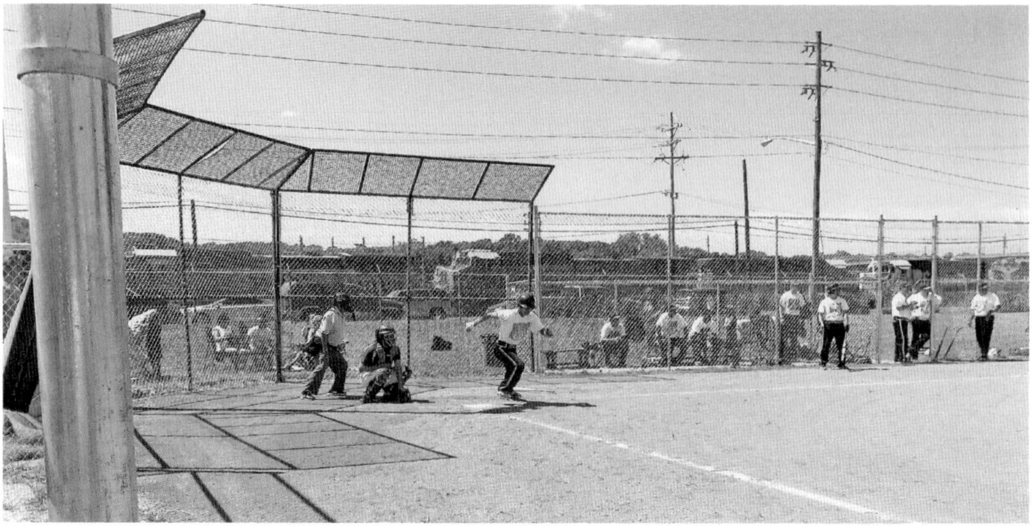

After several years and great effort to obtain Wyandotte County government funds, along with private fundraising by Chris and Eric González and the Women's Auxiliary of the American Legion Post 213, led by Irene González, the Eagles Nest field was in use for the 2017 softball season. In this photograph, the Kansas City Indios and the Kansas City Bandidos battle it out on a field that feels like home. In the summer of 2018, the Eagles Nest will host many more teams and tournaments. (Courtesy of Gene T. Chávez.)

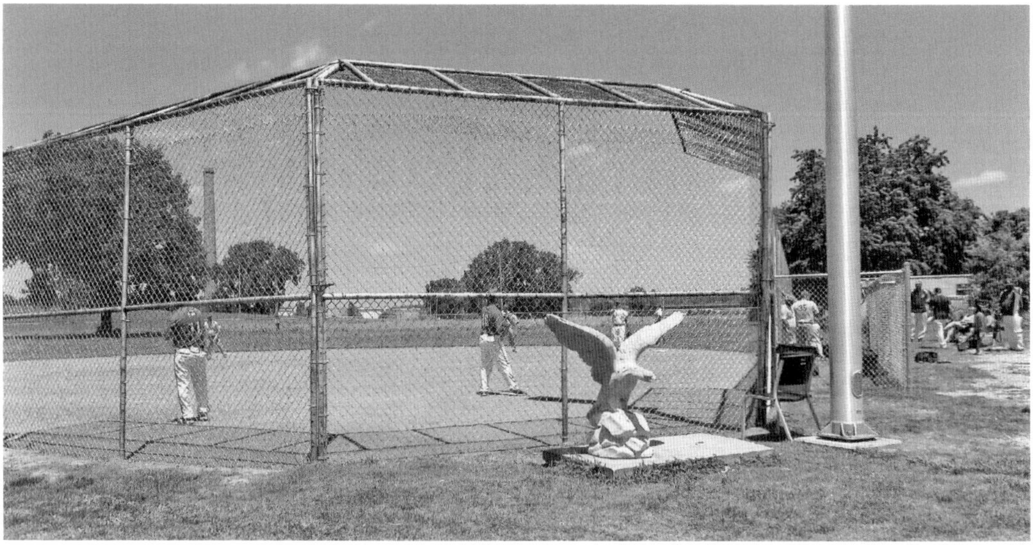

Starting in April 2017, four Mexican American men's fast pitch softball teams played in the Mexican American Softball Association: the Kansas City Indios, Stateline Locos, Kansas City Angels, and Kansas City Bandidos. The teams played at the newly renovated Eagles Nest in Argentine, Kansas. MASA league play lasted throughout the early summer and ended in a Saturday tournament on July 28. Plans for continued improvements to the field include bleachers and field lights to extend the hours of operation and usefulness. In this photograph, the Indios and the Angels enjoy the new field. (Courtesy of Gene T. Chávez.)

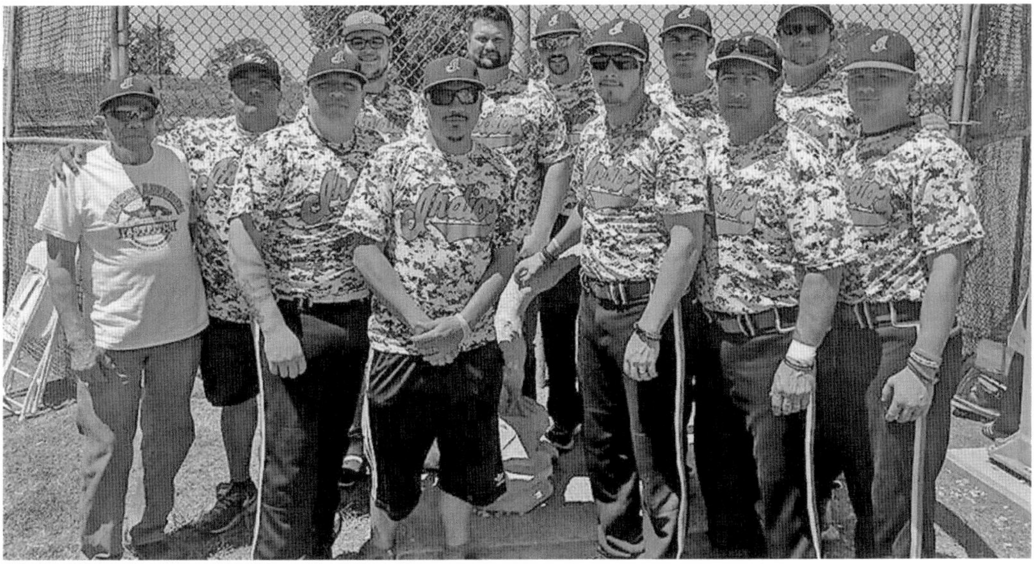

The Kansas City Indios men's fast pitch softball team have been playing since the 1970s. The first Indios took pride in their team name, because their hometown team was the Juarez Indios. They also take great joy in four generations of García family members who have helped develop a team known for winning throughout the region. Indios at the renovated Eagles Nest on July 28, 2017, are, from left to right, (first row) Adán García, Rico García, Lou Ramírez Jr., Lou Ramírez Sr., and Dominic García; (second row) Arturo García Sr., Louis Oropeza, Joséph García, Brandon Sisk, Arturo García III, Jordan García, and Jaime García Sr. (Courtesy of Gene T. Chávez.)

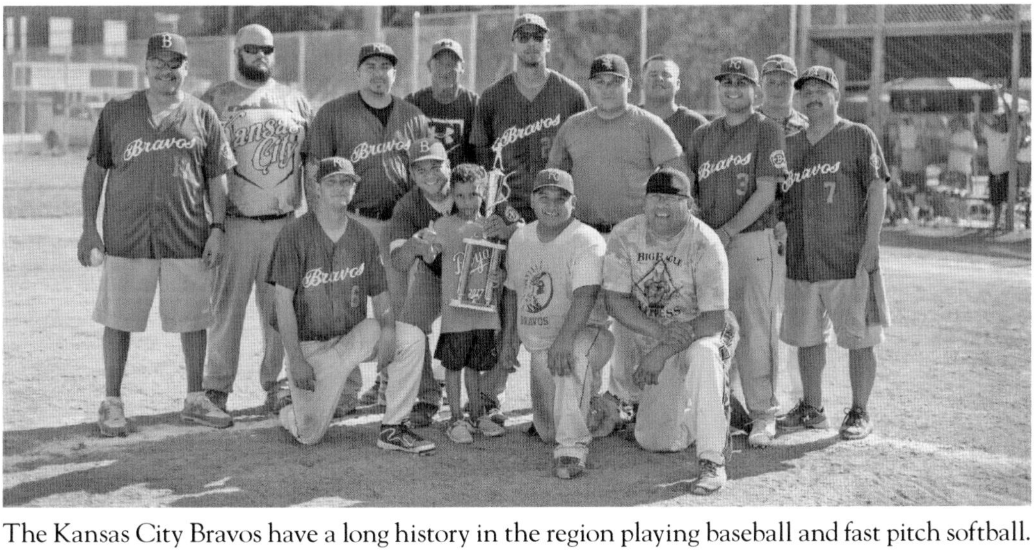

The Kansas City Bravos have a long history in the region playing baseball and fast pitch softball. Originally formed in the West Side in the 1940s, the team was a dominant force in the Mexican American leagues. In July 2017, members of the reconstituted Bravos are, from left to right, (first row) four unidentified and Tony Díaz; (second row) Robert Olvera, unidentified, Eric García, Tony Peeples, Mike Aguirre, Brian Gómez, Julien Miller, Thomas García, Nick Wilson, and Jim Reyes. (Courtesy of Gene T. Chávez.)

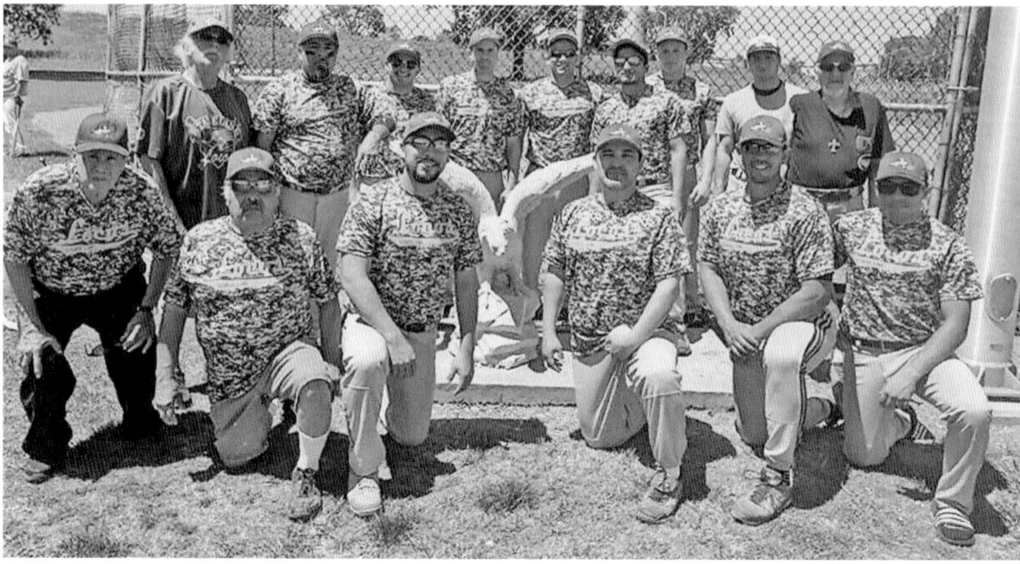

The Stateline Locos have a long history playing men's fast pitch softball. In 1947, Carlos Móntez got a group of young men together at Shawnee Park in Kansas City, Kansas. In this 2017 photograph at the Eagles Nest Tournament, the players are, from left to right, (first row) Tony Talavera Sr., Larry García, Lalo Sandoval, Anthony Oropeza Jr., Greg Escobar Jr., and ? Ramírez; (second row) John Hernández, George Frías, David Frías, Charles Herrington, Manuel Talavera, Ralph Sánchez, Nick Wilson, Andrew Schider, and Albert Alcanter. (Courtesy of Gene T. Chávez.)

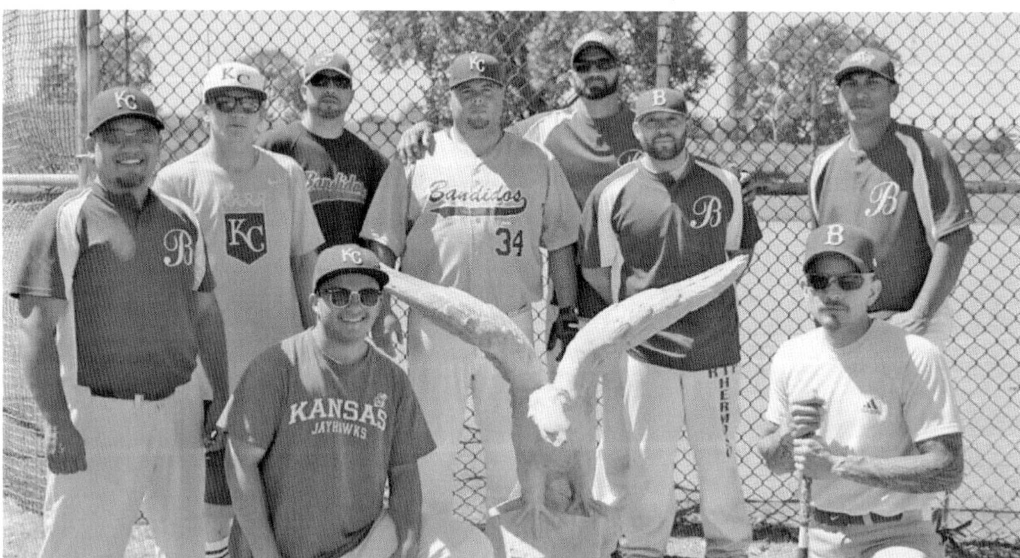

Los Bandidos started in 2008 and competed in many summer men's fast pitch softball tournaments around the region. The hope is to strengthen the team in the near future in order to compete successfully in the MASA League. Players at the 2017 Eagles Nest Tournament are, from left to right, (first row) Gabriel Frías and Danny Trejo; (second row) Hugo Melgoza, two unidentified, Anthony Viegas, Tomás Paez, unidentified, and Vic Hernández Jr. (Courtesy of Gene T. Chávez.)

Brittany García is playing at the Paul "Waxie" Hernández Fields in Kansas City at Penn Valley Park. The occasion was the second annual Los Sabios Commemorative Games sponsored by the Kansas City Museum and MASA in 2016. Teams of the West Side Latina Softball League were invited to play, honoring two legendary sports figures: Waxie Hernández and Anthony "Tony" Aguirre. García is wearing a T-shirt that pays tribute to Hernández. (Courtesy of Michael Alvarado.)

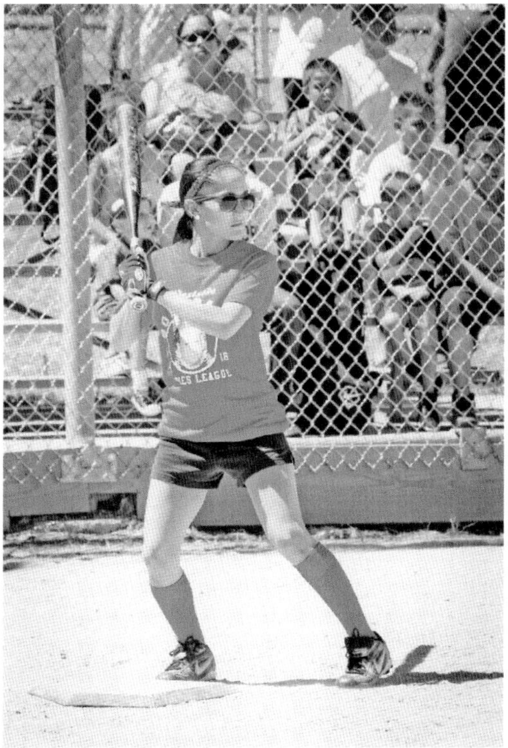

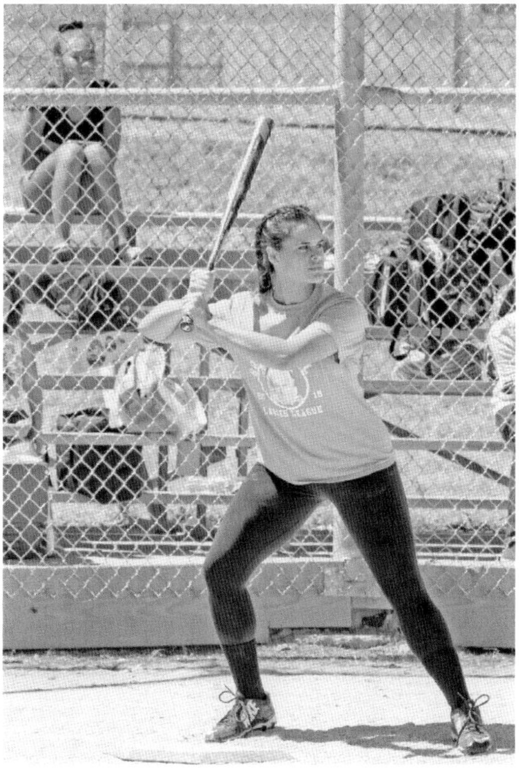

The West Side Latina Softball League was formed by Paul Briones Jr. and his family. Their desire is to honor the wishes of his uncle, Anthony "Tony" Aguirre, who asked Paul to keep the recreational sports ongoing. Aguirre had dedicated his life to helping the Mexican American youth of Kansas City engage in sports. Paul promised his uncle that he would do what he could to keep his legacy alive. Makenzie Nesselhuf wears a T-shirt honoring Aguirre. (Courtesy of Michael Alvarado.)

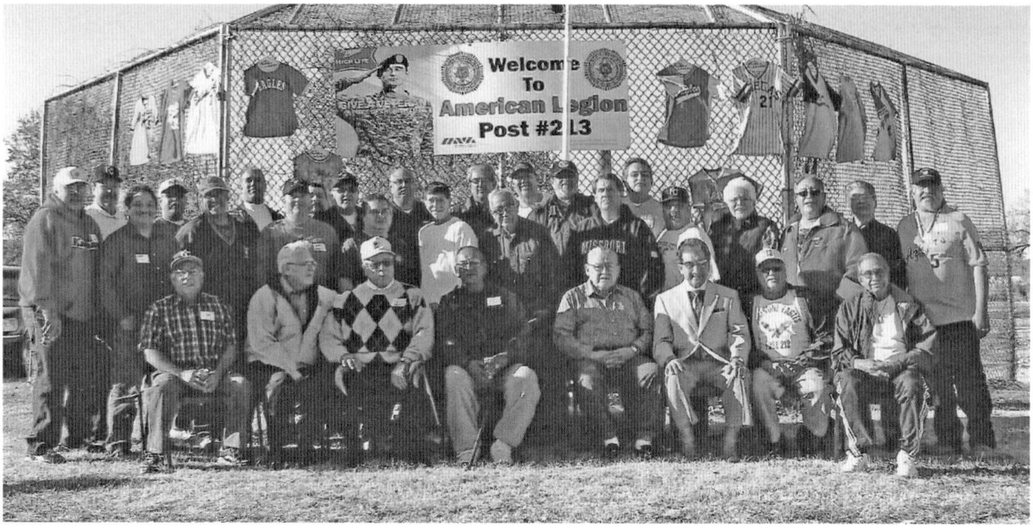

This 2013 reunion of Mexican American fast pitch softball players was held at American Legion Post 213 in Argentine. From left to right are (first row) John Chacón, Harley Ponce, Pete Gómez, Joe Moreno, Frank Solís Sr., Joe Velásquez, Tony Quiroga, and Martín Pérez; (second row) Danny Salas, Manuel Jaso, Frank Solís Jr., Harry Medellín, Eddie Madrigal, Brian Padilla, unidentified, Tommy García, Larry García, Ted Ponce, Frank Guerra, Ray Fernández, and Chris González; (third row) Anthony Scott Gómez, Mario Escobar, Sylvester Bustamante Jr., Tony Talavera Jr., Gilbert Castro, Charlie Rivera, Tony De La Torre, Richard Campos, and Frank Oropeza Sr. (Courtesy of Chris González.)

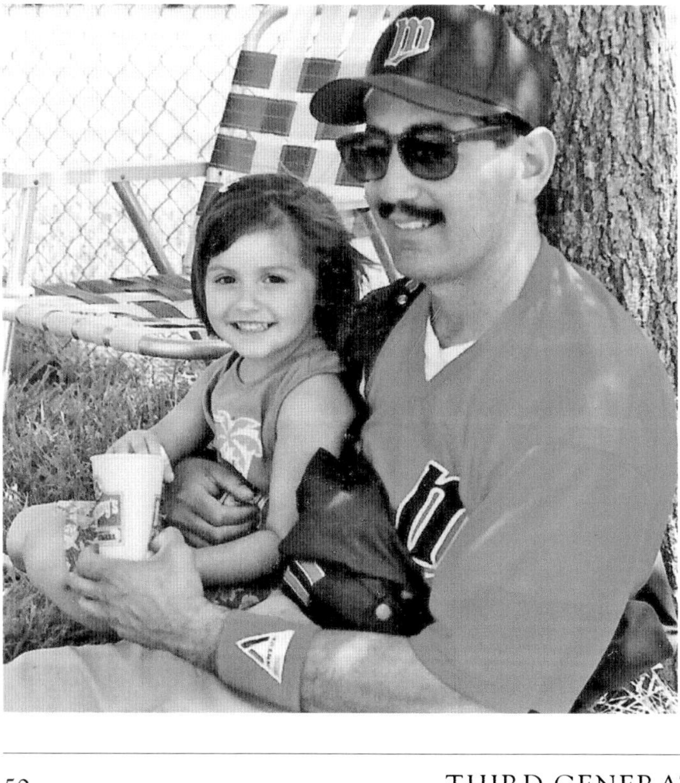

People consistently remark that the closeness, caring, and camaraderie experienced playing Mexican American baseball and fast pitch softball was much like that of family. Ali Solís, shown with Vince Ramos at the Newton Annual Tournament, says that being at the games was like being with family. So many of the players felt like her big brothers. The hometown games and the regional tournament brought Mexican Americans together and helped develop a sense of community solidarity. (Courtesy of Ali Solís.)

John Wayne Proctor was born in 1961 to Michaela "Mickey" Tórrez and Ed Proctor. David, his brother, was born in 1968. They grew up in the Oakland barrio in Topeka, where their uncle Mike Tórrez grew up. The brothers both played for Allen County Community College in Iola, Kansas, after graduating from Topeka public schools. John was drafted by the Philadelphia Phillies in 1981 and played two seasons in the minors. (Courtesy of Michaela Tórrez.)

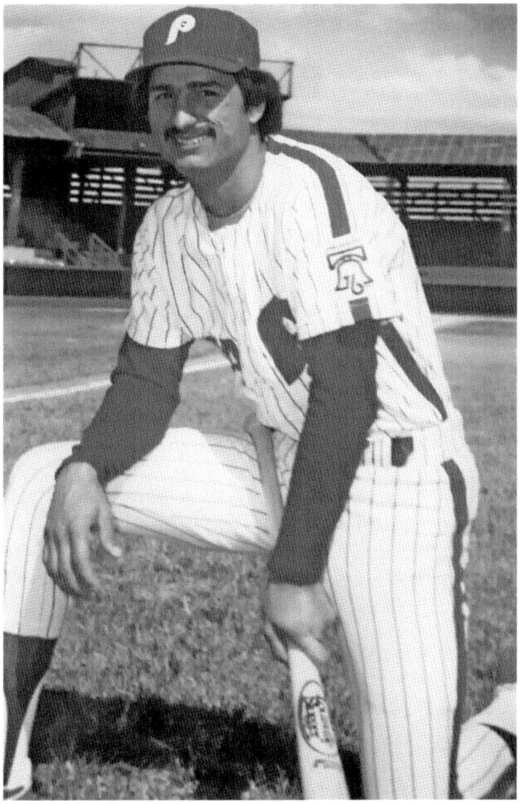

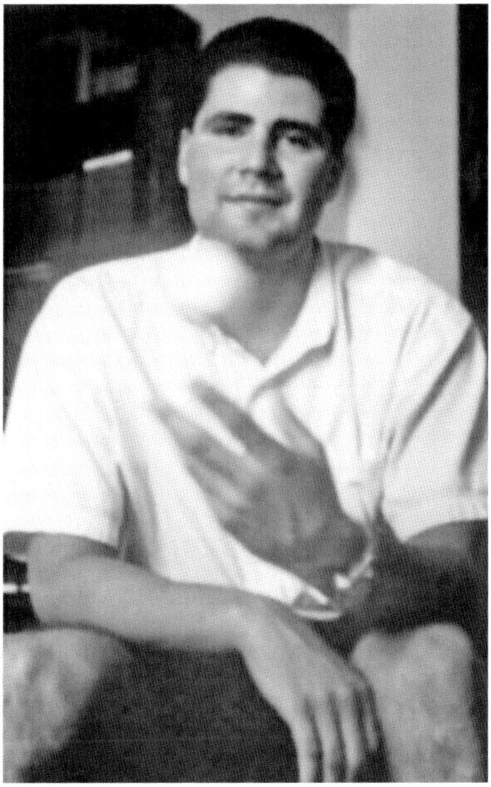

David Proctor was drafted right out of Topeka High School by the Los Angeles Dodgers in 1986 and was signed by the New York Mets in 1988. He and his older brother John are nephews of Topeka hometown hero Mike Tórrez and were inspired to follow in his footsteps. David pitched four seasons (1988–1992) in the Mets organization, going 17-18 with a 3.18 ERA. His best season was arguably in 1989, when he was 7-6 with a 2.36 ERA over 22 games (21 starts) in A ball. (Courtesy of Michaela Tórrez.)

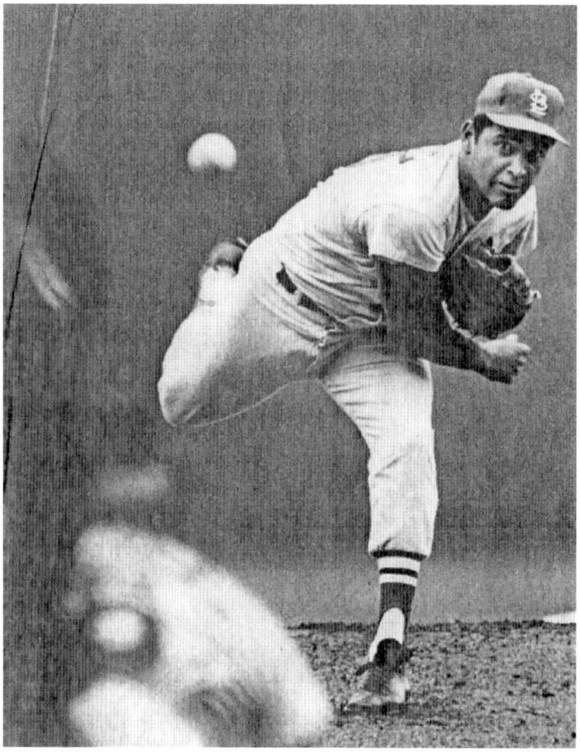

Mike Tórrez grew up near the Santa Fe Railroad yards in the Oakland barrio of Topeka, where many Mexican immigrant families settled. Mike's father found employment with the railroad. To supplement the family income, the eight Tórrez kids worked at local truck farms and gasoline stations, and the girls worked as domestics cleaning others' homes. As a kid, Mike picked potatoes for local farmers and got in plenty of practice pitching by slinging potatoes at targets in the fields. Tórrez was inducted into the Kansas Sports Hall of Fame in 2008, and the Latin American International Sports Hall of Fame in 2018. (Courtesy of Mike Tórrez.)

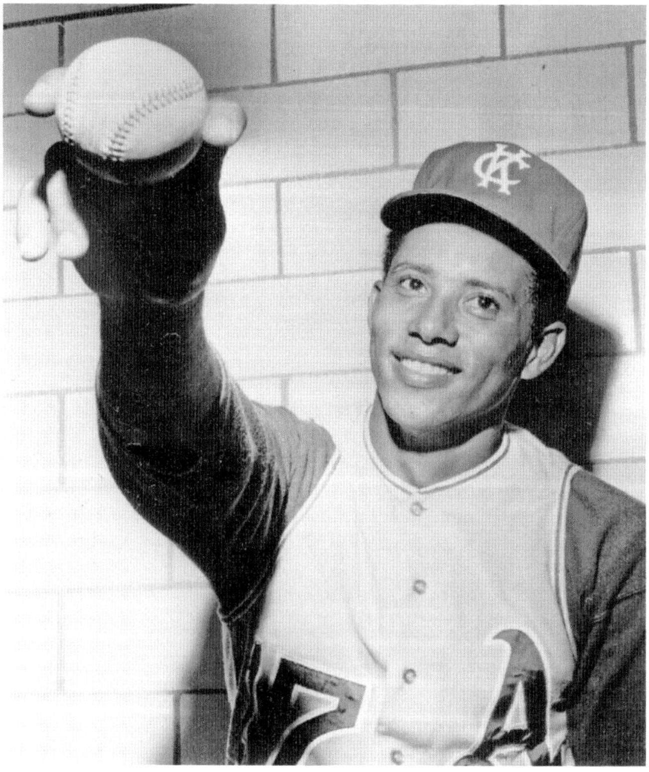

Pitcher Diego Pablo Seguí González was born in Holguín, Cuba, in 1937. He was a forkball specialist who played professionally in Cuba at the time of Castro's takeover. Along with other Cuban players, he was given an ultimatum by Castro to either play for a Cuban national team or leave the country. He decided to leave. He made his major-league debut on April 12, 1962, with the Kansas City Athletics. He went on to pitch for the Washington Senators, Oakland A's, Seattle Pilots, St. Louis Cardinals, Boston Red Sox, and Seattle Mariners. His MLB career lasted for 16 seasons from 1962 to 1977. (Courtesy of Emily Seguí.)

Pictured here are Emily Sauceda and Diego Seguí. Her family was composed of Mexican immigrants who boasted a long line of baseball and fast pitch stars. Upon coming to Kansas City in 1962 to play for the Kansas City Athletics, Seguí connected with the Spanish-speaking communities of the city. He and Emily married in 1963. The Seguís raised their four children in Kansas City, Kansas. Their son David made his debut with the Baltimore Orioles in 1990, continuing to play with various major-league teams until 2004. The other children competed in little leagues and at the high school level. (Courtesy of Emily Seguí.)

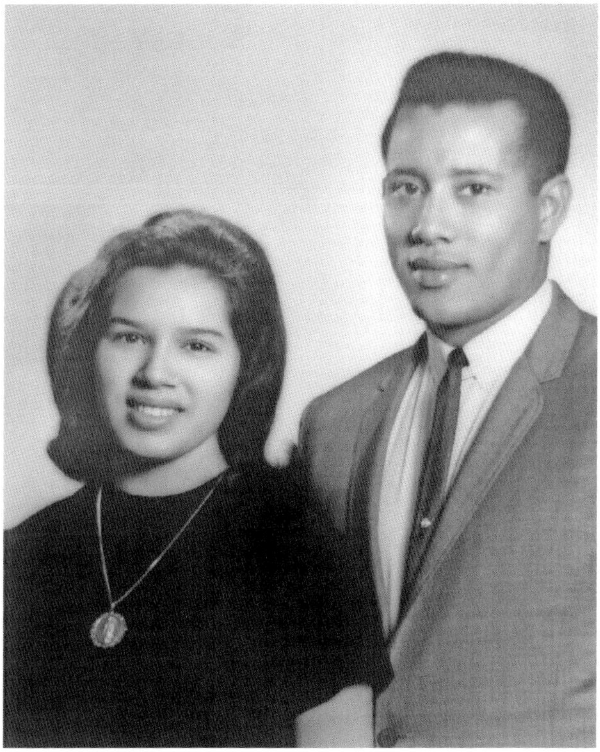

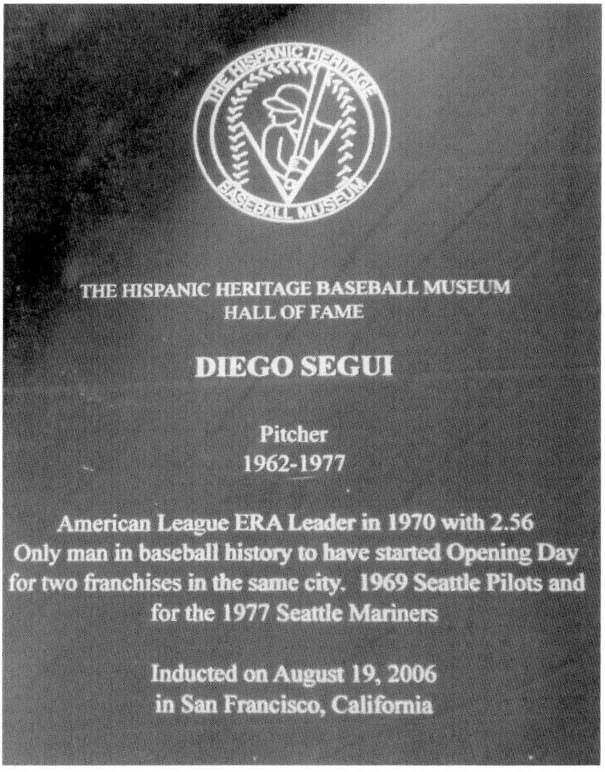

Diego Seguí was inducted into the Hispanic Heritage Hall of Fame in 2006. Because of the low salaries offered by MLB teams in the 1960s and his growing family, Seguí found it necessary to play in the Latin American leagues in the winter. He played in Venezuela in 1962, in Mexico and Puerto Rico from 1963 to 1966, and then again in Venezuela from 1966 to 1983. His unusual pitching stance, the speed of his fastball, and the effectiveness of his forkball earned him many accolades throughout Latin America. (Courtesy of Emily Seguí.)

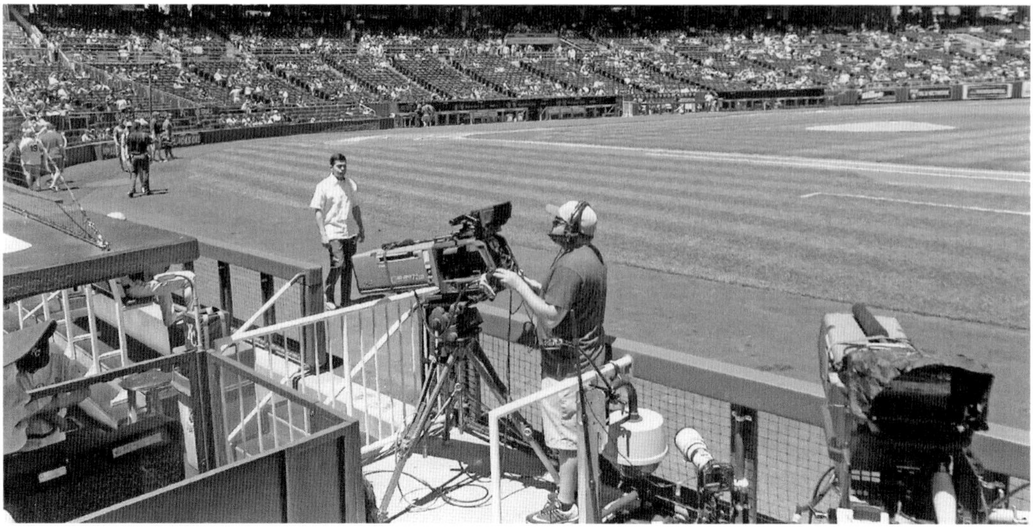

On June 24, 2017, the Mexican consul in Kansas City, Alfonso Navarro-Bernachi, was invited to throw out the first pitch at the Hispanic Heritage Day at Kauffman Stadium, home of the American League Kansas City Royals. The Royals organization and Major League Baseball have sponsored this day for several years and include fan giveaways, musical concerts, and Mexican food specialties and contests. (Courtesy of Gene T. Chávez.)

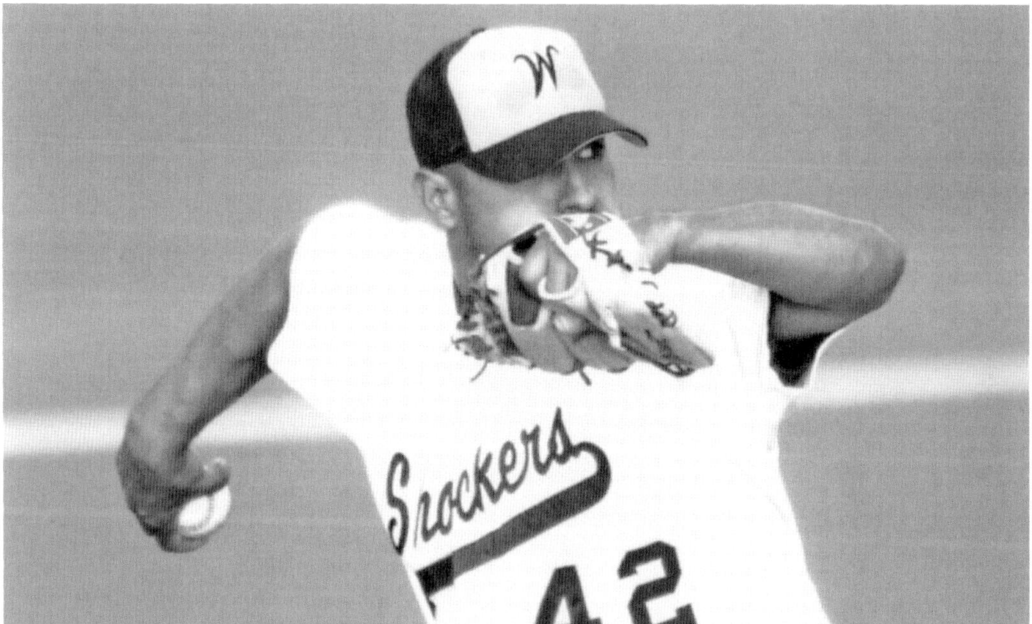

John Tetuan, from the Oakland barrio in Topeka, is the cousin of noted softball pitcher John Tórrez Jr. and major leaguer Mike Tórrez. An all-state high school football player and state champion in both football and baseball, John was an all-American pitcher for Wichita State before playing minor-league ball in the Colorado Rockies organization. Tetuan coaches baseball at Topeka West High School. (Courtesy of John Tórrez Jr.)

Baseball great Diego Seguí lives with his wife, Emily, in a beautiful ranch-style home built by their son David in western Wyandotte County, Kansas. Seguí says that it reminds him of home in Cuba, where he grew up on his parents' farm. In this photograph at his home in June 2015, he sits in the memorabilia room maintained by his loving wife, Emily. The baseball glove he is holding is like another one of his that is on loan to the Smithsonian National Museum of American History exhibition The Nation We Built Together. (Courtesy of Bruce Mathews.)

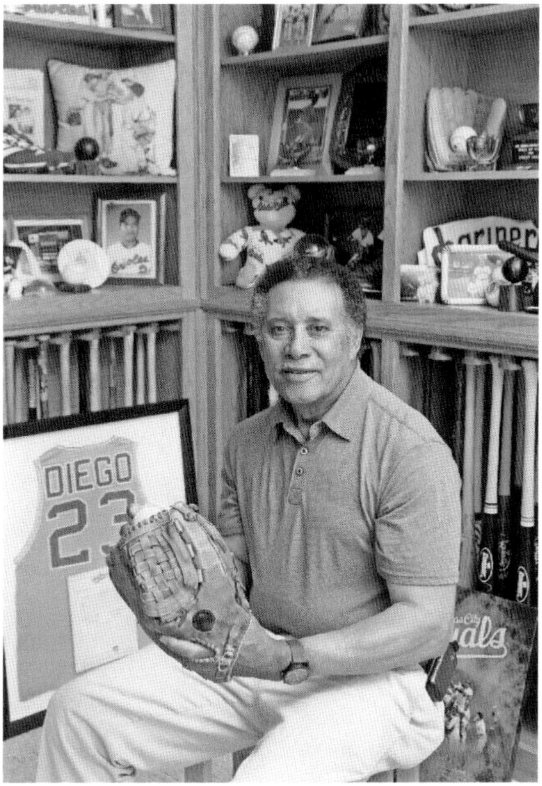

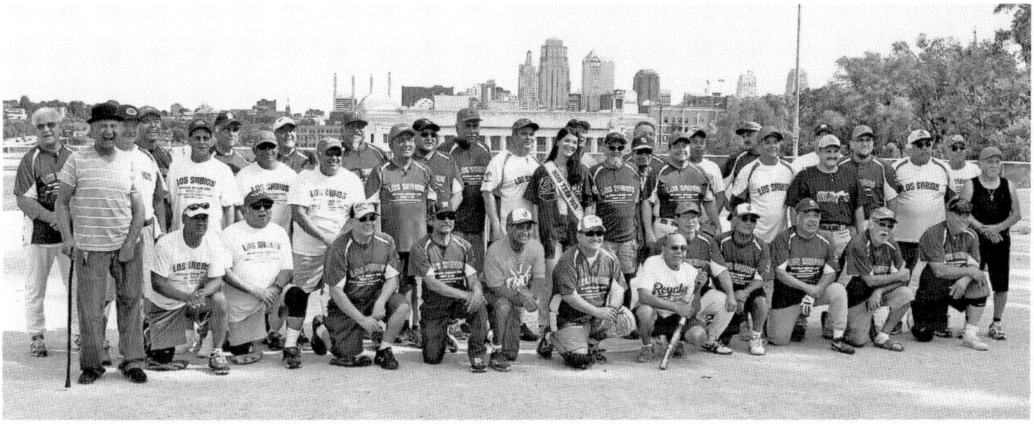

The third annual Los Sabios Games were held at the "Waxie" Hernández Fields on August 12, 2017. From left to right are (first row) Paul Hernández Jr., Edward Ramírez, Ronnie Escobar, Gator ?, Barney Torres, Steve Jaso, Manuel Jaso, Richard Moreno, Jesse García, Ray Jaso, Larry García, John Hernández, and Harry Medellín; (second row) Hank Carrillo, Anthony Scott Gómez, Brian Padilla, Richard Toledo, Richard Escobar, George Jaso, Sophía Domínguez (Miss Teen Missouri 2016), Albert Alcanter, Art Ruíz, Mike Quiroga, Jimmy Reyes, Anquilleno Villegas, Danny Salas, and Ralph Pacheco; (third row) Dave Rodríguez, John Tórrez Jr., Ruben López, Chris González, Gilbert Castro, Paul Vega, Eddie Aguirre, unidentified, Gary Estrada, Javier Marrón, J.D. Amayo, Ron Porras, and Mario Escobar. (Courtesy of Michael Alvarado.)

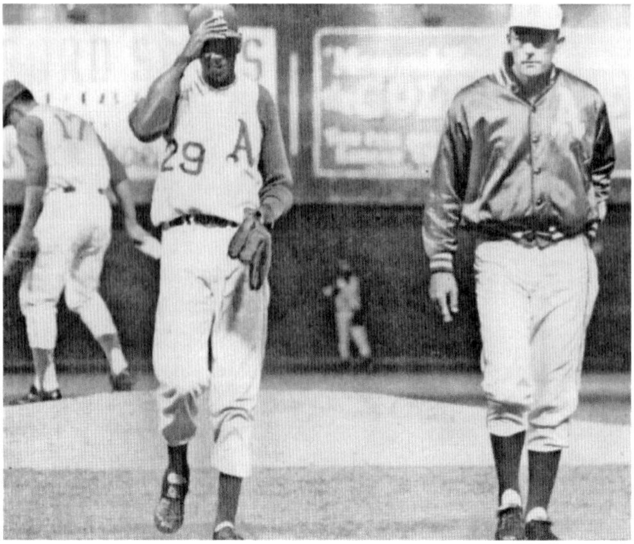

In 1965, the Kansas City Athletics brought former Negro Leagues star Satchel Paige out of retirement to pitch three innings. After the third inning, Paige was relieved by Diego Seguí (No. 17, on mound). Seguí considers this a highlight of his career. On that night, September 25, 1965, on a major league mound at Municipal Stadium in Kansas City, the paths of the Mexican American Leagues, the Negro Leagues, and the major leagues met. (Courtesy of Emily Seguí.)

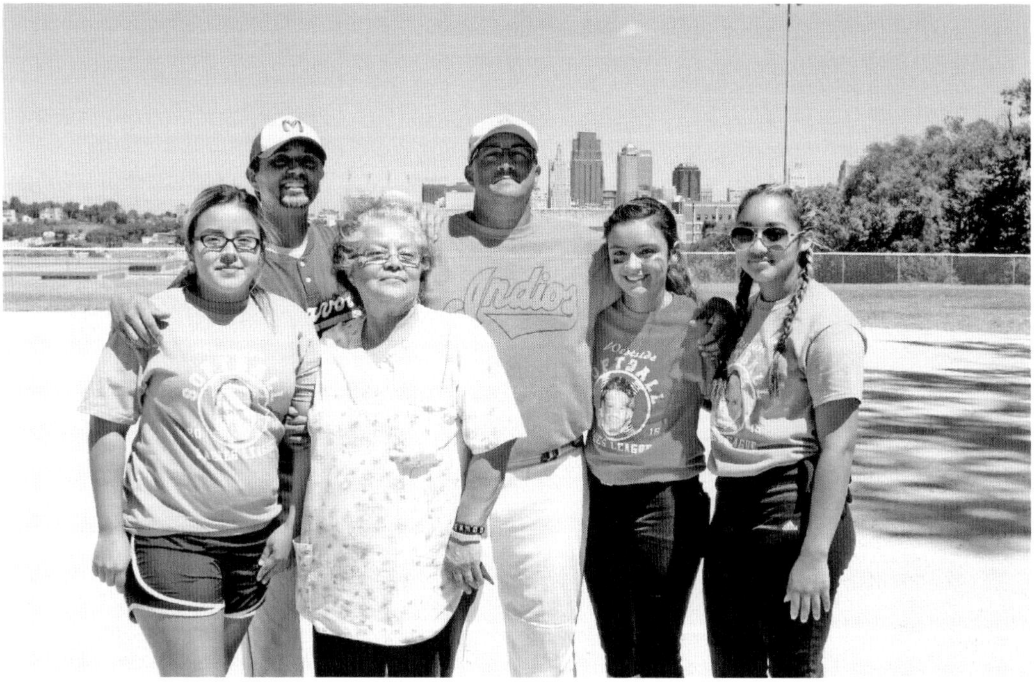

The Kansas City Museum started an annual tradition of hosting commemorative community softball games in 2015. The 2016 Los Sabios Games at the "Waxie" Hernández Fields were part of its collaboration with the Smithsonian's national collecting initiative entitled Latinos in Baseball: In the Barrios and the Big Leagues. This photograph shows the involvement that Mexican American families continue to have in baseball and softball. The Oropeza family are, from left to right, (first row) Marissa Sánchez, Lupe Escareño Oropeza, Mariah Sánchez, and Andrea Oropeza; (second row) Anthony Oropeza and Louis Oropeza. (Courtesy of Michael Alvarado.)

4

Newton Softball Tournament

In 1905, a newspaper in Newton, Kansas, reported Mexican laborers passing through town. Later, workers recruited by the Santa Fe Railroad were provided housing in Newton. The housing units were christened El Ranchito (the little ranch) by the residents, who later built Our Lady of Guadalupe Church in 1920. Newton's baseball roots can be traced directly to the Ranchito and its 1930s Cuauhtémocs team.

Throughout the United States, young Mexican American men and women set aside their bats and gloves while serving in the military and defense plants during World War II. After the war, softball replaced baseball as the most popular form of ball. Newton's team reorganized and participated in the competitive yet segregated city league. The Our Lady of Guadalupe team was often referred to as the Mexican Catholics in box scores. On July 3, 1946, a local press story reported a daylight softball tournament sponsored by the Mexican Catholics at Athletic Park for the Fourth of July weekend. Two local clubs and teams from Topeka, Wichita, and Hutchinson participated in the single-elimination event. Though the first tournament was small, it has grown each year with the exception of two, earning the title "Home of the Oldest Fastball Tournament in the Country." In 2018, the tournament will celebrate its 70th successful year.

The early tournaments were held at Athletic Park until a new ballpark was built on the property of Our Lady of Guadalupe in 1963. At that point, the tournament was managed and guided by the Holy Name organization. In 1995, the Fourth of July softball tournament left the sponsorship of Holy Name and reorganized as the Newton Mexican American Athletic Club, returning to Athletic Field, where it continues to this day. The successful tournament extended beyond the borders of Kansas by inviting teams from Oklahoma, Missouri, Colorado, Nebraska, and Texas.

Extraordinary players and powerful teams excited and delighted admiring fans by showcasing their flair on the field, high-octane hustle and bustle, mastery of the game, sensational home runs, breathtaking throws, and daring base-running skills. The fierce pitching duels, colossal home runs, and jarring collisions at the plate make for profound memories in the hearts and minds of those lucky enough to have witnessed these remarkable athletes, coaches, umpires, scorekeepers, sportswriters, batboys, and ground crews.

Besides the games, the tournament serves as the annual Fourth of July reunion, bringing together generations of families, friends, fans, ballplayers, and countless others to reconnect, reminisce, laugh, drink, dance, and enjoy being part of this magnificent tradition. Never far away are the everlasting gratitude and fond recollections of the original Ranchito inhabitants of so long ago.

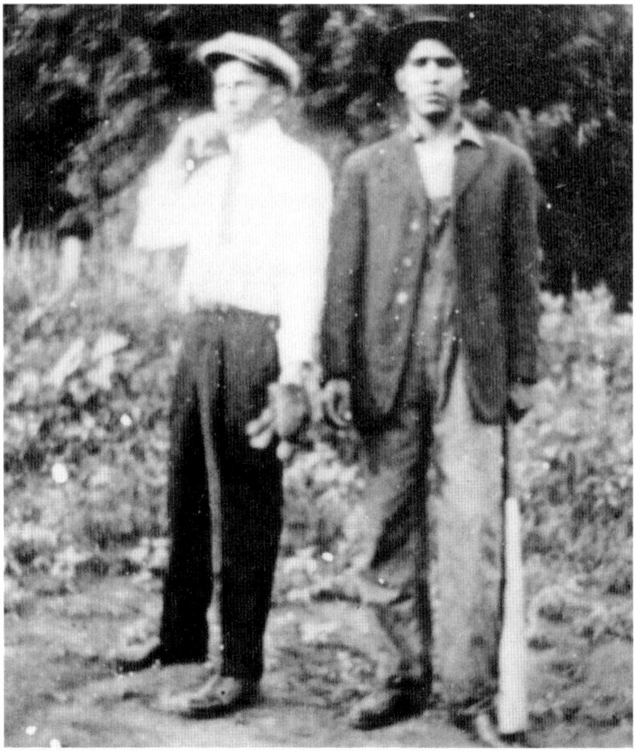

Raymundo Jaso (left) and an unidentified teammate pose with a bat and gloves in 1919. Baseball was adopted throughout the United States, and Raymundo and his brother, Magdaleno, participated while growing up in El Paso, Texas. After moving to Newton, Raymundo continued his love of the game by organizing teams to play against each other. In 1927, he chose a team of outstanding players to compete against Wichita teams. Raymundo later played with the 1930s Cuauhtémocs, coached for the 1940s Mexican Catholics, and helped establish the Fourth of July softball tournament. (Courtesy of Raymunda Jaso Flores.)

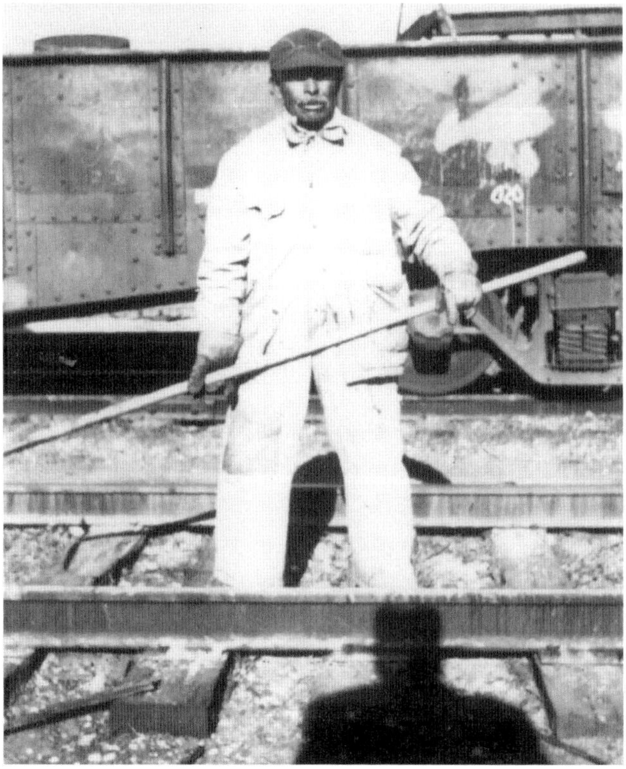

Canuto Jaso, patriarch of the Jaso baseball dynasty, arrived in Newton in 1919 with his sons Magdaleno and Raymundo, where they found work with the Santa Fe Railroad. Canuto coached his sons in early teams playing against Wichita teams. Magdaleno played first base, while Raymundo played second base. Raymundo later played with the 1935 Cuauhtémocs, and after he quit playing, he continued coaching the Mexican Catholics and worked as a force in the annual tournament's formation and success. Canuto Jaso's many descendants have continued playing and organizing the annual tournament over the decades. (Courtesy of Raymunda Jaso Flores.)

Railroad companies served as a factor in bringing Mexicans to the United States, especially to Newton. Local communities began adopting "Americanization" programs to better assimilate these new arrivals, offering them a faster route to becoming productive citizens. Participation in baseball and other sports inevitably led to their gradual acceptance, albeit after suffering years of segregation and discrimination. The identified players in this 1919 photograph are Isabel Romero (second row, center) and Camilo Ávila (second row, far right). (Courtesy of Raymunda Jaso Flores.)

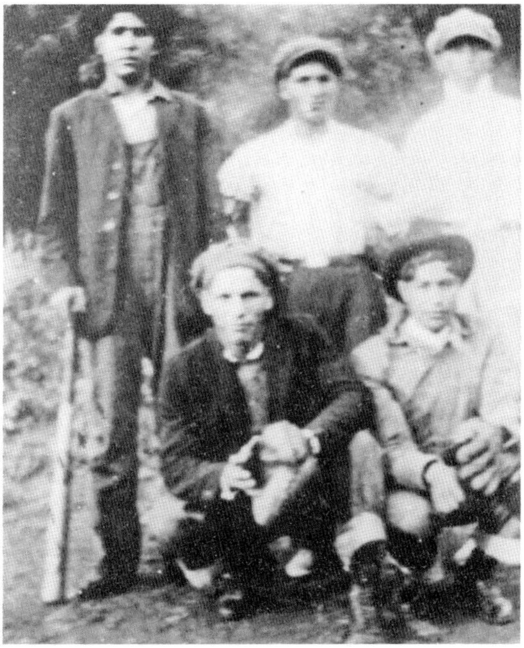

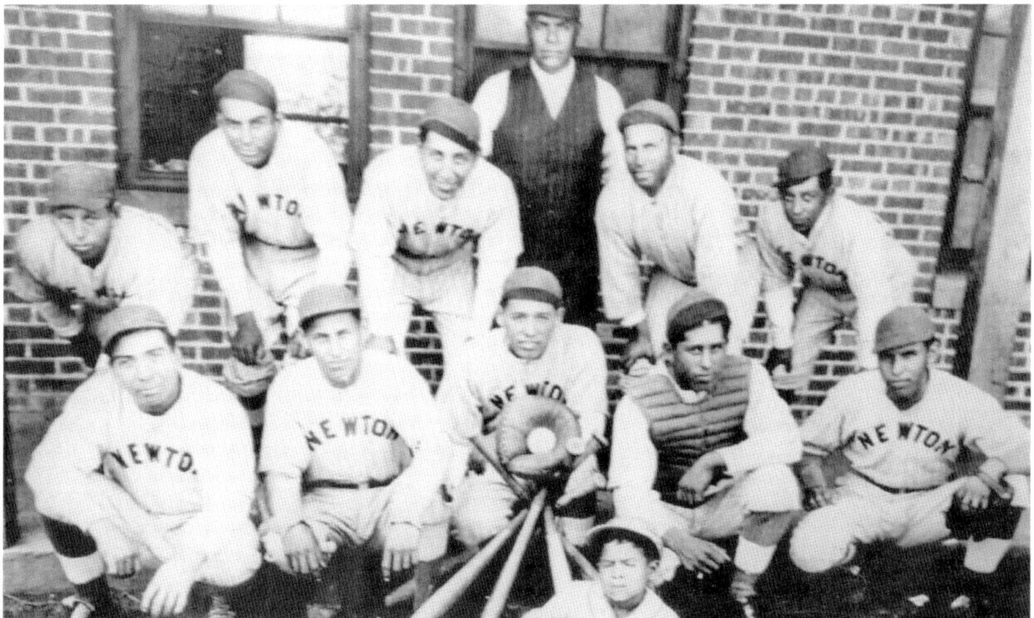

Los Cuauhtémocs competed against other Mexican teams such as Los Nacionales of Wichita, and Los Cometas and Los Piratas of Topeka. The 1932 Cuauhtémocs from El Ranchito are, from left to right, (first row) David Ceballos, Epifanio Arellano, Frank Lujano, Ramiro Carrión, Ramón Pedrosa, and batboy Ángel Ávila; (second row) José Cuellar, Juan Arellano, Ramón Hernández, manager José Ávila, Raymundo Jaso, and Martín Sauceda. The brick facade behind them provided a more pleasing view for train passengers passing by the Ranchito on the main line. (Courtesy of Reynaldo González.)

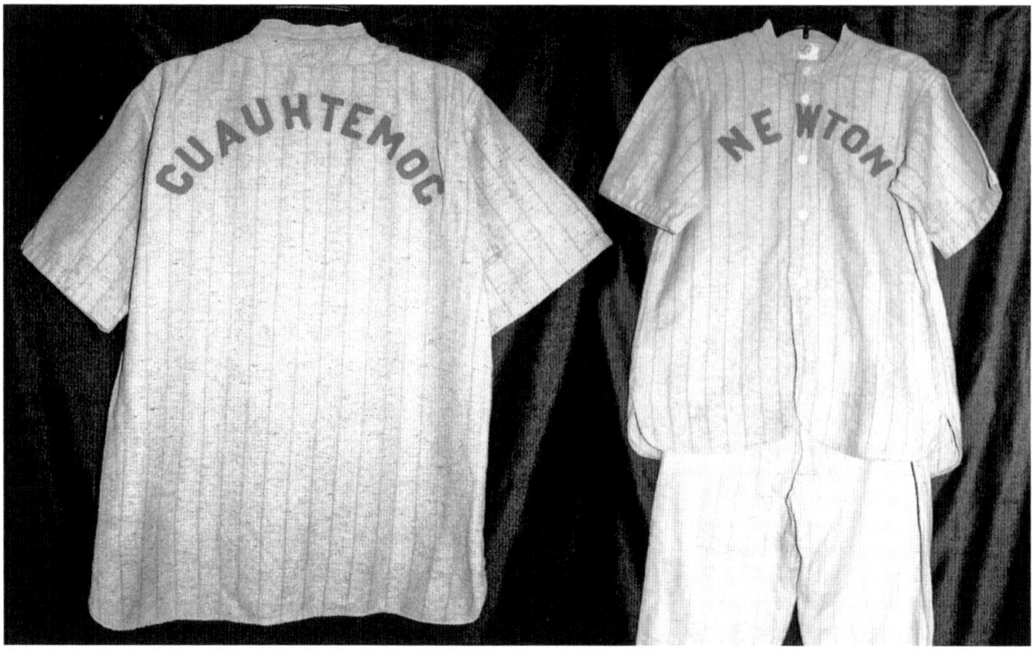

Ramón Pedrosa's wool 1930s Cuauhtémoc uniform was a valuable keepsake kept in excellent condition by his descendants for years. One early remembrance of the Cuauhtémocs was when they accepted a challenge from a team in Alma, Kansas, because word had spread that Newton had "one hell of a team." The players pitched in for gasoline for Don Santo Romero's Model T. Arriving in Alma, they were surprised that no one had mentioned that the Alma team played baseball, while the Cuauhtémocs had softball equipment. Nevertheless, play continued. (Courtesy of the Sylvia Pedrosa family.)

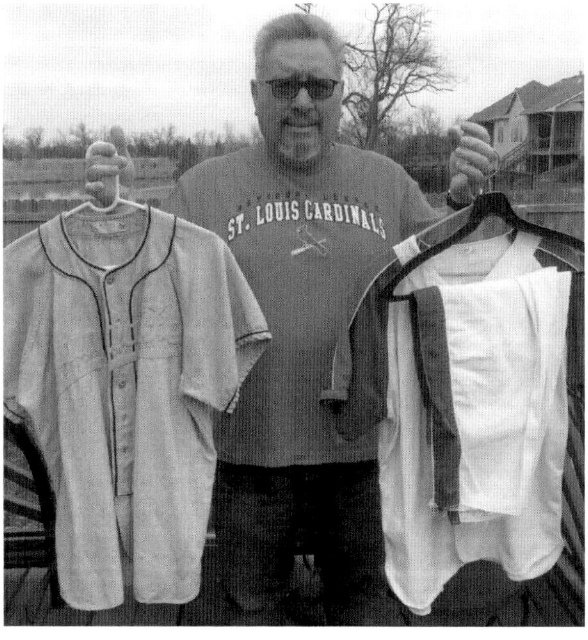

Eduardo Gómez, son of Margarito Gómez from Newton, is holding his father's two uniforms. One represents the Santa Fe Railroad, and the other represents the Newton Texaco Oilers. The Oilers were sponsored by Charlie Newell, a well-known businessman who owned a local truck stop. Margarito began his long fast pitch softball career after World War II in 1945 through the 1960s with the Santa Fe Railroad, the Texaco Oilers, and Our Lady of Guadalupe Church. The team, known as the Mexican Catholics, was part of the Newton Softball League, which included an African American team. (Courtesy of Eduardo Gómez.)

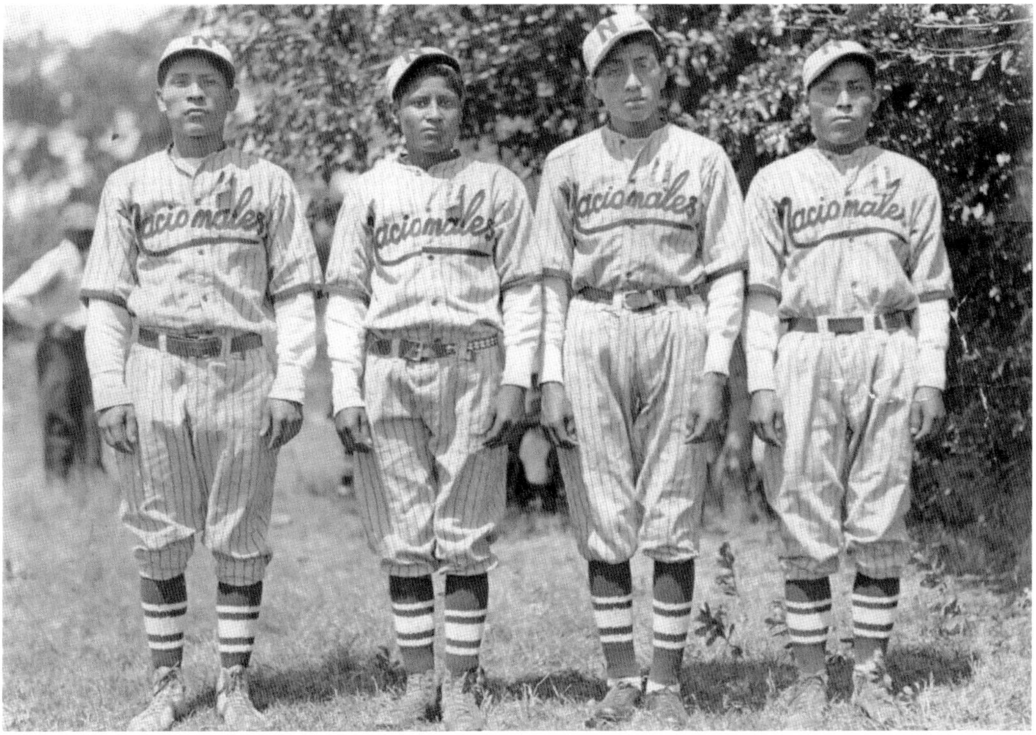

Los Nacionales played baseball in Wichita in the 1930s. Though no records have surfaced documenting their games, they were the contemporaries of Newton's Cuauhtémocs and other Mexican teams throughout Kansas. Los Nacionales players came from Wichita's north-end barrio, El Huarache, and the south-end Ranchito. El Huarache became the cultural focal point for the community, home to railroad laborers, and now provides meatpacking jobs for new urban immigrants. (Courtesy of Al Hernández and *El Perico*.)

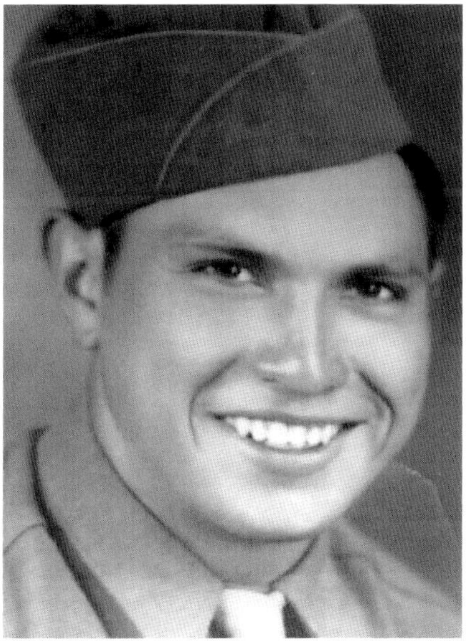

US Army Air Corps technical sergeant Margarito Gómez from Newton, Kansas, entered the service in 1943, and was awarded two Bronze Stars with clusters for his service in building airfields on the Burma Road. He was discharged in 1945, returned to Newton, and in 1947, found employment with the Santa Fe Railroad and immediately joined the company's softball team. He also played for the Newton Texaco Oilers and Our Lady of Guadalupe Church from the 1940s through the 1960s. Due to discrimination, the Catholic team was forced to build its softball field on the grounds of Our Lady of Guadalupe Church. In 1949, the St. Louis Cardinals offered Margarito a contract, but he turned it down because of family obligations. Baseball and softball were his passion. (Courtesy of Eduardo Gómez.)

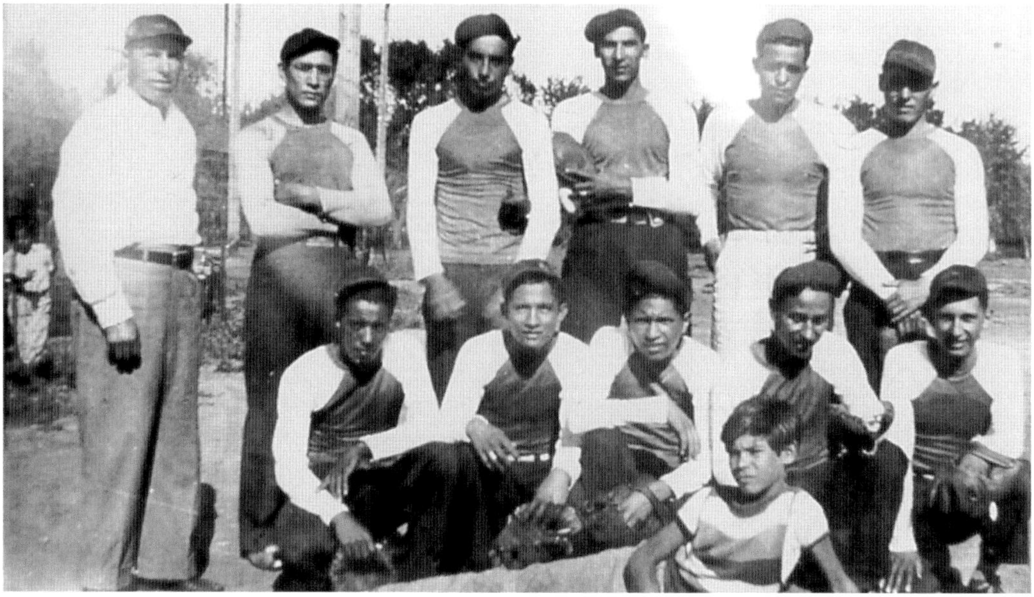

The Mexican Catholics organized the first Newton tournament at Athletic Park in July 1946, as documented by the *Evening Kansan-Republican*. In 1920, Our Lady of Guadalupe was built on the Ranchito grounds. Unwelcome by the main Catholic church in Newton, residents built the chapel to serve this devoted and growing congregation. This c. 1946 Mexican Catholics team, is, from left to right, (first row) Curly Rodríguez, Nick Jaso, Maggie Gómez, Bill Lujano, John Florez, and batboy Lee Piña; (second row) Raymundo Jaso, Frank Florez, Ángel Rodríguez, Elmer Vega, Lalo Viramóntes, and Frank Lujano. (Courtesy of Raymunda Jaso Flores.)

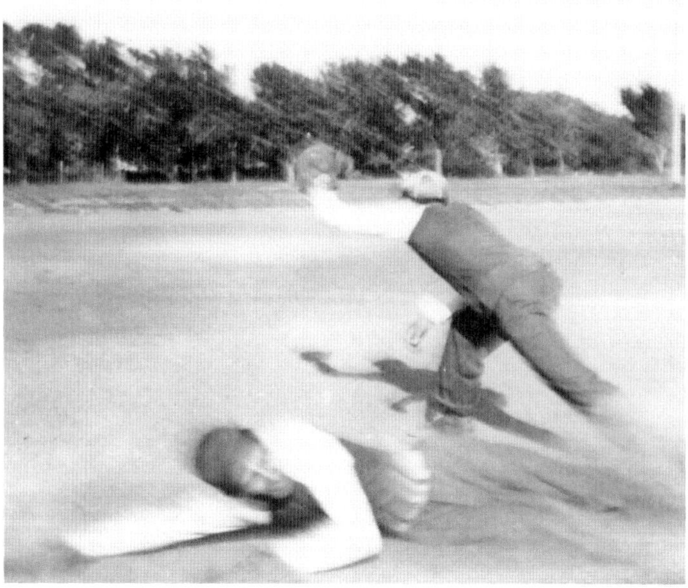

The Mexican Catholics team practices before a game at Athletic Park in Newton. While being the founders of the Fourth of July tournament, the Mexican Catholics participated in Newton's City League. The teams were segregated but were allowed to play against each other. White teams included the Junior Chamber of Commerce, Wiley-McCall, Candyland, and the Lutheran church, and an African American team, the Hot n Tots. (Courtesy of Raymunda Jaso Flores.)

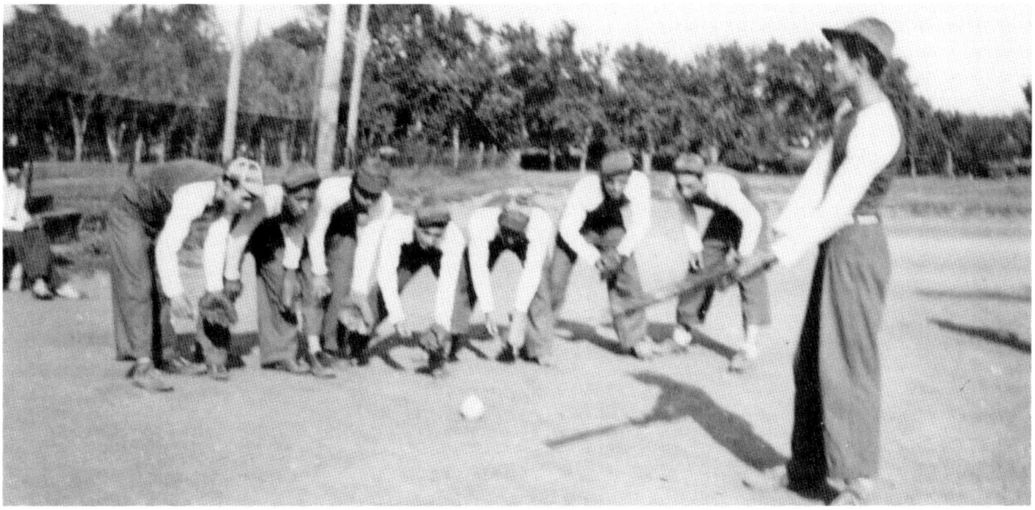

A c. 1940s Mexican Catholics team warms up for a City League game at Athletic Park, the main diamond for the Newton tournaments until the construction of Guadalupe Park in the 1960s. Veterans from World War II continued playing ball upon their return from service. Military service, considered a duty and obligation, demonstrated their allegiance to their country. The military service of Newton's eight González brothers, including five who served during World War II, is a fine example of commitment and honor. (Courtesy of Raymunda Jaso Flores.)

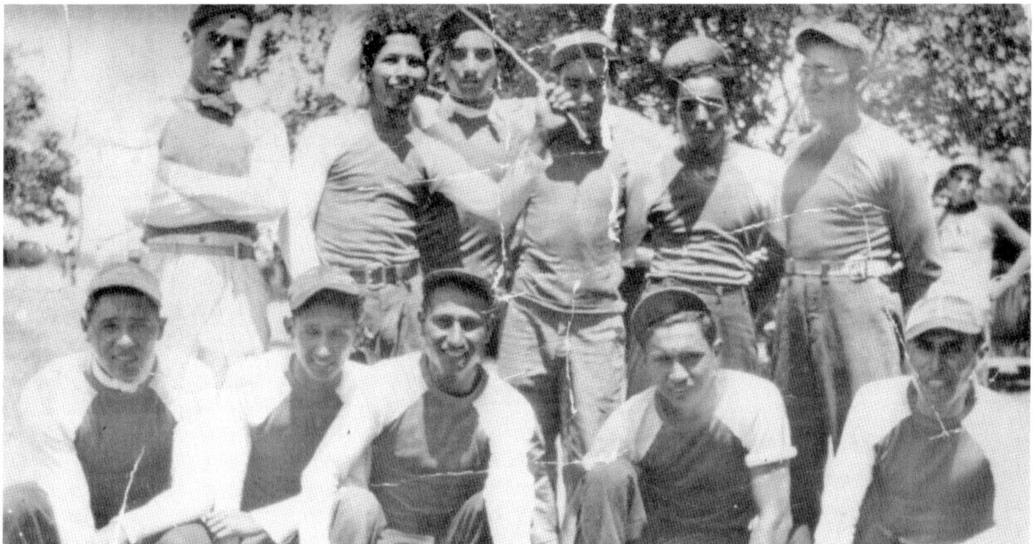

Mexican Catholics around 1946 are, from left to right (first row) Frank Lujano, John Flores, Bill Lujano, Margarito Gómez, and Raymond Pedrosa; (second row) Bacho Rodríquez, unidentified, Ángel Rodríquez, unidentified, Frank Rodríquez, and Frank Flores. The Catholics are one of several softball teams from Newton, including Los Cuauhtémocs, Los Rayos, Newton McGees, Holy Name, Our Lady of Guadalupe, Newells Oilers, the Merchants, the Varsity, Los Gallos, J-Train, and the Newton Metros, along with pickup teams playing for fun prior to the official games. (Courtesy of the Raymunda Jaso Flores.)

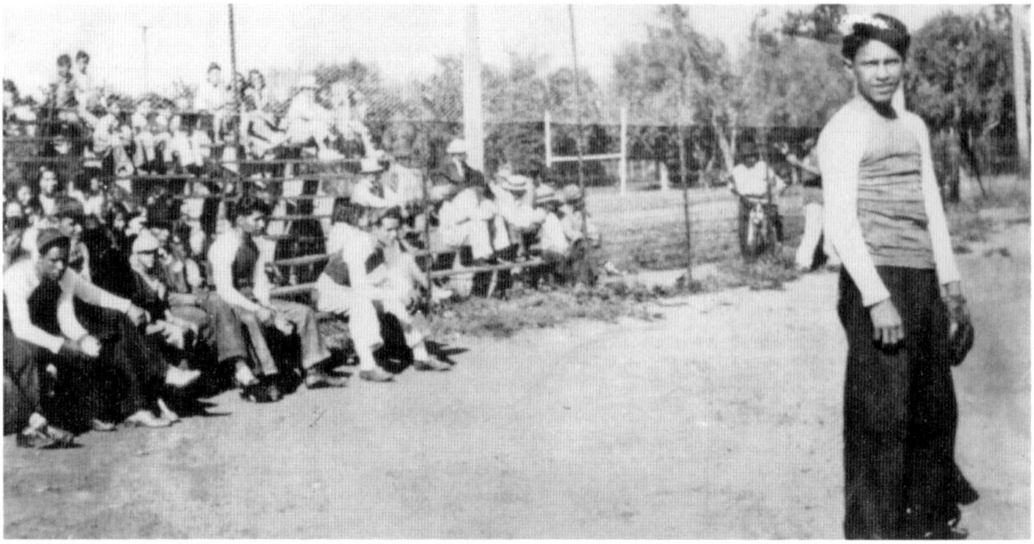

The Mexican Catholics team is pictured at Athletic Park around 1947. From left to right on the bench are Frank Rodríguez, Manuel Perez, Lidio Jaso, and Lalo Viramóntes. Margarito "Maggie" Gómez is on the field. Gómez was offered a tryout with the St. Louis Cardinals in the early 1940s but declined due to lack of sponsorship. In 1946, he was part of the first Mexican American fast pitch team in Newton, which hosted the tournament. Gómez hitting the long ball is legendary. He homered in the first championship game against Topeka, along with Joaquín Estrada and Ángel Rodríquez. (Courtesy of the Raymond Olais collection.)

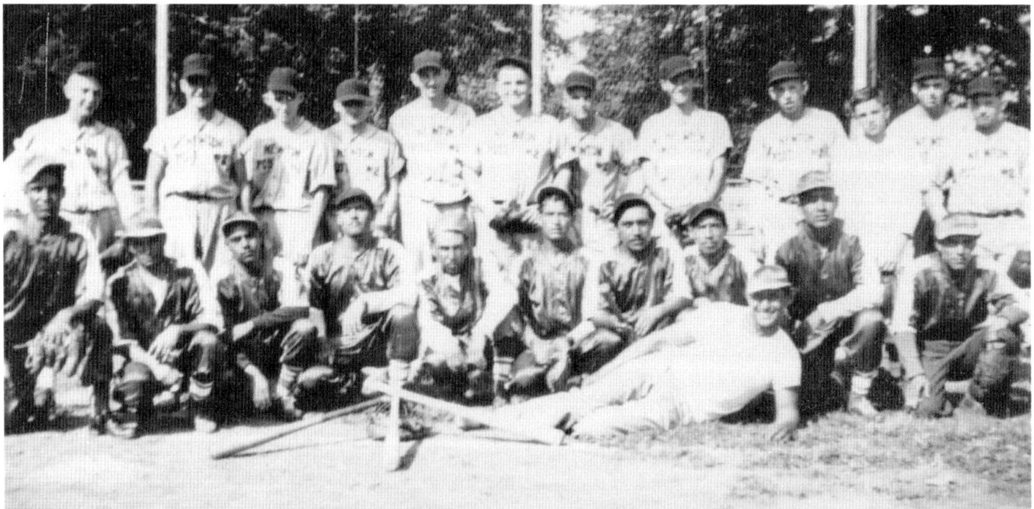

This baseball team was comprised of imported Mexican railroad workers known as *braceros* during World War II. The white players from Newton and surrounding area comprised the opposition team. The braceros ("arms") were imported to replenish the dwindling Mexican workforce, since Newton's railroad workers were serving in the military. The bracero team was managed by Elmer Vega, who was bilingual and worked with the braceros on the railroad. He was a member of the Mexican Catholics and later played with the McGees team. (Courtesy of the Raymond Olais collection.)

Softball Tournament

A day-light softball tournament sponsored by the Mexican Catholics also is scheduled for Thursday at Athletic park. In addition to two local clubs, teams from Topeka, Emporia, Wichita and Hutchinson are expected to compete in the single elimination event. Games will start at 10 a. m., and continue throughout the day.

July 3, 1946

The July 3, 1946, *Evening Kansan-Republican* reported a softball tournament sponsored by the Mexican Catholics. This was the tournament that started the annual Fourth of July Mexican softball fast pitch tournament. Competing teams included two local clubs and visiting teams from Emporia, Topeka, Hutchinson, and Wichita. The Fourth of July fell on a Thursday that year, with a daylong tournament and a dance afterwards. The results were published in the city newspaper the next day. (Courtesy of Newton Public Library Archives.)

Mexicans Win Own Softball Tournament

The Newton Mexican Catholics, host club in a four-team softball tournament staged at Athletic park Thursday, carried off the title by defeating Topeka, 15 to 5, in the final game.

Newton eliminated Hutchinson, 16 to 5, and Topeka put out the Wichita entry, 6 to 5.

Flores and Estrada divided the pitching duties for the locals, the latter allowing three hits in the final four innings of the championship contest. He also got a home run, along with fourbaggers by M. Gomez and A. Rodriguez. Newton collected seven homers in the two games.

July 5, 1946

This newspaper clipping from July 5, 1946, announced the host team winning its own tournament. The Mexican Catholics claimed the title by defeating the Topeka team 15-5 in the final game. In the earlier rounds, Newton defeated Hutchinson 16-5, while Topeka eliminated Wichita by the score of 6-5, advancing to the championship game. Flores and Estrada divided the pitching, while Estrada, M. Gómez, and A. Rodríquez each homered for the Catholics. (Courtesy of Newton Public Library Archives.)

Mexican Teams In Softball Meet

Mexican softball teams from Wichita, Hutchinson, Lyons, Emporia, El Dorado and Newton will compete in a tournament at Athletic park tomorrow, sponsored by the Latin American club of Newton.

Wichita and Hutchinson will clash in the opening game at 11 a. m. There will be a small admission fee.

As an added attraction, three girls teams also are scheduled to appear. Lyons will play Wichita and the Newton girls will oppose the winner.

July 3, 1947

The July 3, 1947, *Evening Kansan-Republican* highlighted a meeting of Mexican softball teams from Wichita, Hutchinson, Lyons, Emporia, El Dorado, and Newton. Three girls' teams were included. The girls' team from Lyons played Wichita, with the winner facing the Newton team. Participation by women was short-lived due to the raising of new families following World War II. Veterans took advantage of the GI Bill, affording them opportunities despite discrimination. Newton, like other Mexican communities, organized a GI Forum chapter to confront discrimination and address issues central to the Mexican community. (Courtesy of Newton Public Library Archives.)

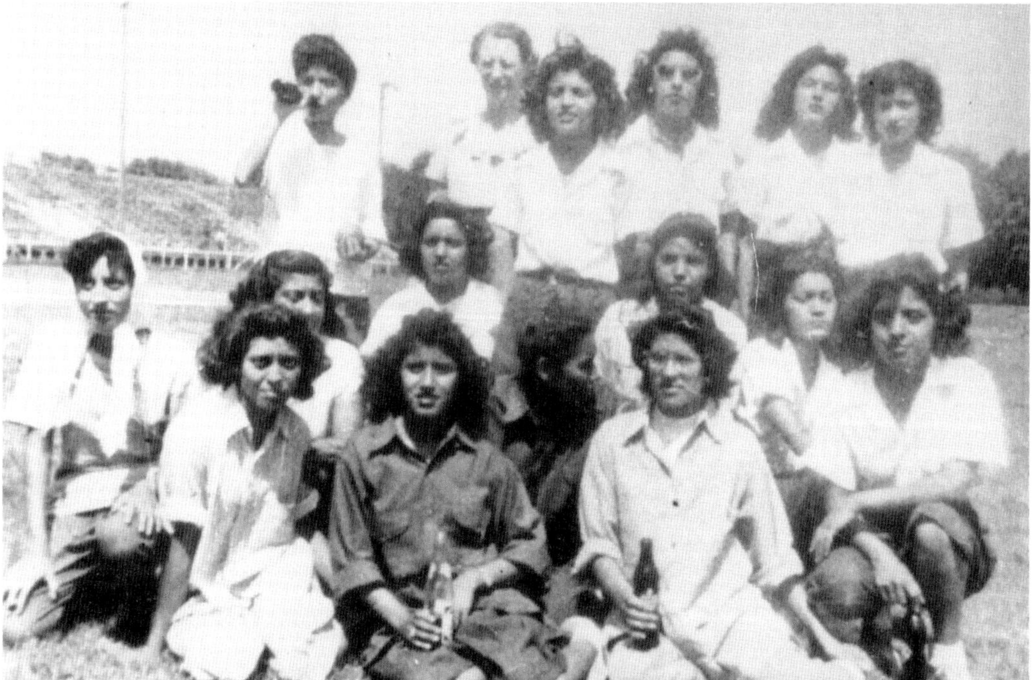

The 1947 Newton City Cab was Newton's girls' team that played against Mexican ladies' teams from Lyons and Wichita as added spice to the tournament games for the appreciative fans. The women's teams played between the men's games in the 1947 and 1948 tournaments. From left to right are (first row) Alice Gallardo, Esperanza Terrones, and unidentified; (second row) Maggie Gallardo, unidentified, Julia Jaso, Sally Hernández, Loretta González, Carmen Llamas, and Lorenza Terrones; (third row) Catherine Jaso, unidentified manager, Frances Nuñez, Fifi Sifuentez, Henrietta Rodríguez, and Carol Martínez. (Courtesy of the Raymond Olais collection.)

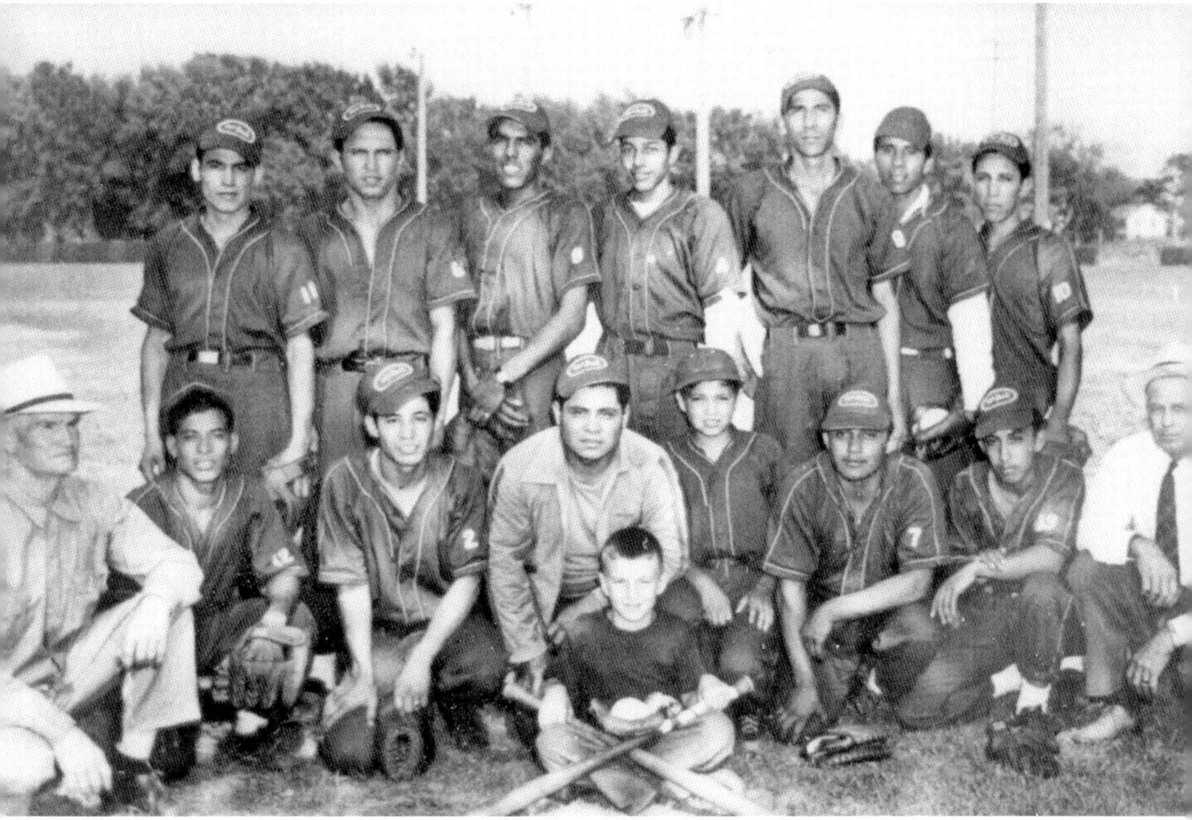

Tournament records list the 1948 McGees team as the winners of the Fourth of July tournament. The McGees also participated in Newton's fast pitch city league during the late 1940s. This black-and-white photograph does not do justice to their beautiful red uniforms. From left to right are (first row) Jack Snyder, Nick Sauceda, Senon Palacioz, Joaquín Estrada, Julian García, Ángel Torres, Phillip Cervantes, ? McGee, and batboy Bobby Snyder; (second row) Ángel Monares, Maggie Gómez, Tony González, Ralph Pérez, Elmer Vega, Ángel Juárez, and Robert Hernández. (Courtesy of the Raymond Olais collection.)

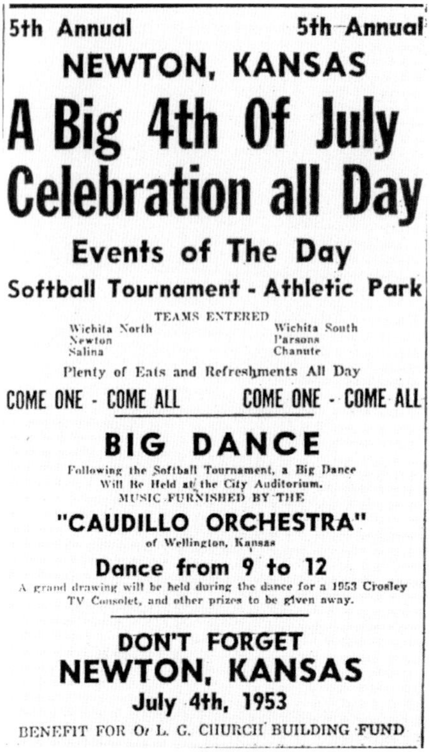
5th Annual 5th Annual

NEWTON, KANSAS

A Big 4th Of July Celebration all Day

Events of The Day

Softball Tournament - Athletic Park

TEAMS ENTERED

Wichita North	Wichita South
Newton	Parsons
Salina	Chanute

Plenty of Eats and Refreshments All Day

COME ONE - COME ALL COME ONE - COME ALL

BIG DANCE

Following the Softball Tournament, a Big Dance Will Be Held at the City Auditorium.

MUSIC FURNISHED BY THE

"CAUDILLO ORCHESTRA"

of Wellington, Kansas

Dance from 9 to 12

A grand drawing will be held during the dance for a 1953 Crosley TV Consolet, and other prizes to be given away.

DON'T FORGET

NEWTON, KANSAS

July 4th, 1953

BENEFIT FOR O. L. G. CHURCH BUILDING FUND

This newspaper advertisement announces the fifth annual Newton "Big 4th of July All Day Celebration" in 1953. The festivities included a softball tournament at Athletic Park and an evening dance at the city auditorium after the tournament featuring the Caudillo Orchestra. Proceeds benefit the Our Lady of Guadalupe building fund. The Newton tournament plays the same cultural role as pre–World War II games in the Mexican American community—family, friendship, and community unity. There are picnics, dances, games, and amusement for the children, and an opportunity for renewing old acquaintances. The post-war period also saw the hiring of Mexican American umpires and officials in city leagues, and the active participation of Mexican American youth on Little League, Pony, Colt, and Babe Ruth Leagues, and on high school and college teams. (Courtesy of the Newton Public Library Archives.)

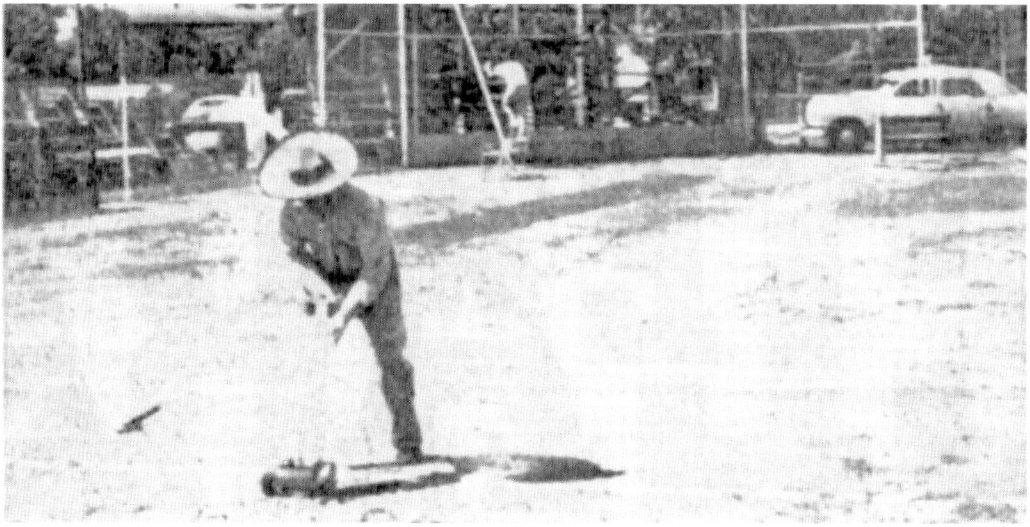

Reynaldo González prepares the infield of Our Lady of Guadalupe's new ballpark, built behind the church grounds. In the background are shaded bleachers and dugouts protecting the fans from the summer heat and allowing a better vantage point behind home plate. Years later, the outfield fence was painted with advertisements of local sponsors, while the church's Altar Society prepared food in the hall and kitchen for weekend activities and dances. A snack bar, restrooms, and a well-stocked beer garden were constructed onsite along with adequate parking. (Courtesy of the Newton Public Library Archives.)

This announcement for the 16th annual softball tournament on July 6 and 7 at Guadalupe Field highlights both Kansas and Missouri teams. On Saturday night, guests danced to the music of Pedro Caudillo at the National Guard armory. Newton's rich musical history can be traced to the 1920s and an earlier band formed by Raymundo Jaso, who played the violin. Other band members, who also played at fiestas and weddings, included Leonardo Estrada, guitar; Nat Flores, bass; Camilo Ávila, guitar; Isabel Romero, mandolin; and Refugio Vásquez, trumpet. (Courtesy of the Catholic Advance Archives.)

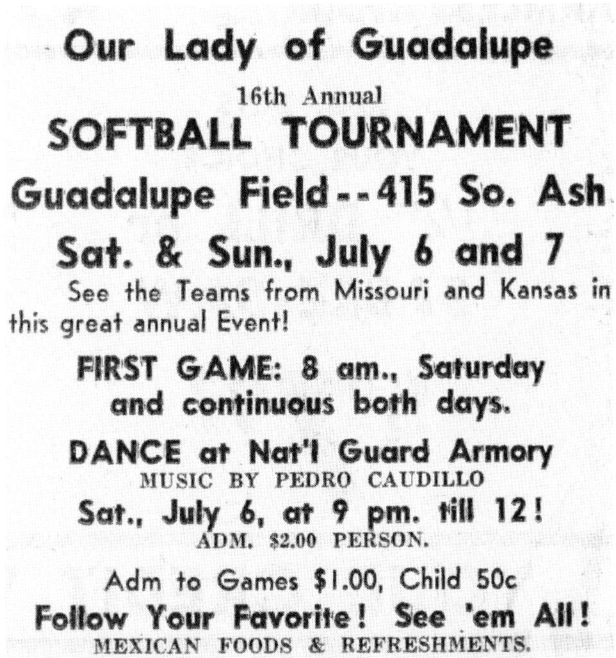

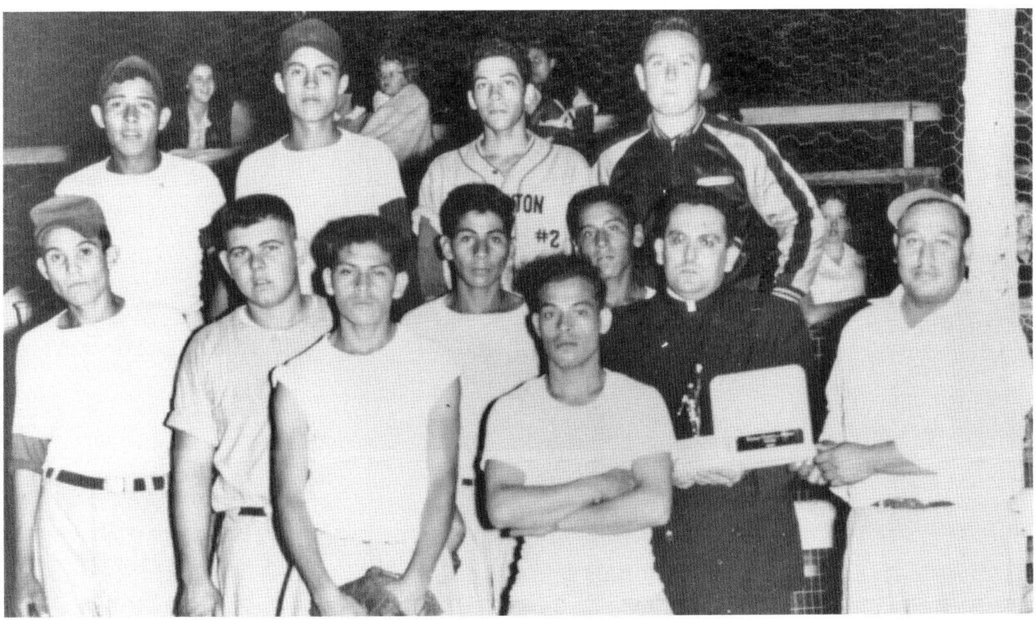

The Wichita Diocese's *Catholic Advance* highlighted its three 1953 championship teams. The St. Mary's team (pictured) defeated St. Mark's and was crowned minor-league champions. From left to right are (first row) Peter Estrada, Henry Sauceda, Fr. Joséph Abraham, and coach Bill Lujano; (second row) Robert Arellano, Leroy Younger, Julián Arellano, and Rubén Carrión; (third row) Ray Arellano, Louis Sandoval, Alfonso Pérez, and Ted Sadowski. Not pictured are Jesse Arellano and Willie Monarez. Members of this team played in the Newton tournament with Our Lady of Guadalupe's Holy Name team or other teams. (Courtesy of *Catholic Advance* Archives.)

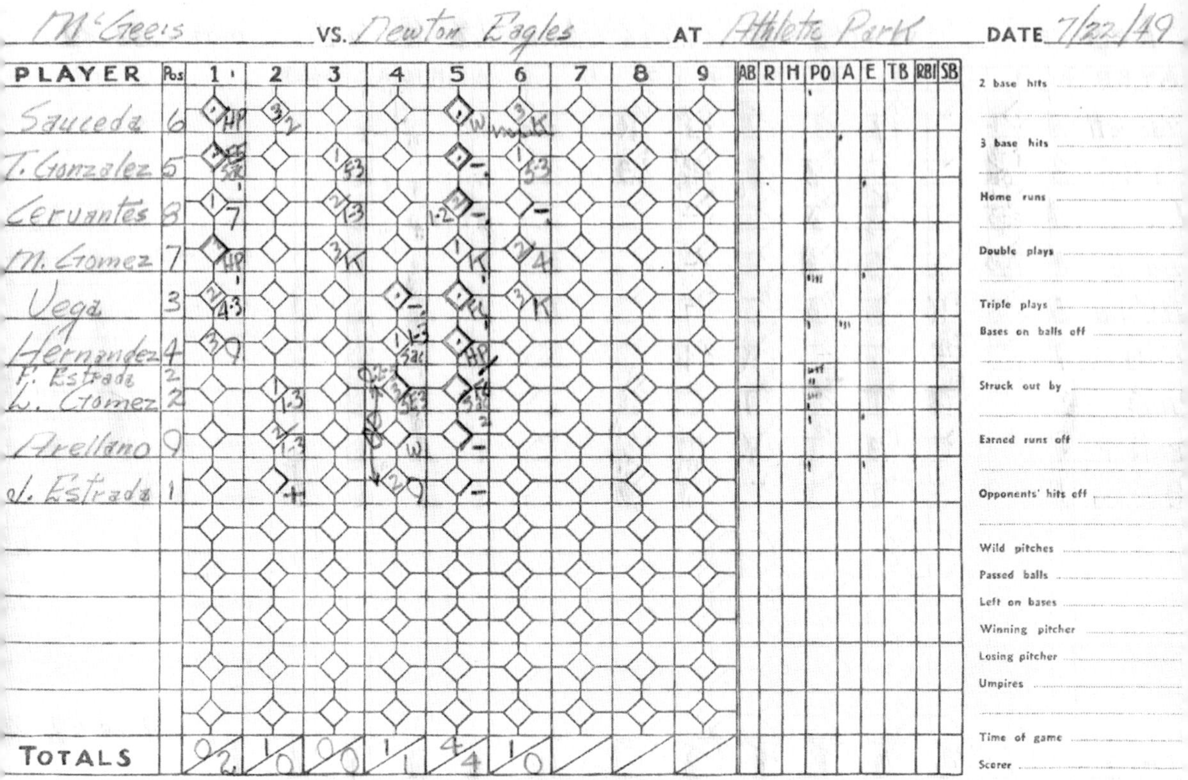

This scorecard is from a game between the McGees and the Newton Eagles at Athletic Park on July 22, 1949. The McGees won the 1948 Fourth of July tournament, and also participated in Newton's city league. This scorecard lists the names of players from the 1948 team. (Courtesy of Roger Gillispie.)

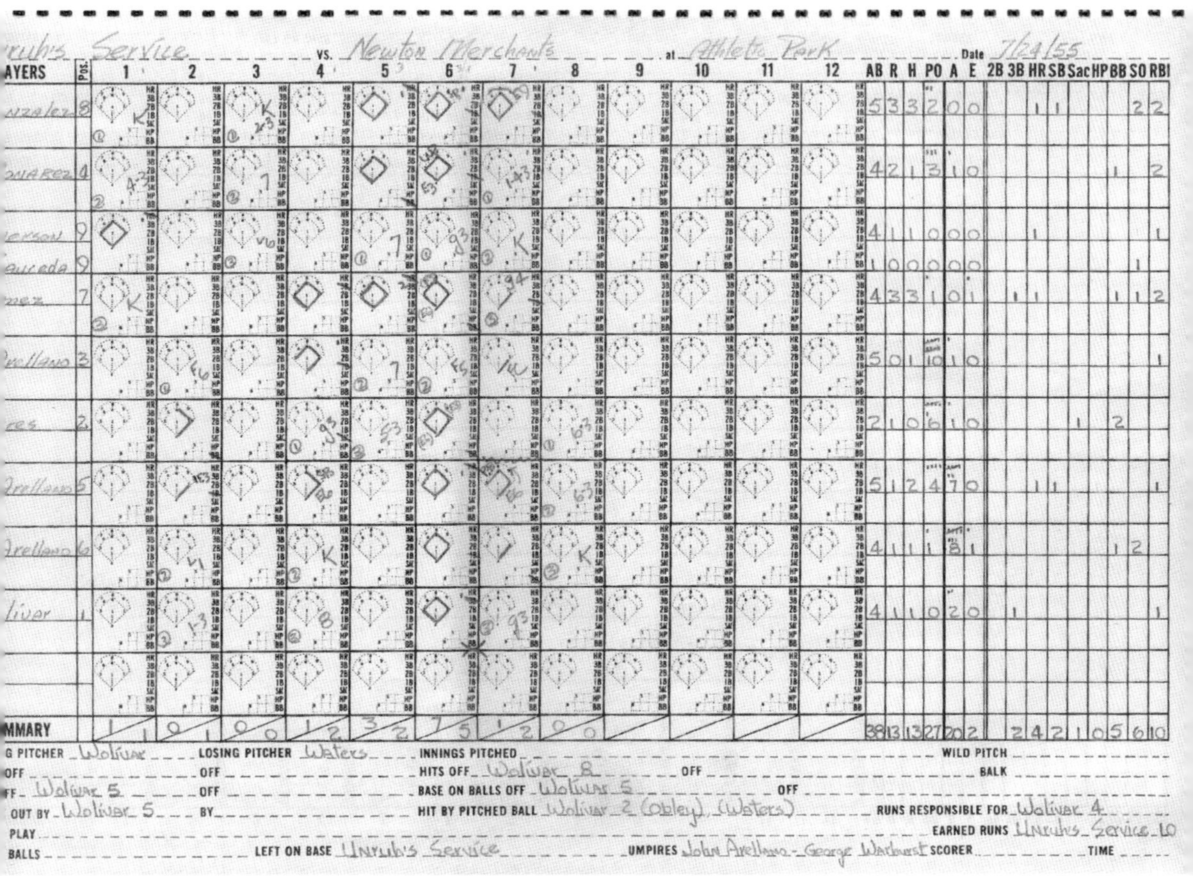

This scorecard documents a game between Unruh's Service and the Newton Merchants at Athletic Park on July 24, 1955. Mexican teams continued in Newton's city league into the 1950s, preserving their batting and fielding skills even though segregated sports activities were the norm. Jesse Arellano played for Unruh's Service team, and is considered a great pitcher, to the extent that he was recruited for the powerhouse Ramsey's Dairy team in Ottawa, Kansas. The scorecard notes that John Arellano, father of Jesse, served as one of the umpires for the game. (Courtesy of Roger Gillispie.)

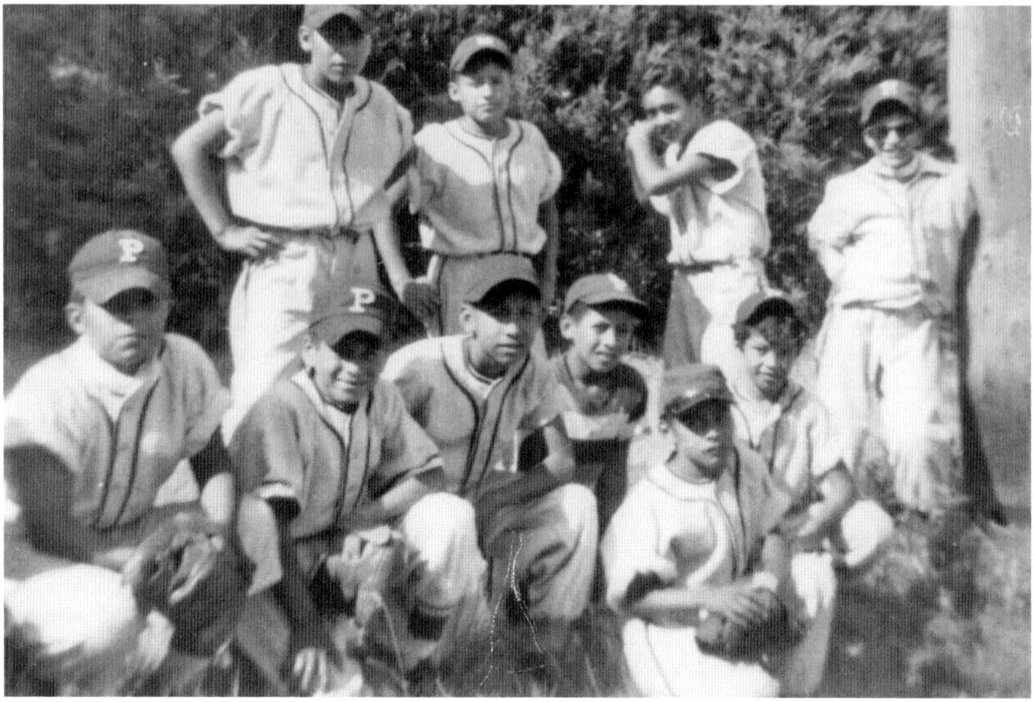

The 1951 Knot Hole League Pirates played at Tenth and Ash Streets. John Arellano organized the team and was an early pioneer of Mexican sports as a player, coach, and umpire. Players included Paul Vega, Marino Lujano, Louie Carrión, Freddy Martínez, Celio Sandate, Albert Arellano, Tino Monarez, and Bobby Jaso. Fred Martínez coached the Pirates. The Knot Hole league integrated in 1952 along with the local high school teams. Ralph Pérez played on Newton's Mexican basketball team, winning three consecutive state championships in Wichita. The Mexican girls, sporting their Railroader sweaters, served as cheerleaders. (Courtesy of Paul Vega.)

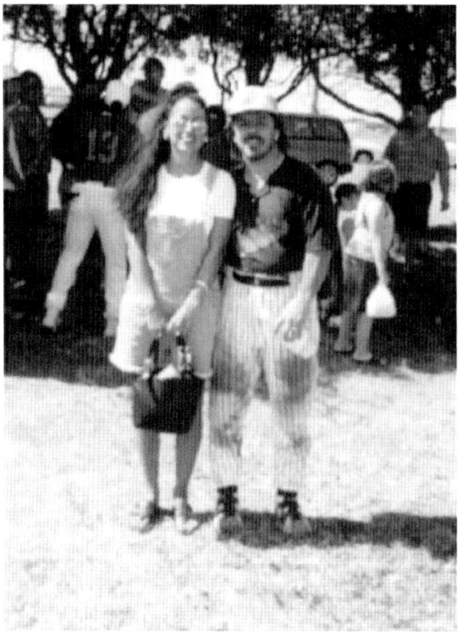

Javier Del Castillo, an inductee in both the Kansas and Missouri Mexican American Fast Pitch Halls of Fame as a catcher, is seen here with his daughter, Anna Del Castillo Harris. Javier served with the Marines in Vietnam. He played with the Wichita Padres. Many outstanding players have come from Wichita's North End and El Guarache barrio to play in the Newton tournament, including Ramon Del Castillo, Chris Rodríguez, Larry Ramírez, Chico Rizo, Louie Ramírez, Stephen Ramírez, Chris Del Castillo, and Freddy Martínez. In 2002, five Vietnam veterans were inducted into the Kansas Hall of Fame: K.P. Sánchez, Joe Solís, Chris Rodríguez, Javier Del Castillo, and Steve Reyes. Most of the Wichita players attended school at Our Lady of the Perpetual Help Church. (Courtesy of Ramon Del Castillo.)

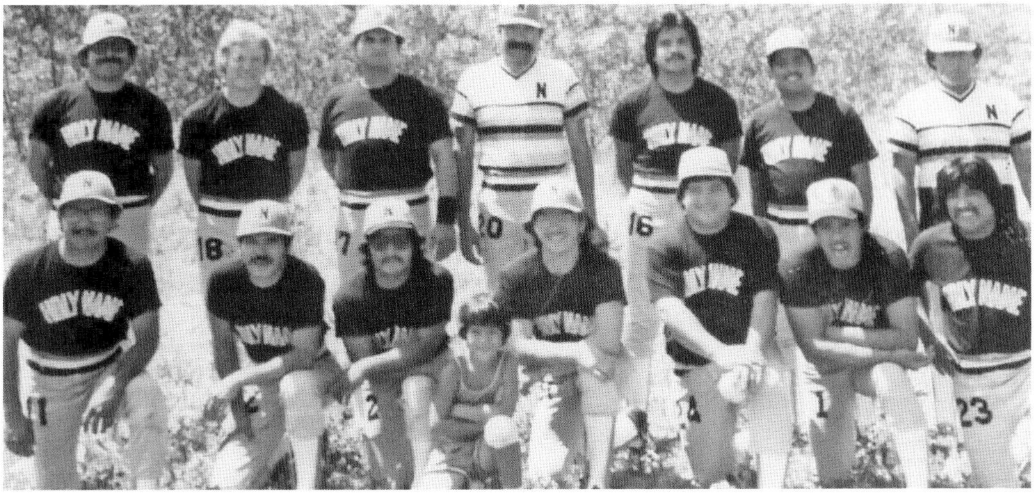

This 1970s Holy Name team is, from left to right, (first row) Tony Sandate, Joe González, Raymond Jaso, batboy Roman Vega, Eddie Ybarra, Manuel Jaso, Steve Scott, and Steve Jaso; (second row) Robert Lavenant, Fred Smith, Mario García, Paul Vega, Rick Camargo, George Jaso, and Patrick Torres. Newton's Our Lady of Guadalupe Church sponsored teams since the 1940s, beginning with the famous Mexican Catholics. Later teams, playing under the banner of Newton OLG and Newton Holy Name, won numerous tournament championships in the 1960s and 1970s. (Courtesy of Jesse Arellano.)

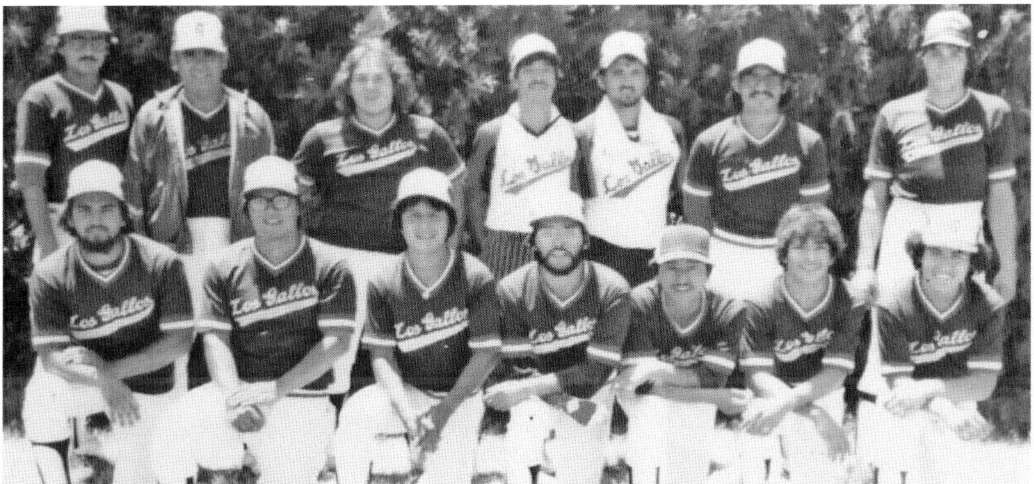

Los Gallos (the Roosters) were coached by Jesse Arellano, who participated in the tournament as a pitcher along with his three sons, Jimmy, Rick, and Steve. From left to right are (first row) Jimmy Arellano, coach Jesse Arellano, Manuel Romero, Pat Sauceda, Julian García, Rick Arellano, and Vince García; (second row) Victor García, Greg Montaño, Mike Álvarez, Ernie Lujano, Phillip Nuñez, Danny Sauceda, and Steve Arellano. The 1970s team played in the Newton tournaments and tournaments in Hutchinson, Wichita, El Dorado, Chanute, Parsons, Emporia, Salina, Kansas City, Pueblo, and Colorado Springs. Jesse's wife, Amelia Arellano, described their trips as summer vacations. (Courtesy of the Jesse Arellano.)

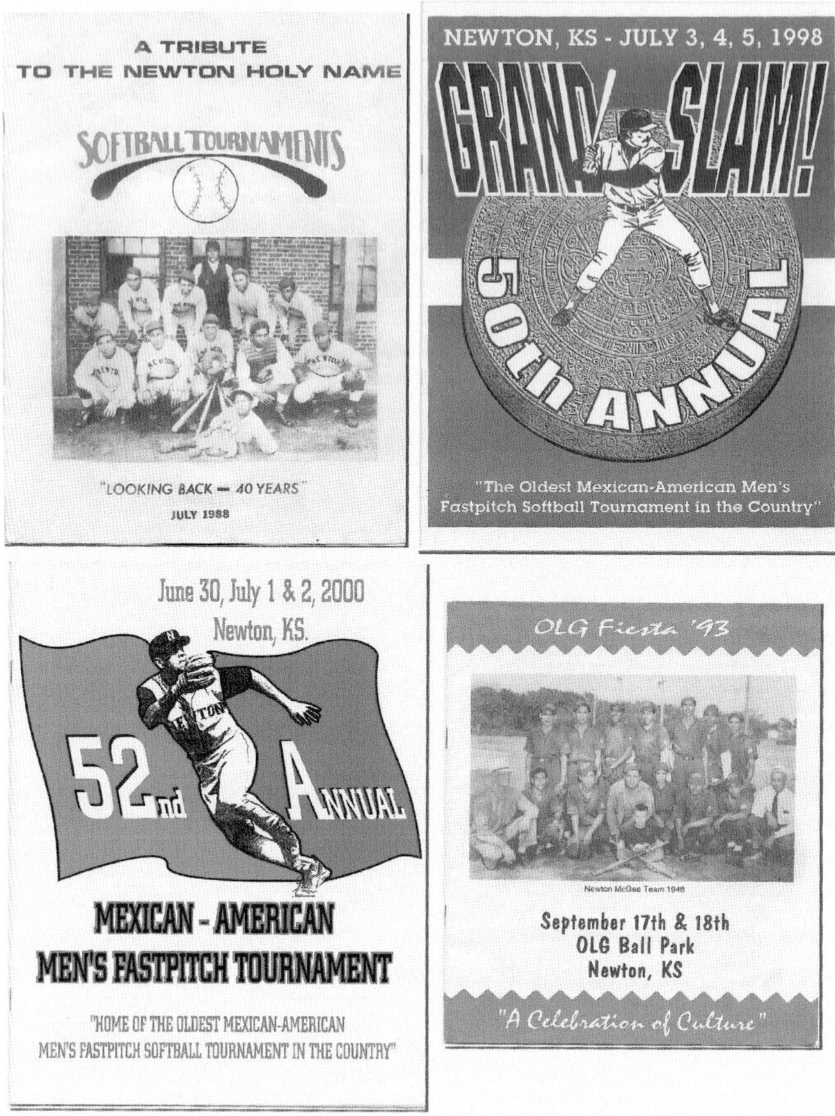

Souvenir booklets promoted Newton's Fourth of July fast pitch tournament as the "Home of the Oldest Mexican-American Men's Fastpitch Softball Tournament in the Country." The 40th-anniversary booklet from 1988, authored by Paula Jasso-Wedel, was titled "A Tribute to the Holy Name Softball Tournaments." The tournament was highlighted in 1993 with an exhibit at the Harvey County Historical Society titled A League of Our Own. A subsequent booklet was produced for the 50th anniversary in 1998. The Kauffman Museum exhibit Recuerdos de Newton (Memories of Newton) also paid tribute to the tournament in 1998. A 1978 mural at the Our Lady of Guadalupe ballpark honored the 30th anniversary by depicting the remarkable history of the Mexican community of Newton. The mural illustrated how the church, the railroad, and the tournament have been integral facets of the community's history. (Courtesy of the Raymond Olais collection.)

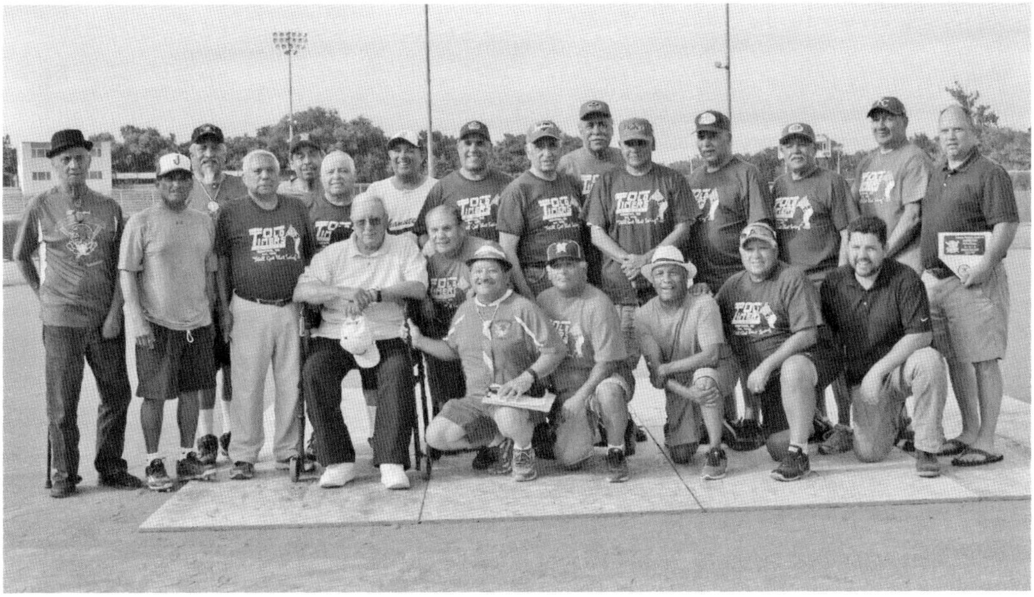

The Newton Mexican American Athletic Club Hall of Famers and Old Timers pose at Athletic Park in 2016. From left to right are (first row) Pete Gómez, Jerry Palacioz (Newton), Manuel Jaso (Newton), Raymond Jaso Sr. (Newton), Donald Díaz, Richard Escobar, and José Ramos; (second row) Paulie Hernández (Kansas City), Steve Jaso (Newton), Chris González (Kansas City), Reynaldo González (Newton), Joe Solís (Newton), Ron Escobar, Tony De La Torre (Chanute), Slyvester Bustamonte, John Tórrez Jr. (Topeka), Paul Vega (Newton), George Ontiberos, Tony Augusto, Mario Escobar, Stan Ramos, and Bryce Buller (Newton). (Courtesy of Robert Sandoval.)

The Kansas City Aztecas drew young players from across the region. Jesse Salas was one of those youthful players who enjoyed the support of his wife, Mary. This sketch, by Argentine, Kansas, artist Anthony Oropeza, depicts the adolescent couple enjoying a day at the park. Wives played a critical part in the lives of the ballplayers; besides being their biggest fans, spouses provided multifaceted family and neighborhood support systems to promote their husband's passion for the game including cleaning their uniforms and raising funds for team equipment and road games. (Courtesy of Anthony Oropeza.)

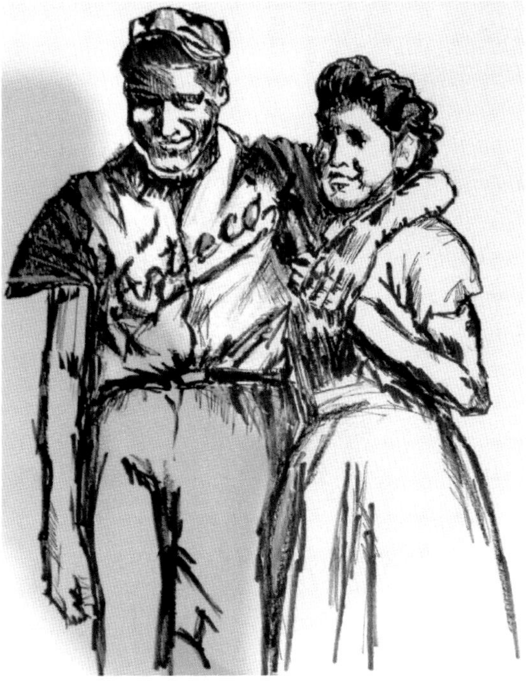

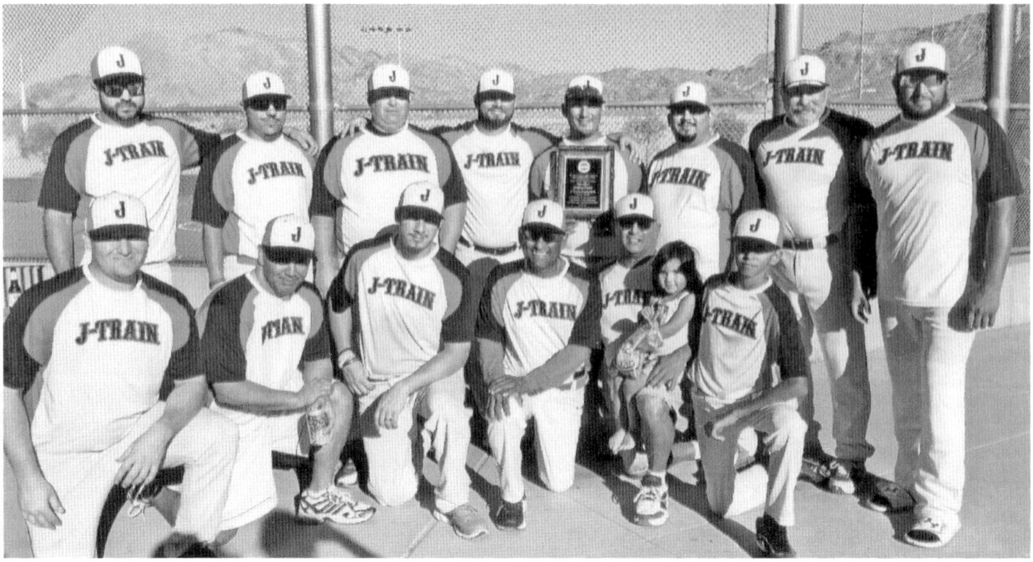

The J-Train, established to play in the 68th annual tournament, continues to this day. The letter J represents the Jaso name, while Train symbolizes why the family came to Newton 100 years ago, to labor on the railroad. The team was recently inducted into the NAFA Hall of Fame in 2017. From left to right are (first row) Johnny Ángel, Tommy Fernández, Luís Ramírez, Steve Jaso, Raymond Jaso Sr., Konner Jaso, and Hadlee Jaso (little girl); (second row) Jorge Rendón, Rico García, Steve Roach, Raymond Jaso, Tony Jaso, Jr., Andy Jaso, Ray Foster, and Shane Campbell. (Courtesy of Raymond Jaso Sr.)

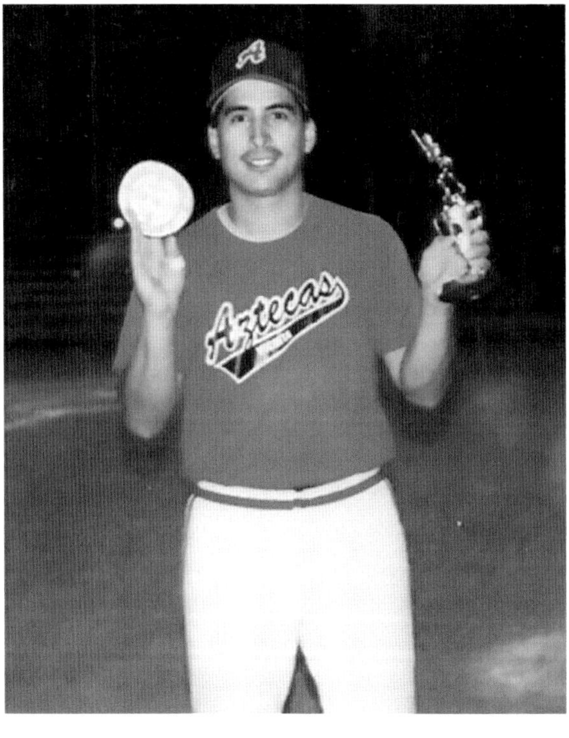

Andy Ramírez, right fielder for the 1989 Wichita Kansas Aztecas, is pictured here. This team competed against Topeka and Ottawa, Kansas, and beat Fort Scott, Kansas, for the 1989 and 1990 fast pitch state American Softball Association Class A championship. Wichita also beat Topeka for the 1991 men's major state tournament, which qualified the team to participate in the four state regionals that included Missouri, Nebraska, Iowa, and Kansas. Andy and his father Louis were inducted into the Newton Hall of Fame. The Aztecas played their games at Westside Athletic Field near the Arkansas River. (Courtesy of Andy Ramírez.)

5

The Sunflower State

The name *Kansas* is derived from the Kansa tribe, which inhabited the land. They were known as the "south wind people." Other indigenous peoples included the Arapaho, Comanche, Kiowa, Osage, and Pawnee—tribes that had occupied the region for thousands of years. In 1541, Spanish conquistador Francisco Vasquez de Coronado y Lujan arrived in Kansas searching for, but never finding, the mythical seven cities of gold of Cibola. "Bleeding Kansas" refers to the 1850s, when anti- and pro-slavery forces battled for territorial control, resulting in violence, death, and massive destruction. Kansas entered the Union in 1861 as the 34th state. One of its many monikers is the "Free State." Kansas also is known as the "Wheat State," because it is the largest producer in the United States of wheat, an important commodity shipped around the world. In 1903, Kansas officially nicknamed itself the "Sunflower State."

Coronado's exploration of present-day Kansas represented a brief but significant introduction of Spanish culture and language more than 60 years before the English settlement of Jamestown, Virginia. Spanish was the first European language spoken in Kansas. Local municipalities are historically connected to Spain, including Alma, Alta Vista, Aurora, Cuba, De Soto, El Dorado, Havana, Lake Quivira, Maize, Montezuma, and Tampa. Quivira is the name Coronado bestowed upon this land while looking for gold, while El Dorado refers to the Spanish legend of a place of fabulous wealth.

Mexicans began arriving in Kansas in the late 19th century. The early 20th century witnessed a tremendous influx of Mexican immigrants, due mainly to the Mexican Revolution. Railroad companies in Kansas employed nearly 15,000 Mexican workers, especially the Santa Fe Railroad by 1912. An often-repeated story is that Mexican Catholics wanted to work for the Santa Fe because its English translation is "Holy Faith." The railroad companies encouraged their workers to recruit family members from Mexico and provided crude houses for their laborers. Mexican *colonias* (colonies) sprang up in Garden City, Dodge City, Emporia, Topeka, Wichita, Copeland, Liberal, Chanute, Hutchinson, Newton, Wellington, Parsons, Kansas City, Salina, Lyons, and countless more towns throughout Kansas.

Discrimination and segregation were harsh realities for the vast majority of Spanish-speaking people. Kansas was once referred to as the "Mississippi for Mexicans." Because of this overt racism, Mexican men and women protected and promoted their own cultural identity in creative ways, including baseball and softball teams. This chapter highlights how baseball and softball were and are important social and cultural instruments promoting and fostering community solidarity as well as labor, civil, gender, and political rights. From sandlots to major league fields, Kansas Mexican Americans have made major contributions to the American pastime, including former major league players Mike Tórrez, Mardie and Nate Cornejo, Dave García LaRoche, and Tyler Ybarra.

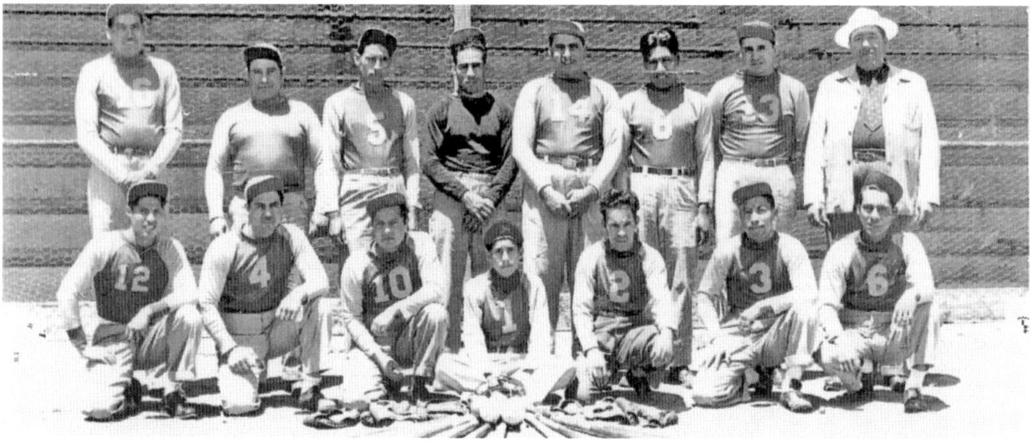

The 1946 Garden City team played at Finney Park. Veterans' groups, including the American GI Forum, Mexican American veterans' clubs, the American Legion, and Veterans of Foreign Wars sponsored teams. From left to right are (first row) Jesse Ávila, Almer Martínez, Ignacio Ávila, batboy Willie Gonzáles, Jessie Orozco, Albert Mesa Sr., and Leo Cervantes; (second row) Rudy Ramírez, Santiago Ramírez, Joe Cervantes, Leonard Perales, Hank García, Andrew Guerrero, William García, and Lupe Guillén (with white hat). By 1913, all the Anglo foremen on the Santa Fe Railroad were issued Spanish dictionaries to communicate with Mexican workers. (Courtesy of Gene T. Chávez.)

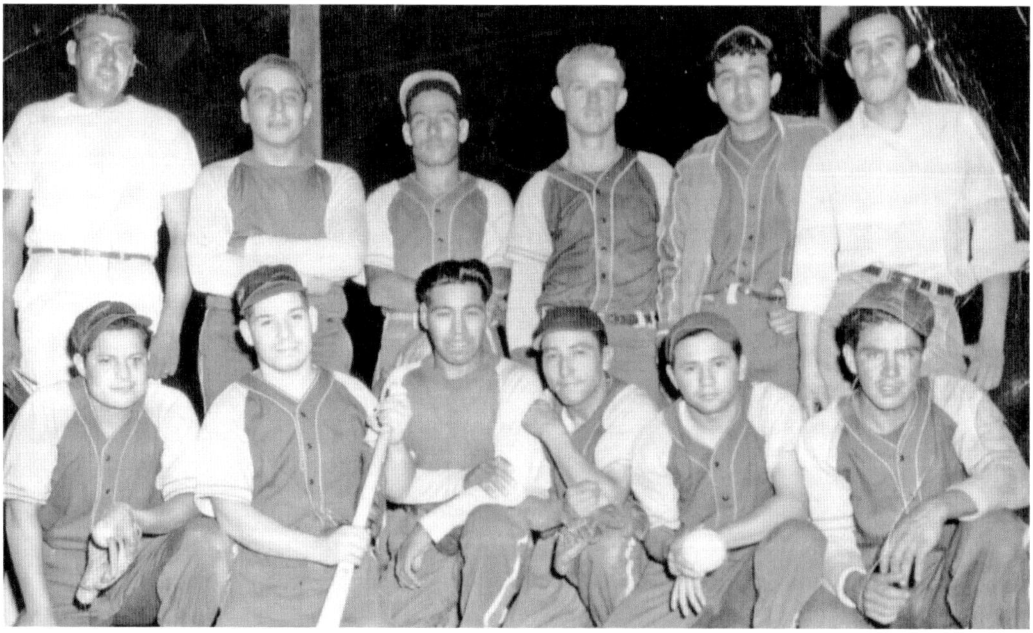

The 1950s Garden City Latin American Club included highly decorated veterans from World War II, but they were confronted with reminders of their second-class status. Their attempt to integrate Garden City's local businesses was met with strong resistance. From left to right are (first row) Buck Ávila, Nick Ortiz Sr., Andrew Guerrero, Albert Mesa Sr., Brigidio Mesa, and Matthew Mora; (second row) Rudy Ramírez, D.C. García, Leonard Perales, Charlie Darling, Joe Delgado, and Daniel Mujica. (Courtesy of Fred Medina and the Finney County Historical Museum.)

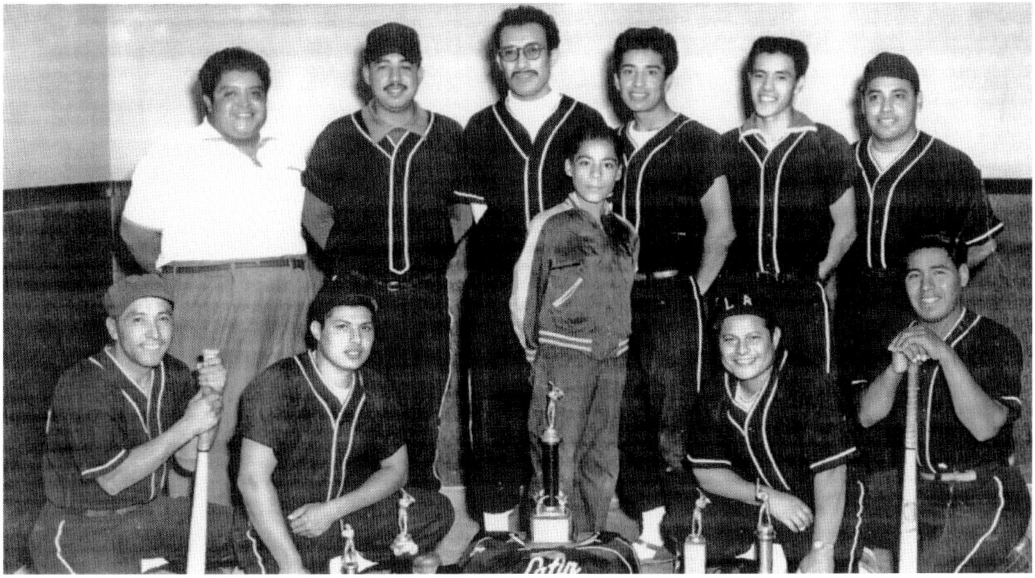

The Garden City Latin American Club fast pitch softball team was created by returning World War II veterans because of the denial of their basic civil rights in Kansas. They formed the Latin Youth group to further their social and political goals. The club existed from 1945 to 1962. By 1920, Kansas had the largest Mexican population of any Midwestern state. From left to right are (first row) Albert Mesa Sr., Jesse Ávila, Benny Guerrero, Buck Ávila, and Andrew Guerrero; (second row) Rufus Delgado, Joe Delgado, Daniel Mujica, Seco García, Paul Hernández, and Rudy Valenzuela. (Courtesy of Fred Medina and the Finney County Historical Museum.)

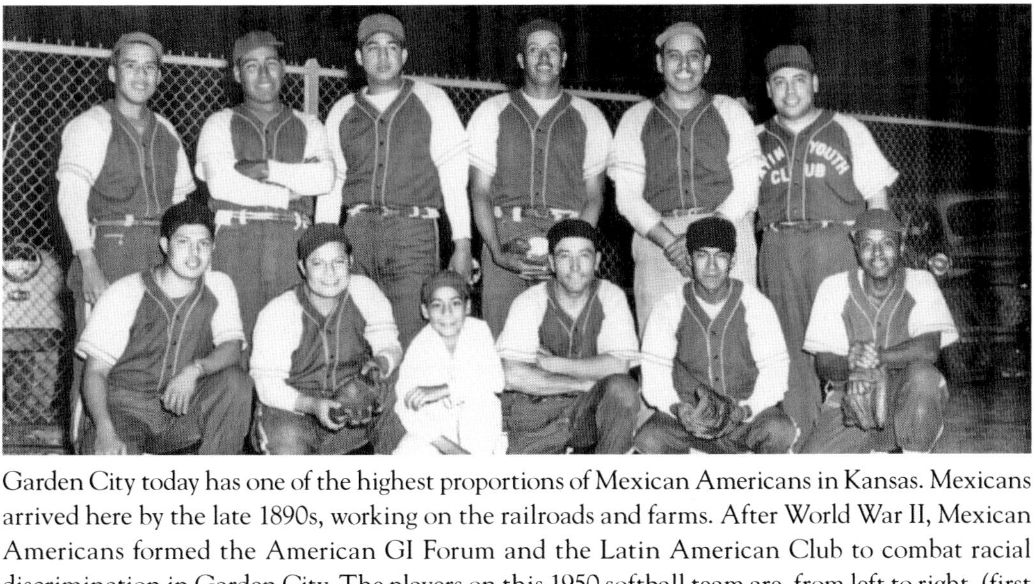

Garden City today has one of the highest proportions of Mexican Americans in Kansas. Mexicans arrived here by the late 1890s, working on the railroads and farms. After World War II, Mexican Americans formed the American GI Forum and the Latin American Club to combat racial discrimination in Garden City. The players on this 1950 softball team are, from left to right, (first row) Ignacio Ávila, Nick Ortiz Sr., Andrew Guerrero, Albert Mesa Sr., Teek Mesa, and Matthew Mora; (second row) Henry Ramírez, Dionicio García, Leonard Perales, unidentified, Joe Delgado, and Daniel Mujica. (Courtesy of Gene T. Chávez.)

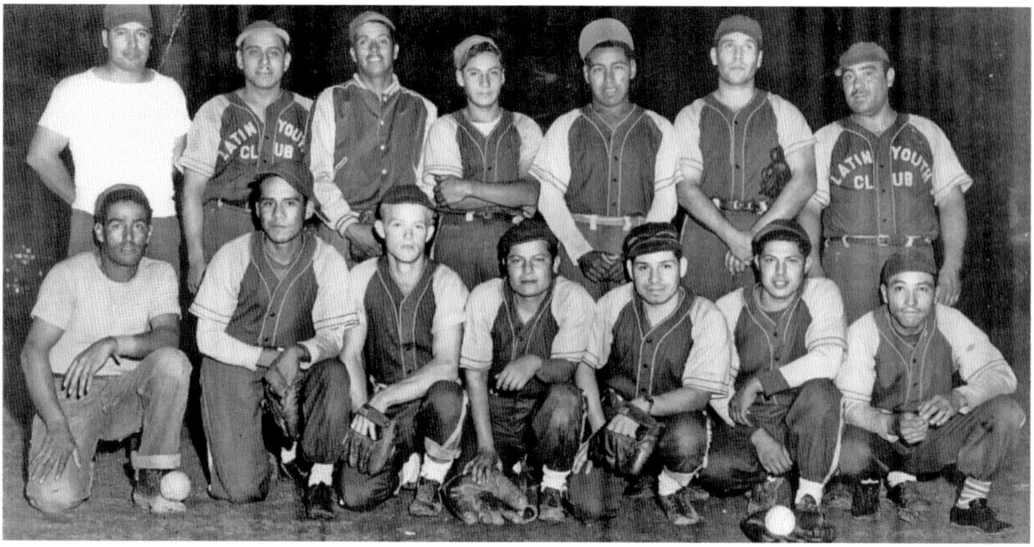

This 1950 Garden City Latin American Club fast pitch softball team was so competitive that it won the subdistrict and the Southwest Kansas District tournament, gaining a berth in the state tournament in Great Bend. A 1952 team placed second in the district tournament. From left to right are (first row) Jesse Ávila, Buck Ávila, Benny Guerrero, Albert Mesa Sr., George Servantz, Oliver Dandridge, and unidentified; (second row) Leo Servantz, Andrew Guerrero, Joe Delgado, Dave Martínez, D.C. García, Rudy Valenzuela, and unidentified. (Courtesy of Fred Medina and the Finney County Historical Museum.)

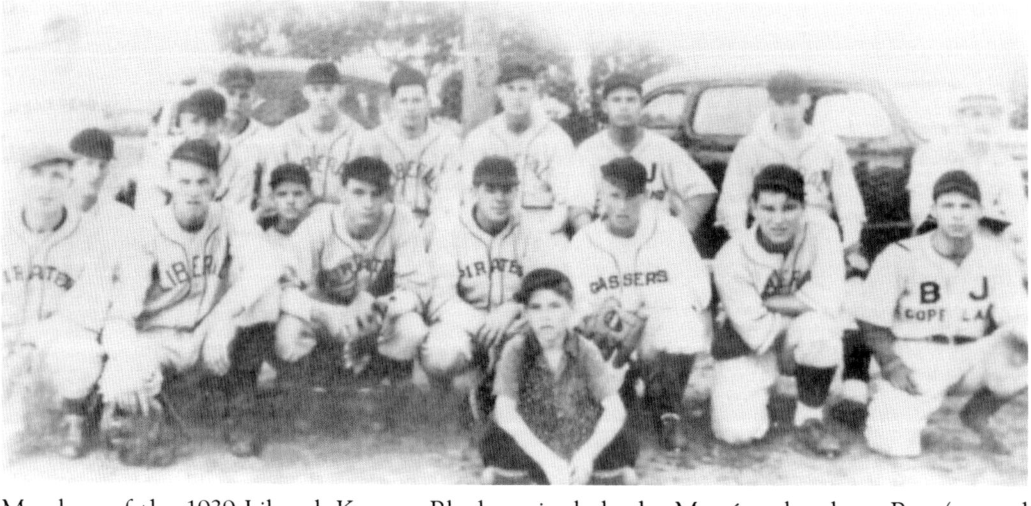

Members of the 1939 Liberal, Kansas, Blacksox include the Martínez brothers, Ray (second row, third from left) and Jay (first row, far right). Ray and Jay were born in Copeland, Kansas, to immigrant parents; they were the only Mexican family in Copeland. The brothers were extraordinary athletes in high school as four-year lettermen in football, basketball, and baseball. Ray played ball in the Army Air Corps while stationed in England from 1944 to 1945, attached to a fighter squadron. Several Mexican Americans on this team also served in World War II. (Courtesy of Rod Martínez.)

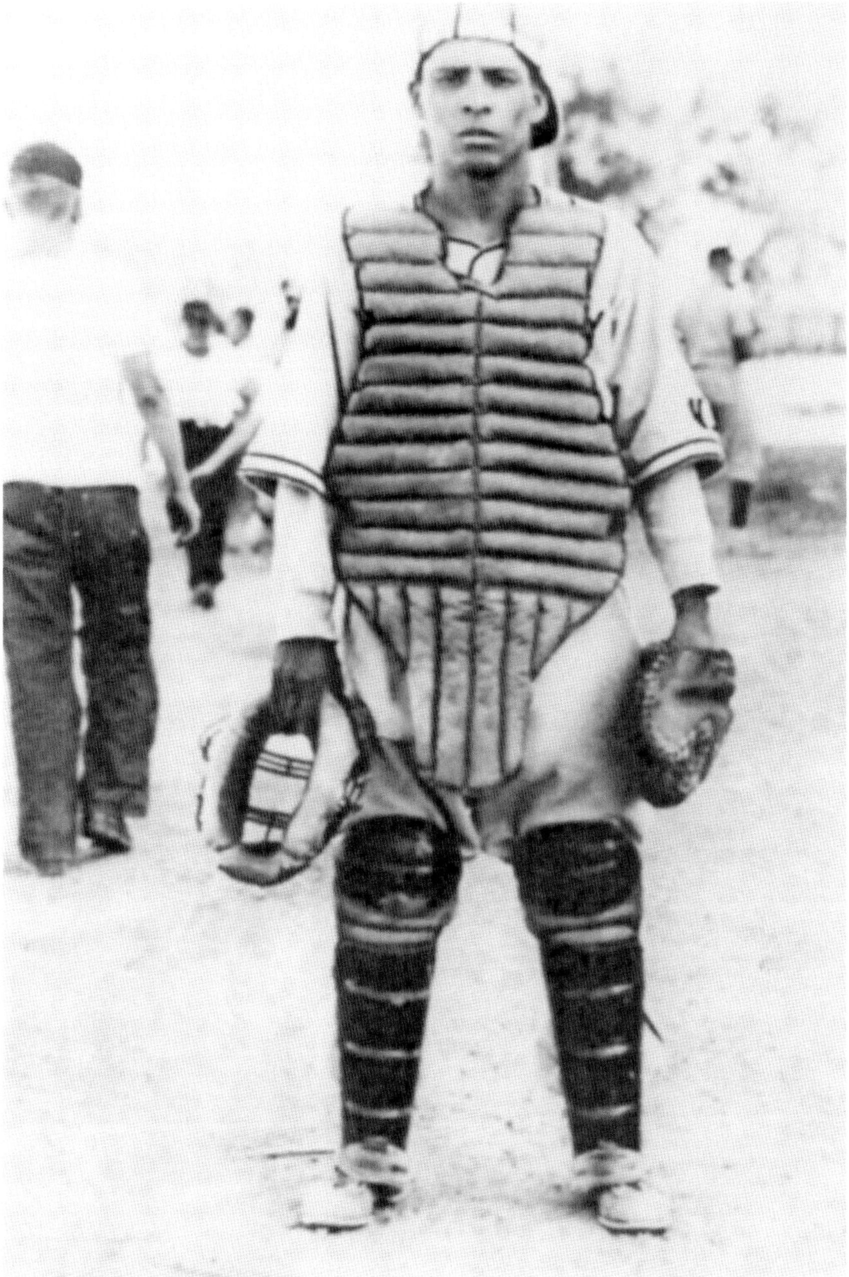

Jay Martínez of Copeland caught for the Dodge City Cowboys in 1947. Jay and his brother, Ray, helped lead another team to success, the Ban Johnson Blacksox of Liberal, Kansas. The Blacksox won the championship of the Western Division of the Ban Johnson League in the team's first year. The Western Division consisted of teams from other Kansas cities, including Dodge City, Garden City, Larned, and Pratt. During World War II, several Mexican families sent sons to war, including the Ramírez family from Emporia, which had six sons who served. (Courtesy of Rod Martínez.)

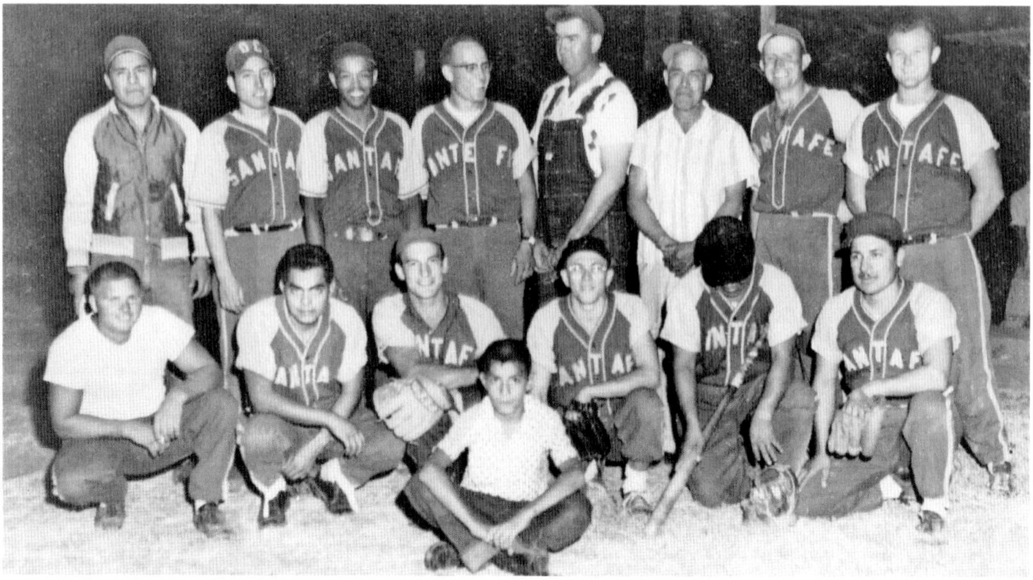

This 1950s Santa Fe Railroad team from Dodge City worked in the roundhouse and repaired tracks and bridges. They lived in the Mexican village on railroad property near the roundhouse at the eastern outskirts of the city. From left to right are (first row) Bob Hudson, Albert González, two unidentified, Marley Espinosa, batboy Louis Sánchez, and Pete González; (second row) Ed Gonzáles, Junior Esquibel, Hubert Bray, Dick Kline, Bill Maskus, coach Domingo González, and two unidentified. The Mexican population was extremely mobile, moving from state to state looking for work. (Courtesy of the Kansas Heritage Center, Dodge City.)

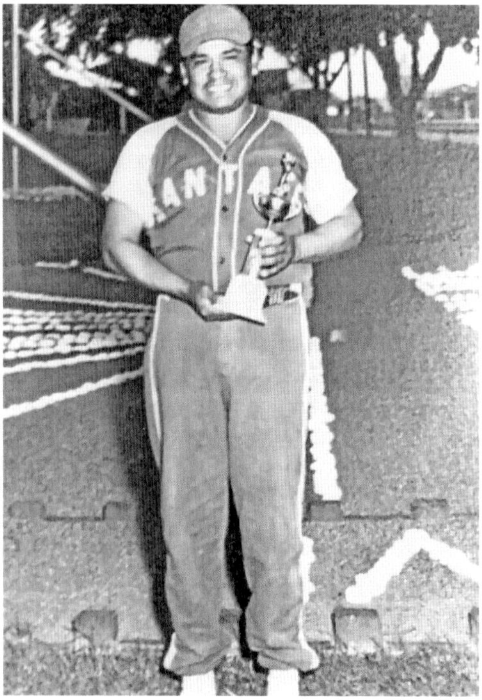

Marley Espinoza, from Dodge City, was a member of the 1952–1953 Railroaders, a Santa Fe Railroad–sponsored softball team that played at Wright Park, near the banks of the Arkansas River. In addition to playing local teams like Kline's Dairy, it was not unusual for the Railroaders to travel 270 miles to Topeka to play the game they loved so much. Marley is standing near the mountain time zone sundial at the east end of the historic Santa Fe depot. By far, the biggest employers of Mexicans in the Midwest were the railroads. By 1908, the Santa Fe and Southern Pacific railroad companies were hiring an average of 1,000 Mexicans a month. (Courtesy of Linda Espinosa.)

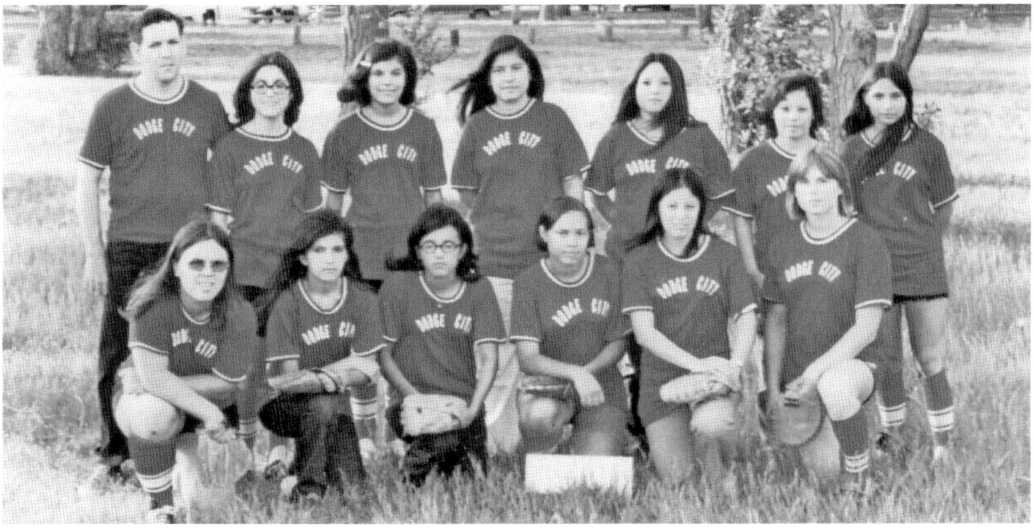

This 1971 Dodge City softball team traveled 52 miles on weekends to Garden City to play. Because Kansas is so sparsely populated, teams from farming communities also traveled to Garden City. Women's league games were played at Fansler Field at Richardson Park. From left to right are (first row) Debbie Locker, Elvira Martínez, Marion Martínez, Florence Robinson, Rachel Sumaya, and Debbie Stoss; (second row) coach Tony Remigio, Dot Remigio, Bobbie Remigio, Vicki Sánchez, Liz Martínez, Bea Sumaya, and Gina Rodríguez. (Courtesy of Advera Remigio.)

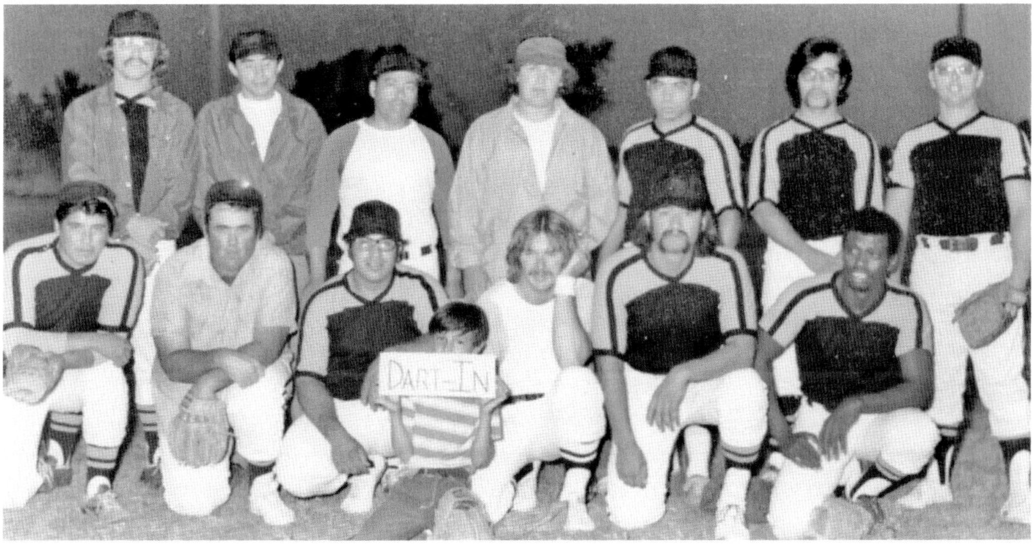

The 1972 Garden City, Kansas, Dart-In softball team was sponsored by Paul Dart, who provided several sets of uniforms and finances for in and out of state tournaments in Denver, Amarillo, Wichita, and Hutchinson. The team's city games were played at Fansler and Clever fields and were supported by the public enthusiastically. From left to right are (first row) Frank Medina, Johnnie Holmes Jr., Robert De La Rosa, batboy Fred Medina Jr., Joe Rangel, Mike García, and Johnnie Johnson; (second row) Ron Whitman, Fred Medina, Benny Guerrero, Walt Donaho, Johnny Guerrero, Bosco Rojas, and Johnnie Holmes. (Courtesy of Fred Medina.)

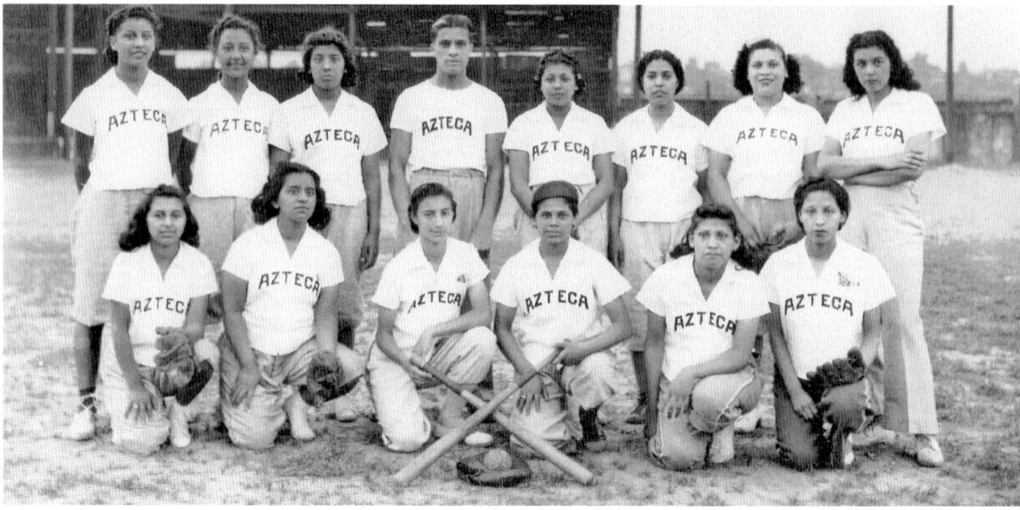

The 1940 Kansas City Aztecas women's team played at Brenneison ballpark located at St. Paul and Scott Streets. Mary Montes (second row, third from right), born in 1918, lived near the diamond, but the family house was demolished due to the construction of the Seventh Street viaduct. There were several surrounding ballparks constructed by businesses where their company teams played, including the Union Pacific Railroad, Rock Island Railroad, Aristo Flour Company, and the Pete Bros. Soap Company. Montes's daughter, Rose Arroyo, also played ball. (Courtesy of Mary Montes Arroyo.)

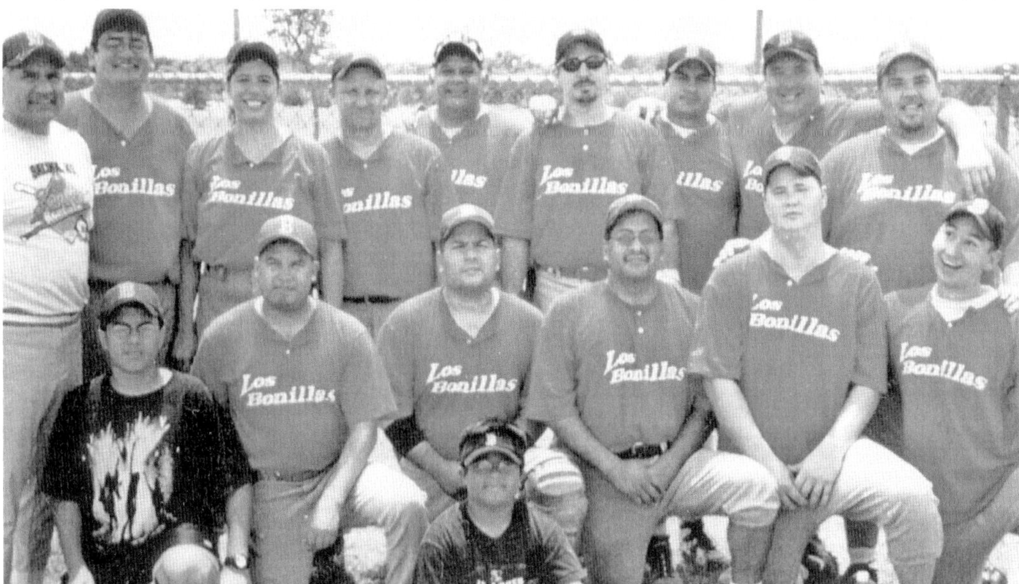

None of the players on this 2003 Los Bonillas fast pitch softball team from Salina, Kansas, are identified. The history of the Bonilla family and fast pitch softball began in the late 1960s, when US Marine Santos Bonilla returned home from Vietnam and formed the Bonilla family team. Prior to the war, Santos was a member of the Our Lady of Guadalupe team. Sadly, the church was purchased and later torn down, making way for an urban renewal project. This injustice led to the formation of the Bonilla family softball team in 1968. (Courtesy of Rodrigo Bonilla.)

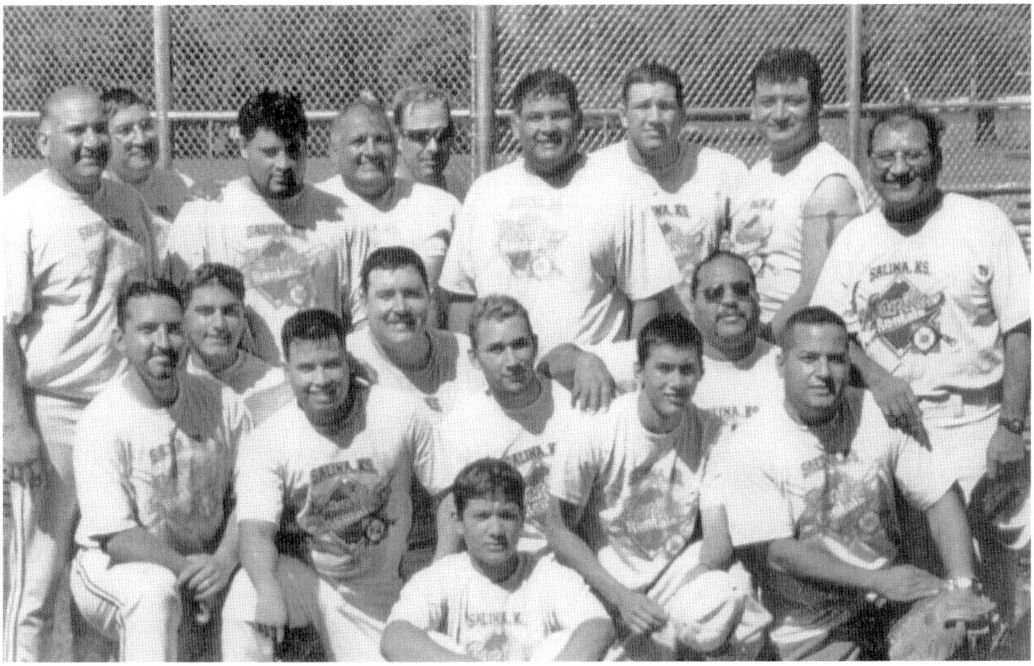

The 1998 Bonilla Rentals fast pitch softball family team from Salina had its beginning when Fortunato Bonilla and Norberta ? migrated from Chihuahua, Mexico, to work the beet fields of southwest Kansas with their parents over 100 years ago. They married in the small town of Deerfield, Kansas, and moved to Salina in 1920. Their family grew, with one daughter and nine sons. Santos Bonilla started the family team in 1968. The team played in two leagues in Salina and Chapman, Kansas. (Courtesy of Rodrigo Bonilla.)

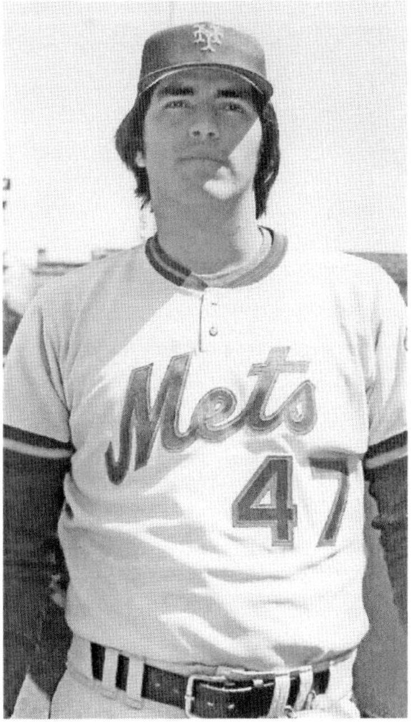

Nieves Mardie Cornejo was born in 1951 in Wellington, Kansas, one of seven children of Nieves and Jessie Cornejo. His father coached him to be a pitcher and shortstop. His Babe Ruth League team went to the World Series in Fairbanks, Alaska, but later lost the championship in New Orleans. He played at the American Legion level and in 1969 was drafted by the Seattle Pilots but decided to attend college. He was drafted by the New York Mets in 1973 and made his major-league debut in 1978 at Shea Stadium, where he defeated the Montreal Expos in 48-degree weather. Mardie has had several highlights and lowlights, like when Pete Rose hit a home run off him during a nationally televised game. Mardie's son, Nate, also played in the major leagues. (Courtesy of Mardie Cornejo.)

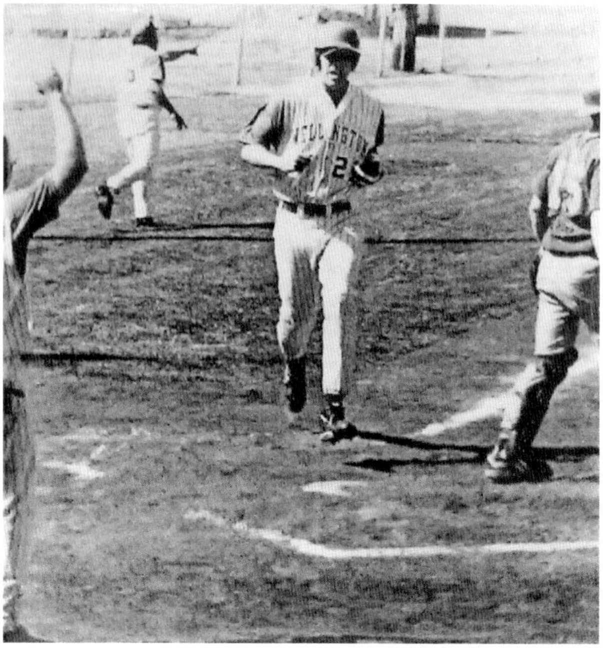

Nathan "Nate" John Cornejo was born in 1979 in Wellington to Teresa and Mardie Cornejo. He pitched in the Continental Amateur Baseball Association World Series, which his team won, and was one of only two freshmen on the high school varsity team, joining his older brother Jesse. Jesse played minor-league ball for the Tampa Bay Devil Rays. Nate was a top major-league prospect in high school due to 96-mile-per-hour pitching. In his senior year, he was the Gatorade Kansas Player of the Year. He made his major-league debut with the Detroit Tigers in 2001. (Courtesy of Nate Cornejo.)

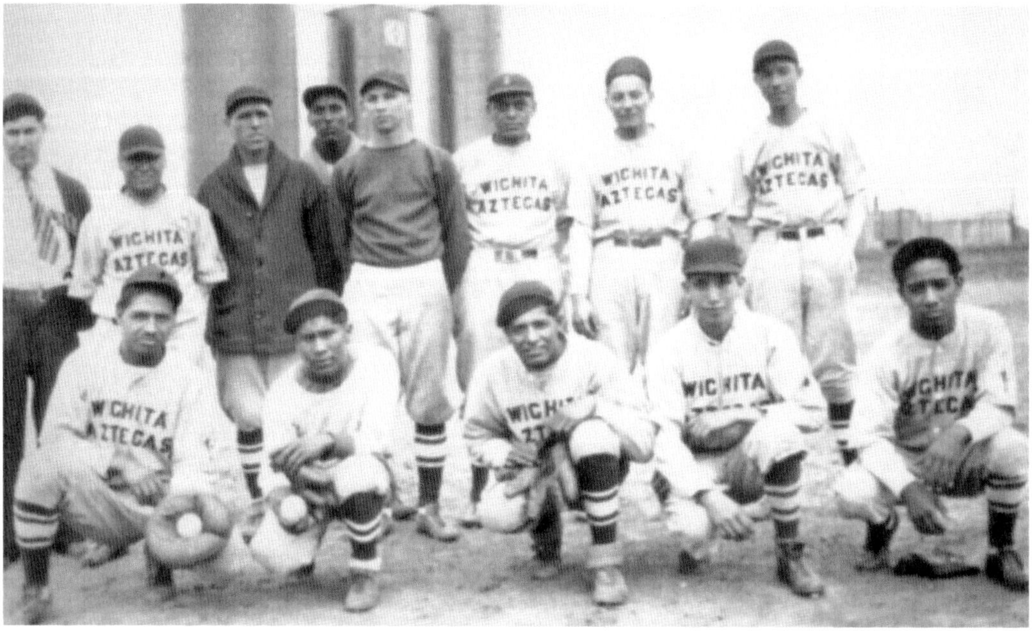

The Wichita Aztecas, like so many other teams, loaded up cars or chartered buses with players, coaches, and families and headed off to their destinations, arriving late Friday night or early Saturday morning to play their archrivals. Sometimes hundreds of fans watched the games and cheered for their homegrown heroes and favorite teams. In the evening, a giant fiesta took place where both teams and their families and fans enjoyed good food, music, dancing, and drink together. On Sunday morning, the weekend guests made the long journey home to start another physically demanding workweek. (Courtesy of the Latino Baseball History Project.)

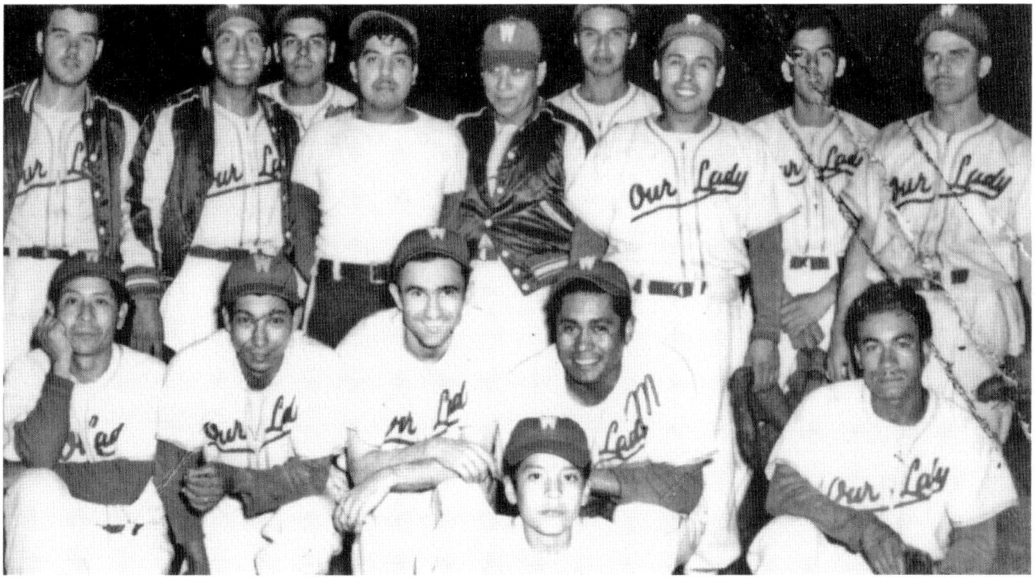

The 1946 Our Lady of Perpetual Help Church fast pitch softball team from Wichita competed in a tournament in Hutchinson, Kansas. The church was built by the team near East Twenty-First and North Broadway Streets. The railroads helped create the north-side barrios through company housing. From left to right are (first row) Tony Solís, Manuel Martínez, Joe Martínez, Manuel Díaz, and Brady Díaz, with batboy Tony Solis Jr. in front; (second row) Louie Castro, Larry Ramírez, Tex Díaz, Tino Rosales, Frank Rosales, Johnny Sánchez, Louie Ramírez, Gilbert Resa, and Frank Morales. (Courtesy of Andy Ramírez.)

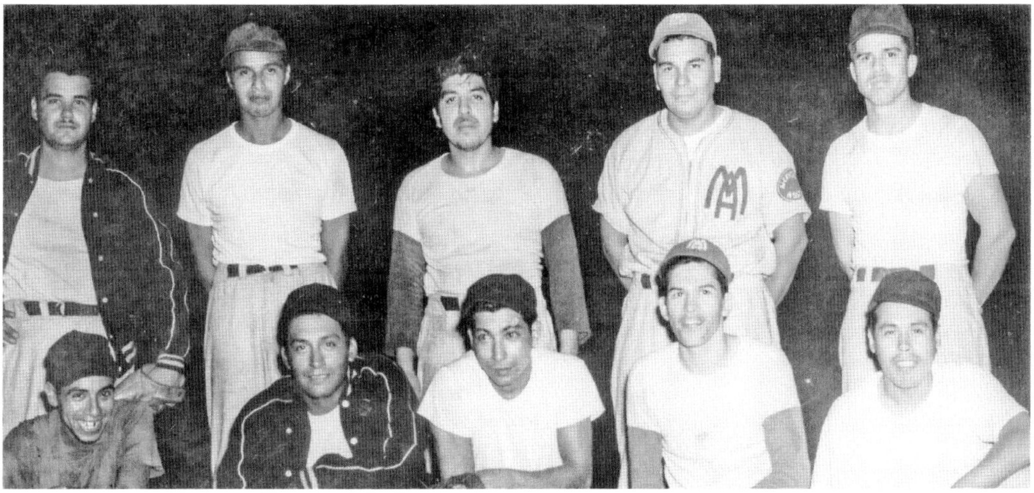

This is the 1948 Mexican Association fast pitch softball team from Wichita. Most of these players were on the 1946 team as well. They lived in El Huarache barrio at the north end of Wichita, east of Broadway Street. Games were played at El Huarache Park, surrounded by fields near the grain elevators and meatpacking plants. From left to right are (first row) Lucas Rodríguez, Larry Ramírez, Manuel Martínez, James García, and Louie Ramírez; (second row) Louie Castro, Johnny Sánchez, Tino Rosales, Tex Díaz, and Frank Morales. (Courtesy of Andy Ramírez.)

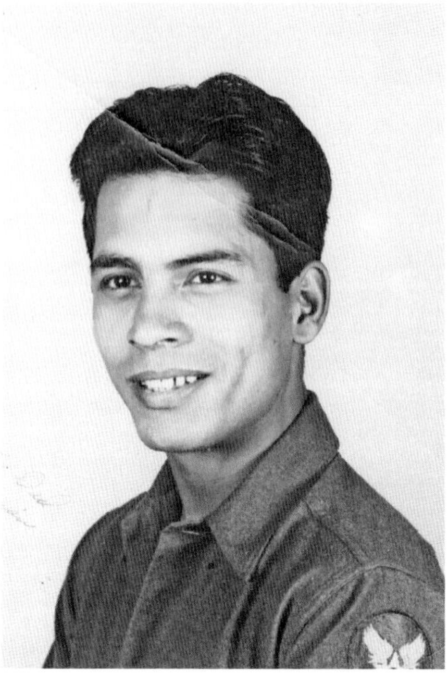

During World War II, Cpl. Ramón Martínez from Copeland, Kansas, was stationed at Wattisham Air Field in England with the 434th Fighter Squadron of the 479th Fighter Group. Ramón's love of baseball was a deep passion from his early years in high school to the battlefields of England to coaching a city league team when he returned home. By 1939, at the age of 17, he began playing semi-professional baseball with the Liberal, Kansas, Blacksox of the Ban Johnson League. That same year, Brooklyn Dodger scout Bert Wells offered him a contract for $90 a month, but Ramón turned down the offer. In 1944, while stationed in England, he helped form a baseball team that won the championship of the 65th Fighter Wing in 1945. Their prize was a week in Edinburgh, Scotland. Back home, his integrated team, the Newton Lions, went undefeated. (Courtesy of Rod Martínez.)

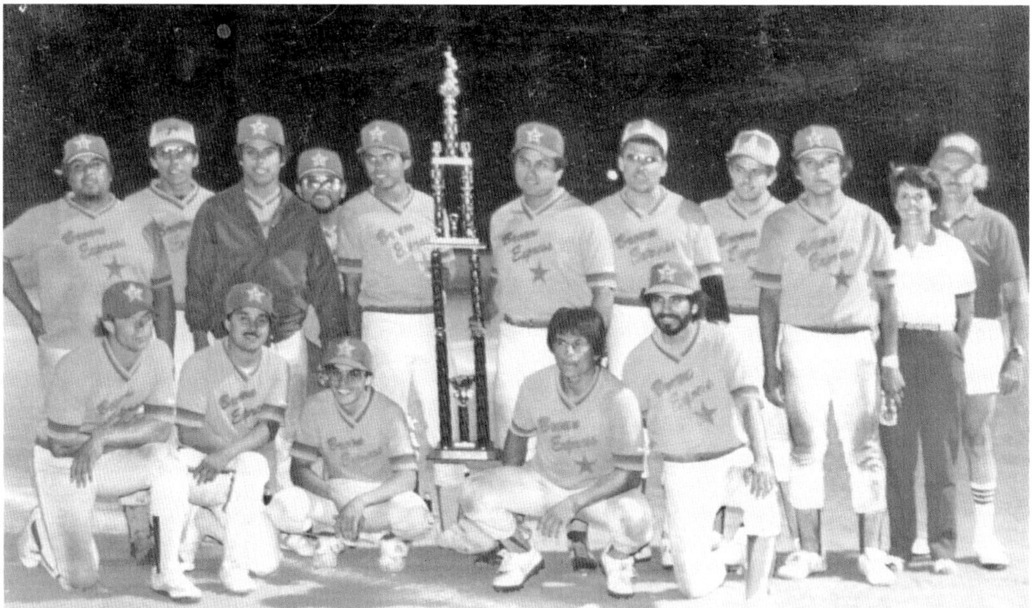

The 1982 Emporia Brown Express softball team was coached by Gilbert Rodríguez. Here they proudly display their first-place trophy at Our Lady of Guadalupe Catholic Church's field in South Hutchinson. David, Chris, and Pete Rodríguez are members of the Mexican American Hall of Fame. From left to right are (first row) Steve Kolmer, Art Tabares, Matt Torres, Fred Águilar, and Steve Cabaral; (second row) Gabriel Rodríguez, Pete Rodríguez, David Rodríguez, Joe Silva, Tippy Martínez, Gilbert Rodríguez, Jeff López, Curt López, Jerry Rodríguez, and two unidentified tournament officials. (Courtesy of David Rodríguez.)

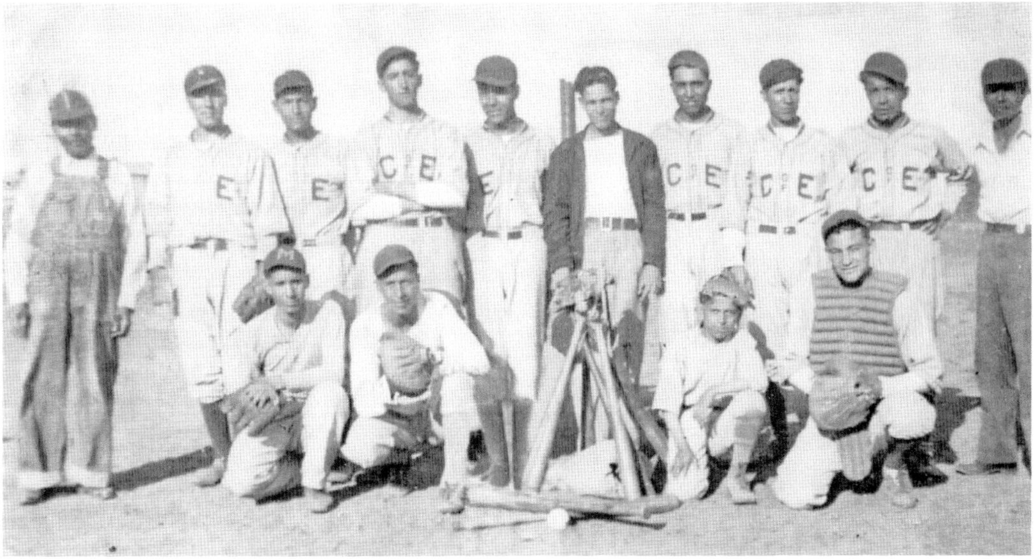

This team from Emporia was formed in 1928. The players are unidentified. During this time, there were outstanding Mexican teams and players from Peabody, Florence, Newton, Garden City, and Coffeyville. In 1920, the Mexican population in Kansas was nearly 14,000, with most employed by the Santa Fe Railroad. These men lived in converted boxcars west of Emporia near the roundhouse in an area known as Little Mexico. Permanent housing was later established in two distinct areas known as Las Colonias and Las Casitas. (Courtesy of David Delgado.)

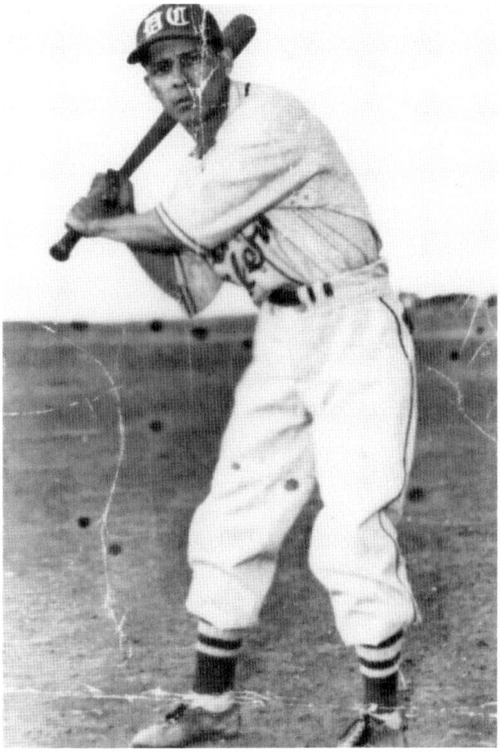

Jay Martínez is seen here in 1950 in Copeland, Kansas. In the late 1930s, he and his brother Ramón were outstanding baseball players in high school. The Liberal, Kansas, high school baseball coach referred to the Martínez brothers as the "two red hot chili peppers." Both boys were subject to racism and were even threatened with death if they played in a football game. Ramón and Jay played for the semi-professional team, the Liberal Blacksox, in the Ban Johnson League and for the Texaco Oilers in Woodward, Oklahoma. Jay was considered an outstanding catcher, and teams rarely ran against him on the bases. It was not unusual to find Jay playing or coaching baseball in Copeland, Dodge City, and Sublette, Kansas. In Copeland, he formed a little league team, building the field himself and passing the hat to pay for balls and bats. (Courtesy of Mark Martínez.)

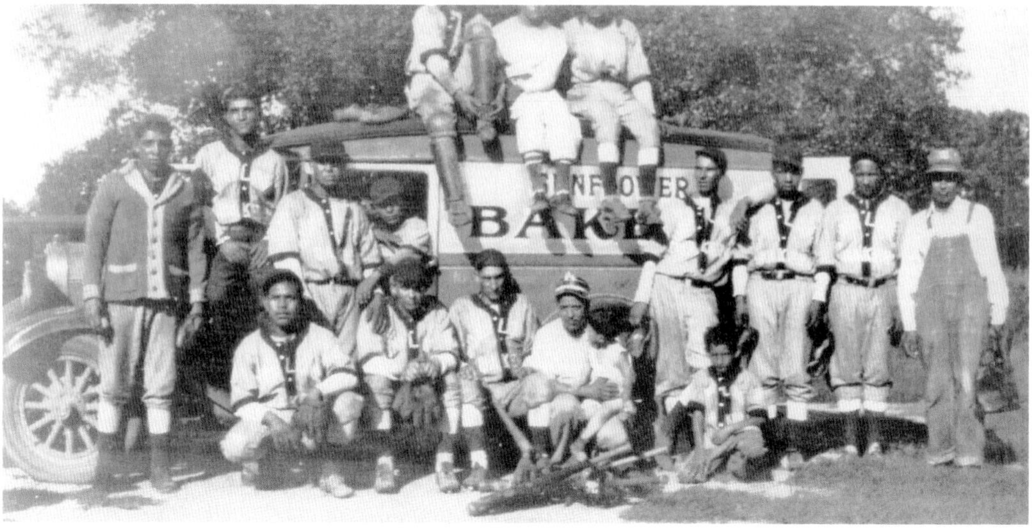

The 1932 Los Bakers team from Topeka made their own fields, frequently in vacant lots or in pastures near the railroad yards, roundhouses, or meatpacking houses. Women sewed the bases from worn-out pillows; sometimes dried-out cow chips were used as bases too. Because Mexicans were often segregated into the less desirable areas of town, like near rivers, several Mexican communities were destroyed by massive floods. Unfortunately, important family documents, precious photographs, and hand-me-down family heirlooms were often lost forever. (Courtesy of Robert and Hazel Gómez.)

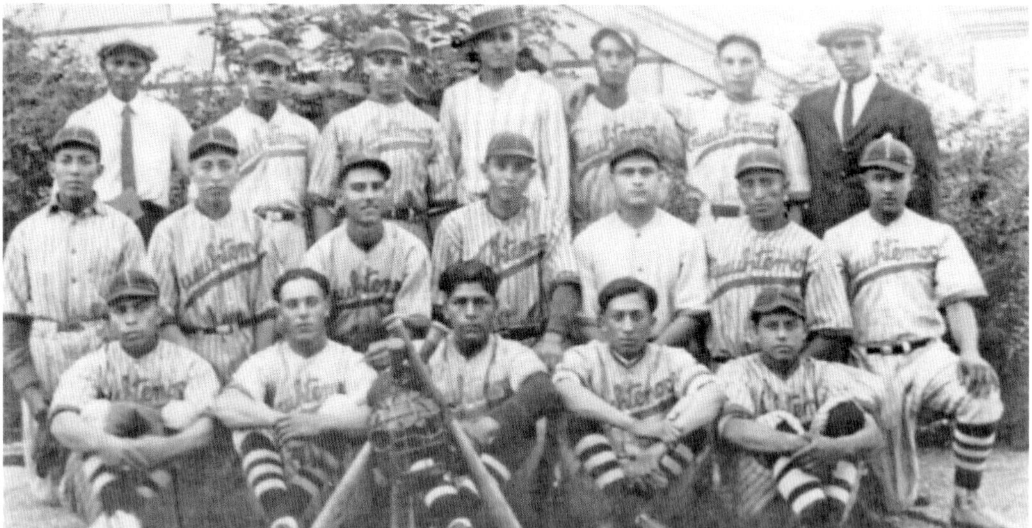

This 1929 Topeka, Kansas, baseball team was one of dozens of Mexican American teams across the United States that adopted the name of Los Cuauhtémocs, a tribute to the last Aztec king, Cuauhtémoc, who ruled from 1519 to 1521, until the Spanish conquest of Mexico. At games, the winners usually received 60 percent of the gate, while the losers took home 40 percent. This increased the intensity of the games. (Courtesy of Robert and Hazel Gómez.)

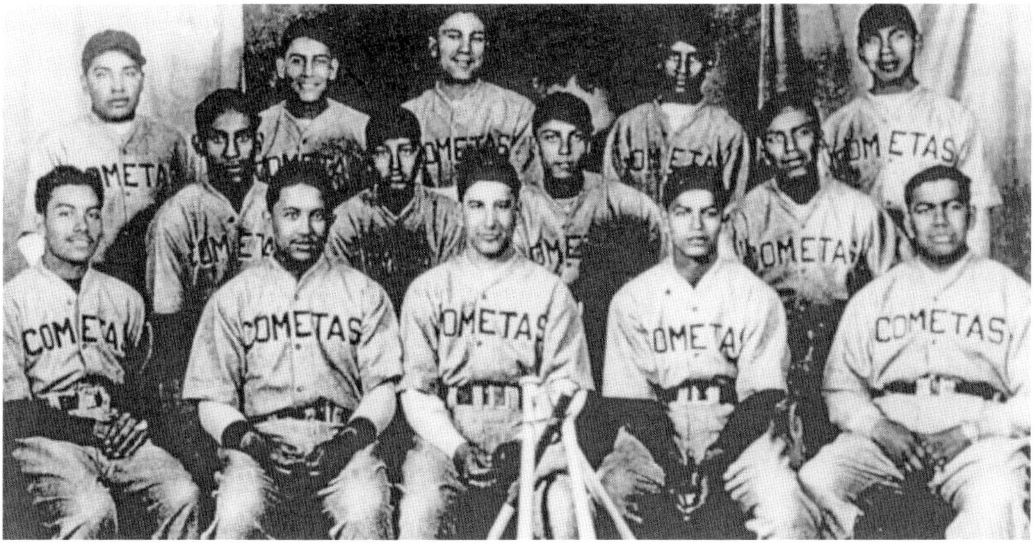

Los Cometas (the Comets), playing in Topeka in 1930, were among countless teams that followed the tradition of adopting names in Spanish, most likely because of the racist exclusion of Mexican Americans from public leagues and parks. As a consequence, Mexican Americans established an elaborate network of community teams, leagues, tournaments, and fields. Adopting Spanish names reaffirmed their language, heritage, and Mexican identity. This reaffirmation of culture and language was reignited by the Chicano movement in Kansas starting in the 1960s, especially on college campuses. (Courtesy of Robert and Hazel Gómez.)

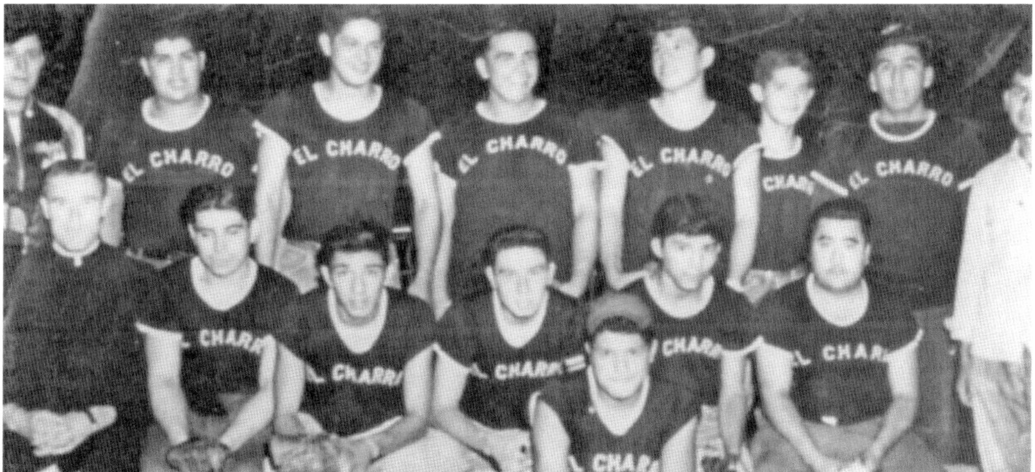

After World War II, softball became very popular within Mexican American communities. In addition to games, annual tournaments were sponsored in several states, bringing together families and fans from many communities, especially in the Midwest. Los Charros (the Horsemen), from Chanute, Kansas, were sponsored by St. Patrick's Catholic Church. The team, seen here in 1951, participated in the Chanute softball tournament from 1963 to 1979, attracting teams from Kansas City, Topeka, Lawrence, Emporia, Newton, Wichita, Parsons, Hutchinson, and Salina. (Courtesy of John and Antonia Alonzo.)

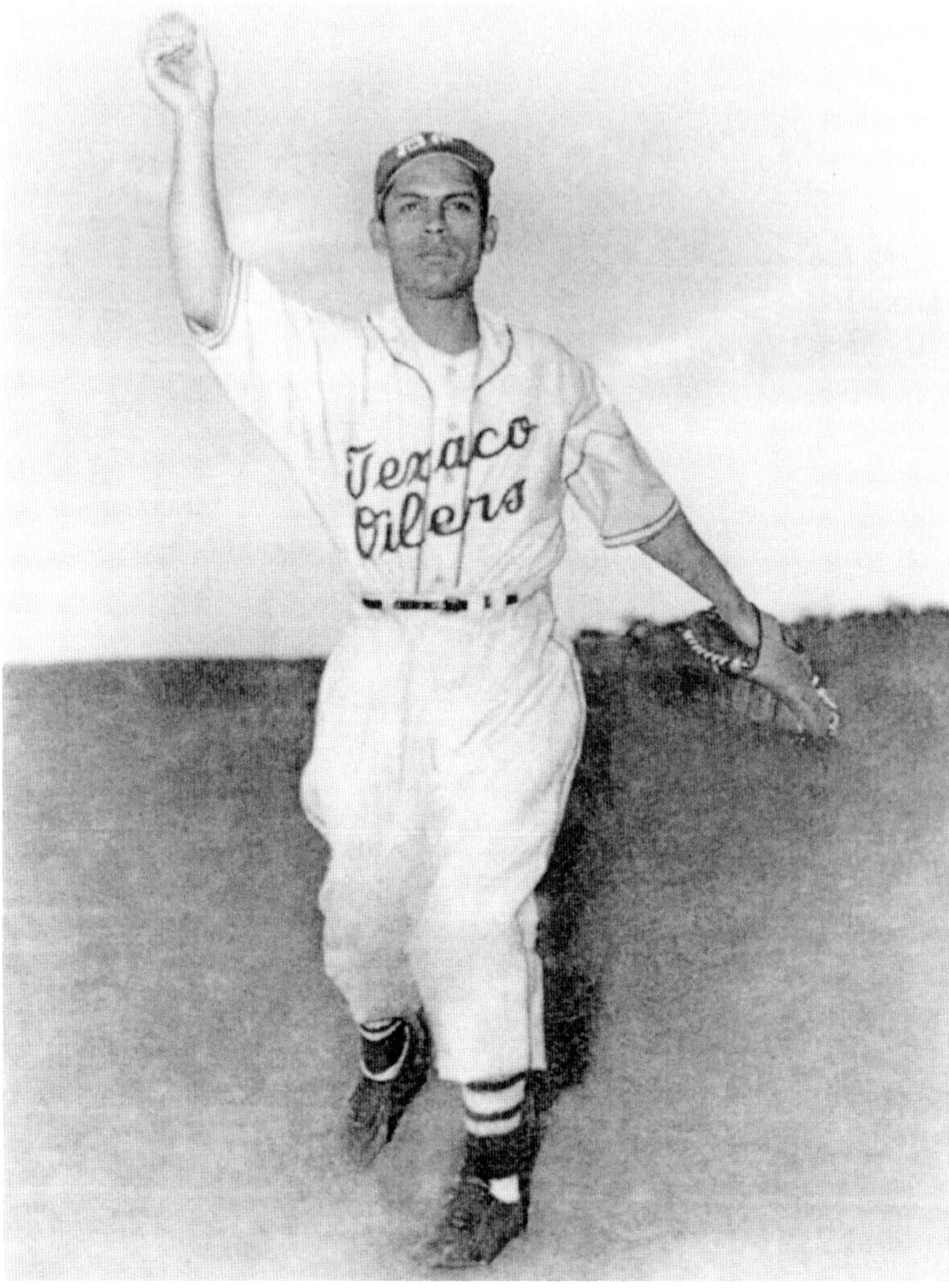

Ray Martínez was a member of the Woodward, Oklahoma, Texaco Oilers. A promising career came his way in 1939 when he was approached by Brooklyn Dodgers scout Bert Wells, who offered him a professional contract for $90 a month plus housing and food. Martínez turned down the offer because he was making more money playing for the Liberal, Kansas, Blacksox. Local community teams paid their players decent salaries and provided good jobs, preventing them from being taken by professional teams. (Courtesy of Rod Martínez.)

6

COAST TO COAST

Mexican Americans are a national ethnic group. They have often been mistakenly viewed as a regional group residing in the Southwest, states that were the territory of Mexico prior to 1848. While the majority of Mexican Americans do reside in California, New Mexico, Arizona, Colorado, and Texas, the truth is that Mexicans are found in nearly every state of the Union. Since the late 1800s and early 1900s, Mexicans have traveled to every corner of the country, seeking work in the Northwest, the Midwest, the East Coast, and the South. By the 1920s, Mexicans were a significant part of the labor force in nearly every industry, including agriculture, railroads, steel mills, auto plants, mining, foundries, farming, dairies, ranching, shipping, tanneries, brickyards, and cement plants.

Since the early 20th century, Mexican communities could be found in Washington, Oregon, Montana, Utah, Idaho, Nebraska, Kansas, Missouri, Iowa, Ohio, Pennsylvania, New York, Florida, Louisiana, Oklahoma, Minnesota, Wisconsin, Indiana, Illinois, and Michigan. Their housing ranged from boxcars to tenements to company housing. Regardless of where they settled, Mexicans and their American-born offspring were confronted by prejudice and discrimination in housing, employment, education, religion, and recreational facilities.

In particular, during the Great Depression, Mexicans shared the horrible experience of the Repatriation Program, a federal-state collaboration to round up and deport Mexicans and their American-born children to Mexico. Nearly 500,000 were deported. The combined social and economic consequences of the Depression and repatriation had a ruinous impact on Mexican neighborhoods, leading to significant depopulation. Especially hard hit were Cherryville and Horton, Kansas; Muscatine, Iowa; Lorain, Ohio; Oklahoma City and Dewey, Oklahoma; Chicago, Illinois; Gary and East Chicago, Indiana; Detroit, Michigan; Kansas City, Kansas and Missouri; and Milwaukee, Wisconsin. The Mexican American community bravely fought back against this expulsion and gave birth to a new generation of leaders who vigorously condemned these racist actions.

Despite numerous floods that destroyed their homes and urban renewal programs that nearly uprooted their neighborhoods, the Mexican people banded together. They rose out of the ashes of the Depression, repatriation, floods, and physical displacement to rebuild, testimony to the depth of the human spirit to survive and to pass on their wonderful history to their children, grandchildren, and great-grandchildren.

Sports, especially baseball and later softball, were a major presence in the lives of Mexicans from California to New York after World War I. More than games, baseball and softball involved nearly the entire community and had political and social importance. At games, people socialized, discussed strategies for social change, and strengthened their sense of racial and ethnic solidarity. Baseball and softball linked every Mexican community together from coast to coast.

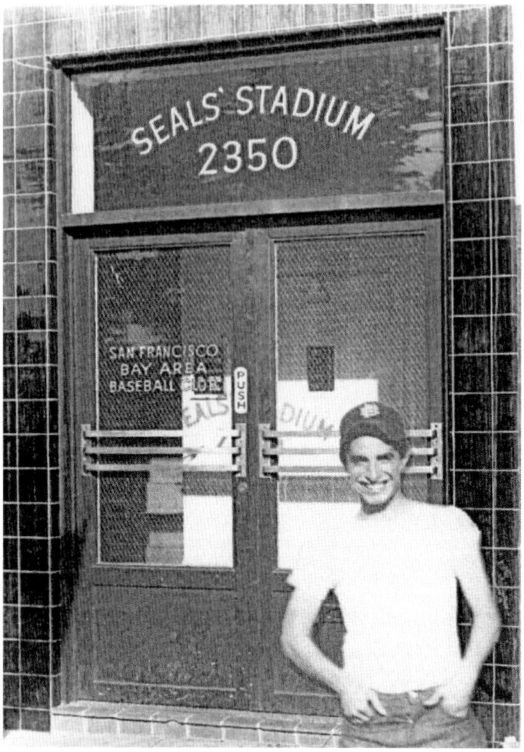

Bill Soto-Castellanos was born in San Francisco in 1935 and raised in West Berkeley, across the bay from San Francisco. He started playing second base and shortstop at Columbus School and James Kanney Park. He attended Berkeley High School, playing for the varsity team. For seven years starting at the age of 15, he worked for the Pacific Coast League San Francisco Seals as both the visitors' batboy at Seals Stadium and clubhouse manager for visiting teams. He has written a remarkable book about his clubhouse and dugout experiences. (Courtesy of Bill Soto-Castellanos.)

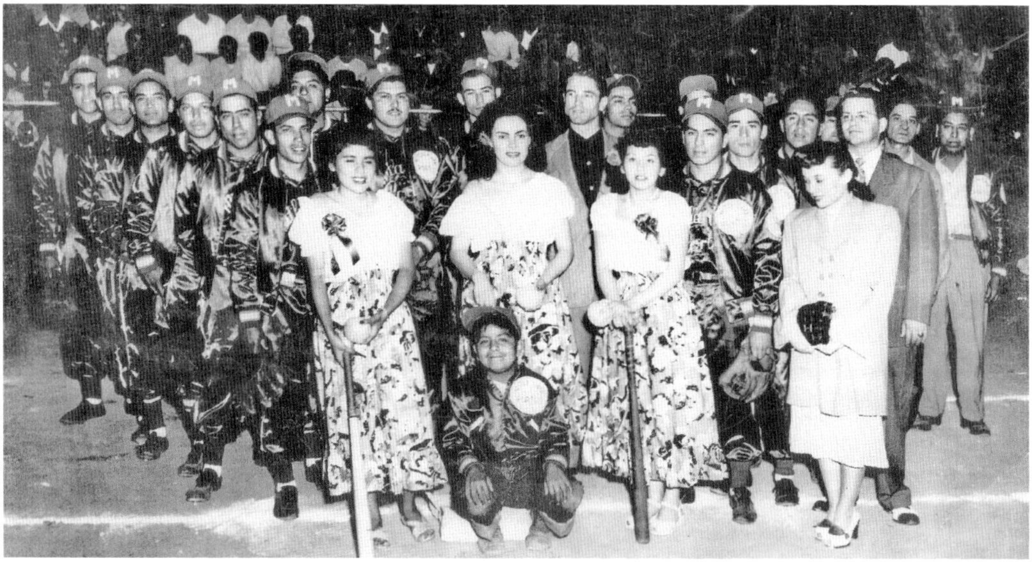

This late 1940s Mitla Café team from San Bernardino, California, poses with beauty pageant contestants from the west-side barrio. Beauty pageant contestants vied to be crowned *la reina* (queen) for the annual Mexican Independence Day parade on September 16. The Mitla Café sponsored this team, displaying the importance of merchant sponsorship in supporting community life. Founded by Lucía Rodríguez in 1937, the Mitla Café is the oldest Mexican restaurant in the Inland Empire region of Southern California. (Courtesy of the Mitla Café.)

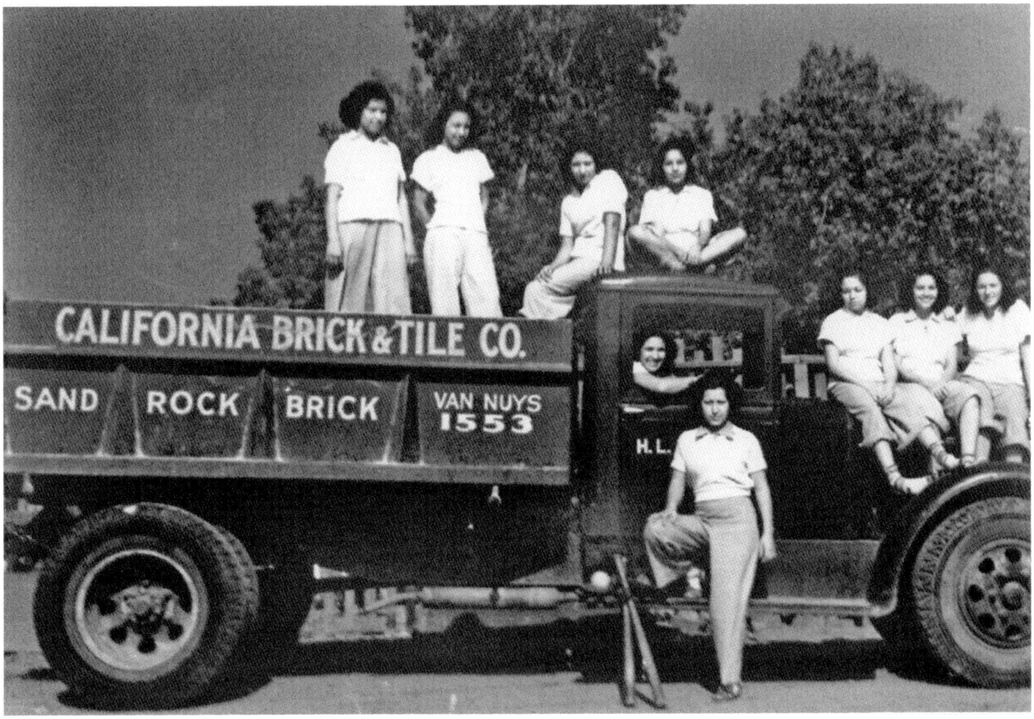

In the 1930s, the California Brick & Tile Company sponsored Van Nuys women's teams. The brickyard was at 6151 Kester Avenue in the Van Nuys barrio. The four players on top of the truck include Phyllis (standing, far left) and Eleanor Martínez (second from right). Other players include Lupe Vásquez, Sophia Vásquez, and Josie Pacheco. Phyllis and Eleanor were the daughters of Ernesto Martínez and Joaquina Bonillas. Their younger sister, Irene Martínez, also played on the Van Nuys Duchesses softball team. (Courtesy of Irene García.)

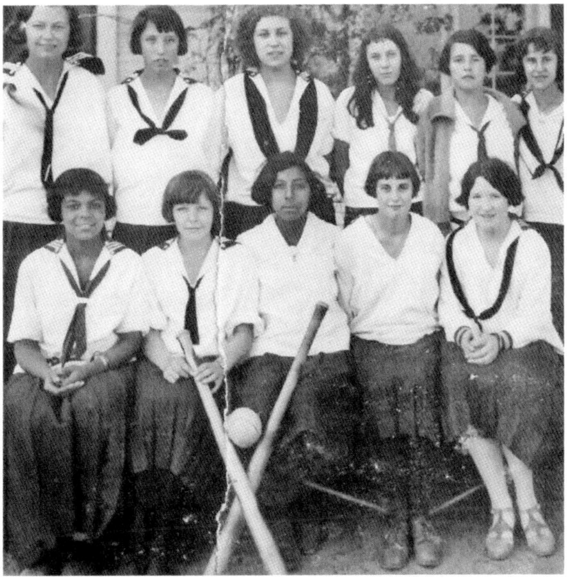

Carmen Almada Tostado (second row, second from right) was born in Mexico in 1909. Her father, Baldomero Almeida, came to Los Angeles in 1912 and served his country for 27 years, including as consul general. At Los Angeles High School, Carmen pitched several no-hitters and was elected president of the Seasonal Sports Club, part of the Girl's Athletic Association. She is seen with a team from Santa Monica. Two brothers, Melo and Louie Almada, were outstanding professional ballplayers. She married Javier Álvarez-Tostado, and they had four children. (Courtesy of Joe and John Tostado.)

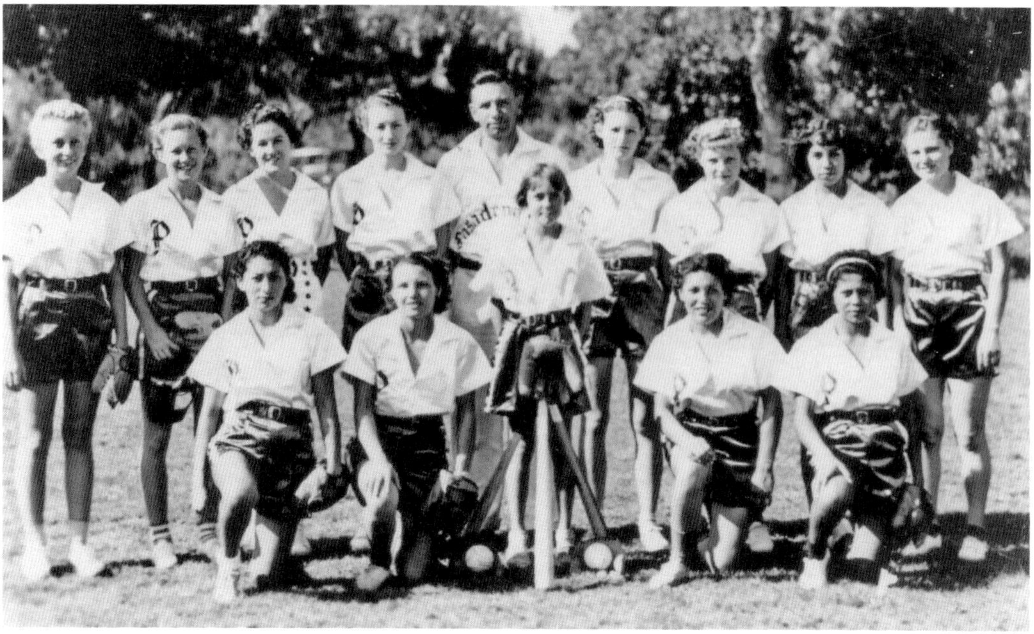

Margaret (first row, far left) and Eleanor Salazar (first row, far right) grew up in an extraordinary baseball family. Their father, Dave, was an outstanding player. The Salazars and their Orozco cousins dominated California baseball from the 1900s through the 1950s. Eleanor and Margaret are seen playing for California's Karl's Shoe Store, barnstorming against the Phoenix Ramblers. They played against the Tolleson Rockets, who featured Elosia "Locha" Díaz, a local legend. The sisters played women's teams from Monterey Park, Montebello, Burbank, and Glendale. Eleanor is the mother of major-league star Darrell Evans. (Courtesy of Carlos Salazar.)

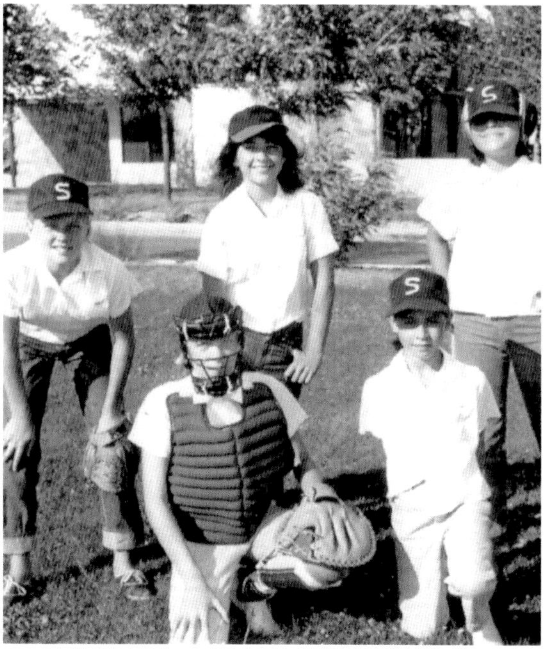

The children of US airmen stationed at Torrejon Air Force Base outside of Madrid, Spain, for several decades played in organized baseball and softball leagues. This 1965 photograph shows girls from two teams. Most of them, including catcher Janet Serros, upper right, played for the Santas (the Saints). Mary Serros Gonzáles, top center, played first base and pitched for the Gitanas (the Gypsies). The girls played in the American enclave known as Royal Oaks, which provided housing for military dependents. The girls' uniforms consisted of white shirts, jeans, and baseball caps. The United States stationed aircraft at the base from 1957 until withdrawing in 1992. (Courtesy of Mary Serros Gonzáles.)

Amelina "Amy" Peralta Shelton's (second from left) career spanned more than 20 years, including 17 with the Peterson Brooke Steiner Wist Ramblers, who earned ASA national championships in 1940, 1948, and 1949. At 23, her pitching and hitting talents lured All-American Girls Professional Baseball League (AAGPBL) scouts. She declined the opportunity because of family obligations. Her athletic prowess aided her journey to college. She earned certificates in softball, baseball, field hockey, volleyball, and track and field while attending Arizona State University, graduated with a degree in physical education, and became a member of the Women's Athletic Association. (Courtesy of Sandra Uribe.)

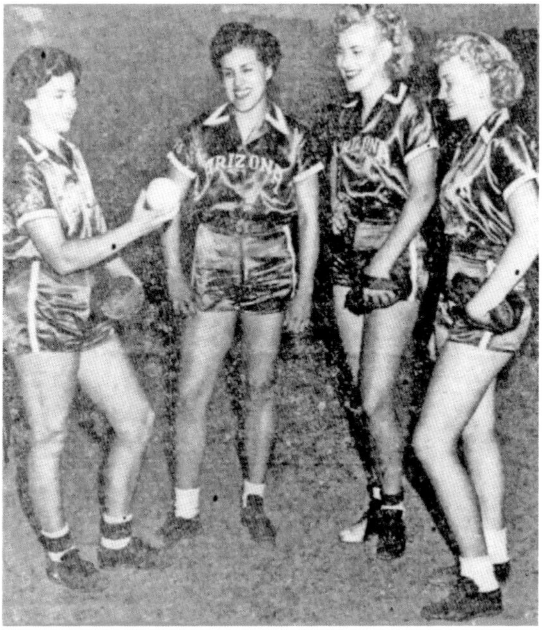

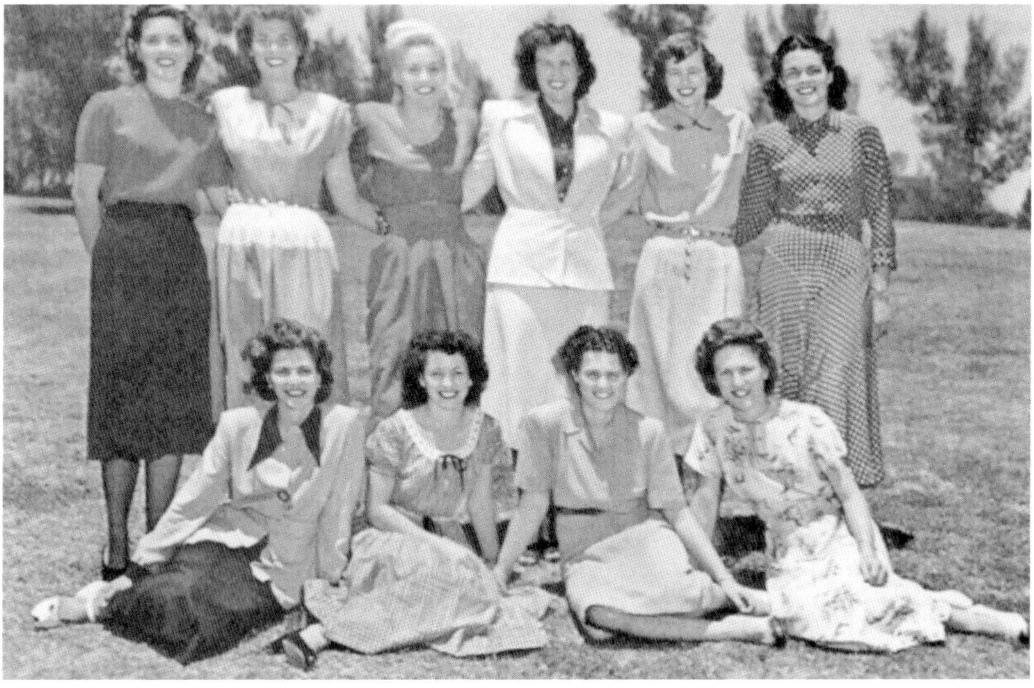

Helene "Chow" Machado Van Sant (second row, far left) of Venice, California, played in the AAGPBL for the Peoria Redwings (1946) and Fort Wayne Daisies (1947). Although a segregated league, it employed fair-skinned Latinas. She was scouted at 19, but her strict father, Porfirio, restricted her from playing until age 20. At nine, along with her four brothers, she played on teams managed by their father. In 1948, she left the league when her father fell ill, but returned in 1949 as an outfielder for the A-1 Queens. (Courtesy of Sandra Uribe.)

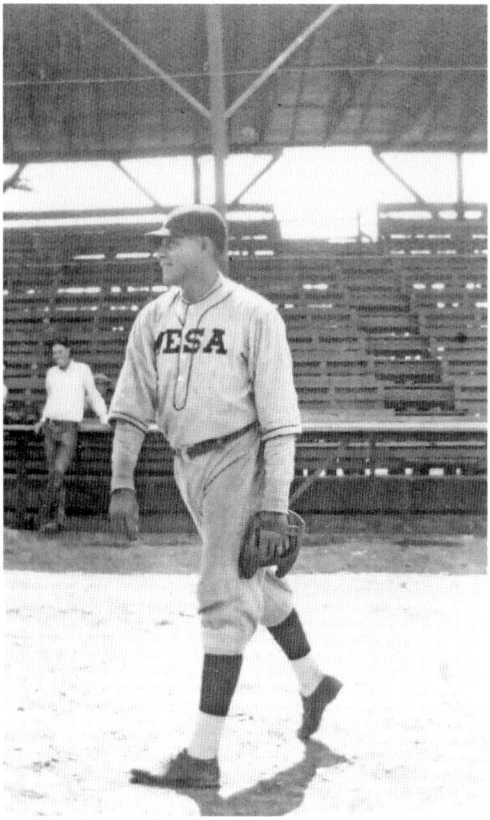

Dave Salazar pitched for the Mesa Orphans in the Arizona League during the 1920s against teams in Globe, Bisbee, Phoenix, Douglas, and Tucson. In 1924, he found time to play for the Pacific Coast League San Francisco Seals, and later played for Nogales in the Texas-Arizona League and with "outlaw leagues" in Phoenix and Tucson. He mentored Jesse Flores from La Habra, California. Flores played with the Pacific Coast League Los Angeles Angels and in the major leagues with the Cubs, Indians, and Philadelphia Athletics, and became a successful scout for the Minnesota Twins. His two sons, Jesse Jr. and Steve, are major-league scouts. (Courtesy of Carlos Salazar.)

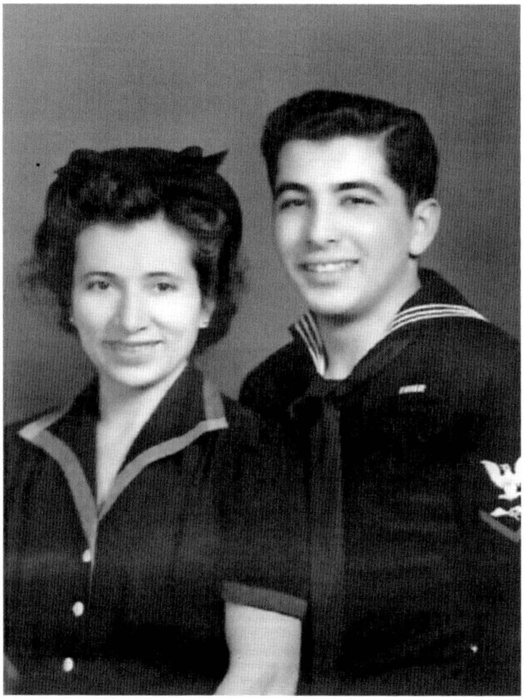

Mario Suárez is seen here with his mother, Carmen Suárez, in Tucson, Arizona. Suárez served in World War II in the Navy and was stationed in Lakehurst, New Jersey, not far from Yankee Stadium. He and his sailor buddies often went to the games to watch the Yankees and did not have to pay admission because they were in uniform. After the war, Suárez attended the University of Arizona, where he met his wife, Cecilia Cota-Robles, both of whom would later be professors at California State University at Pomona. They had three children, Francisco, an attorney; Mario Miguel, an ad executive; and Laura, a school administrator. Both Francisco and Mario Miguel played little league in the city of Rosemead, located in the San Gabriel Valley. (Courtesy of the Suárez family.)

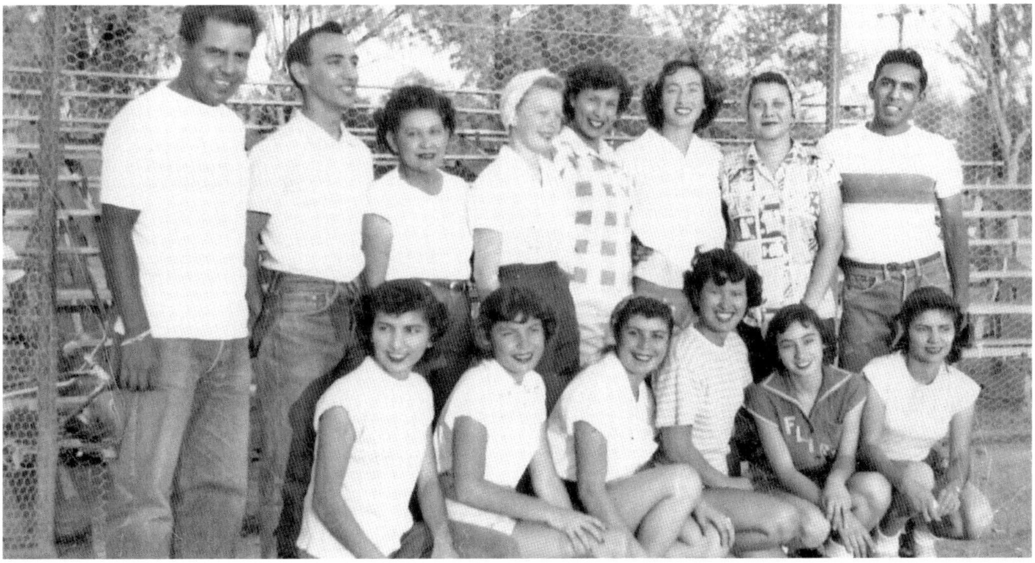

Bertha Félix is seen with a women's softball team in Tucson around 1949. She is wearing her Flirts jersey; she may be substituting for another player or playing for both teams. The Flirts were a women's team in the Tucson city league from 1948 through 1956. After the games, they loved attending dances at the Casino Ballroom. Other Flirts included her sister Esther, sisters Delia and Alice Reyna, Elma Padias, Gracie Pellón, Mary Grace, Lucy Dupont, Betty Mayer, and Nellie Contreras, whose husband, Fabián, was the coach. (Courtesy of Norma Gallego.)

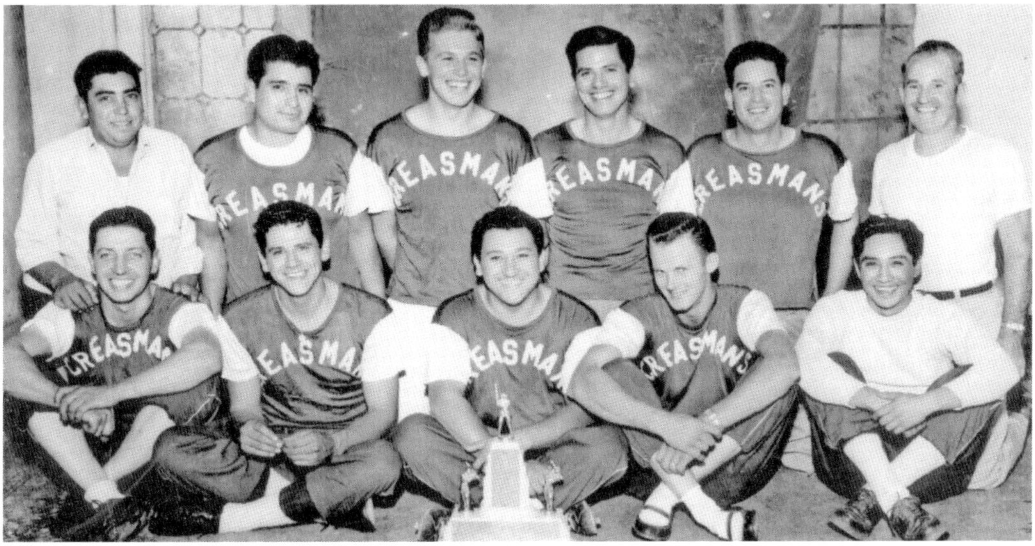

In 1951, Creasman's Firestone Home and Auto Supply in Globe, Arizona, formed a softball team of players from Globe and Miami. From left to right are (first row) Jimmy Troglia, Tommy Arrona, Ignacio "Nacho" Benítez, unidentified, and Gilbert Rivera; (second row) manager Tony Sermeno, Lupe Trujillo Marin, ? Paul, Ray Arrona, unidentified, and Art Van Harlen Sr. Van Harlen, from Superior, Arizona, was a fair and respected umpire and a boxing judge who was inducted into the Arizona Sports Hall of Fame. (Courtesy of Christine Marin.)

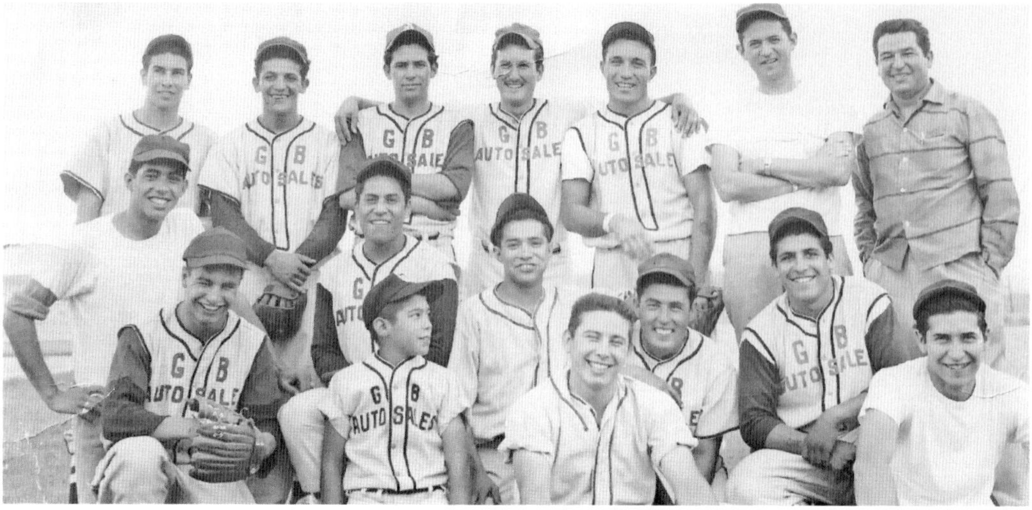

Robert García Lovato (first row, third from left) was born in 1929 in Albuquerque and played for GB AutoSales in 1957. He also played in Sunday leagues. He served in the US Navy and married Eleanor Mello from Boston, moving to Lincoln Heights in East Los Angeles, where his son, Bobby, played at Baldwin Plaza Little League and later at Lincoln High School. Bobby returned to Albuquerque, where he still plays senior ball. He has two grandsons representing a fourth generation of players: Robert in Austin and A.J. in Albuquerque. (Courtesy of Bobby Lovato.)

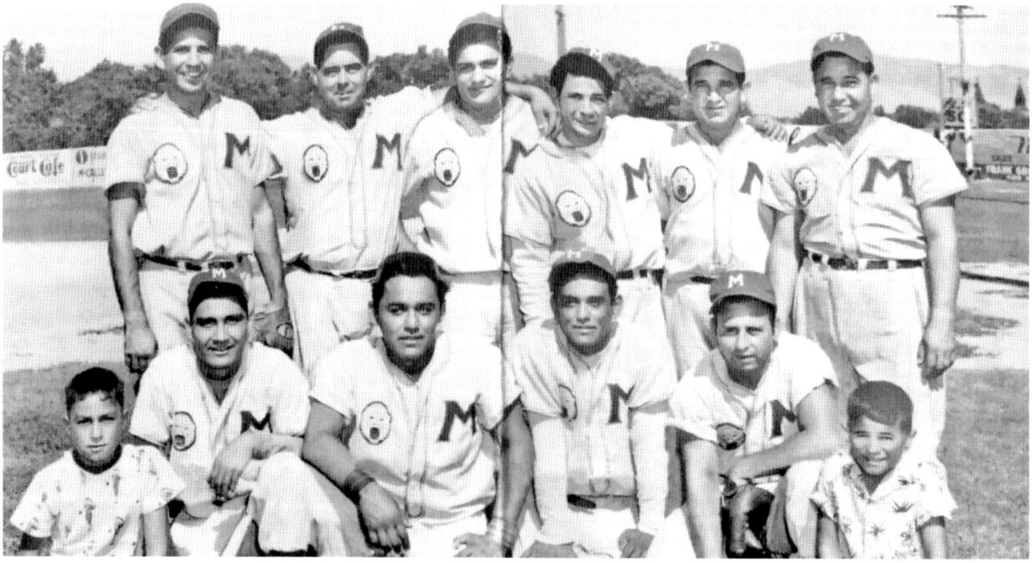

Robert Durán Sr. (first row, far left) was born in Bernalillo, New Mexico. He was an outstanding player known for his remarkable defense. He served in the Air Force. His two sons, Bobby and David, were excellent athletes at Lincoln High School in East Los Angeles. Bobby was all-city in both basketball and baseball and played baseball at East Los Angeles Community College and UCLA. Bobby was a big part of developing a championship program at Lincoln High School, winning the California Interscholastic Federation Division II championship in 2015, the school's first since 1935. (Courtesy of Bobby Durán.)

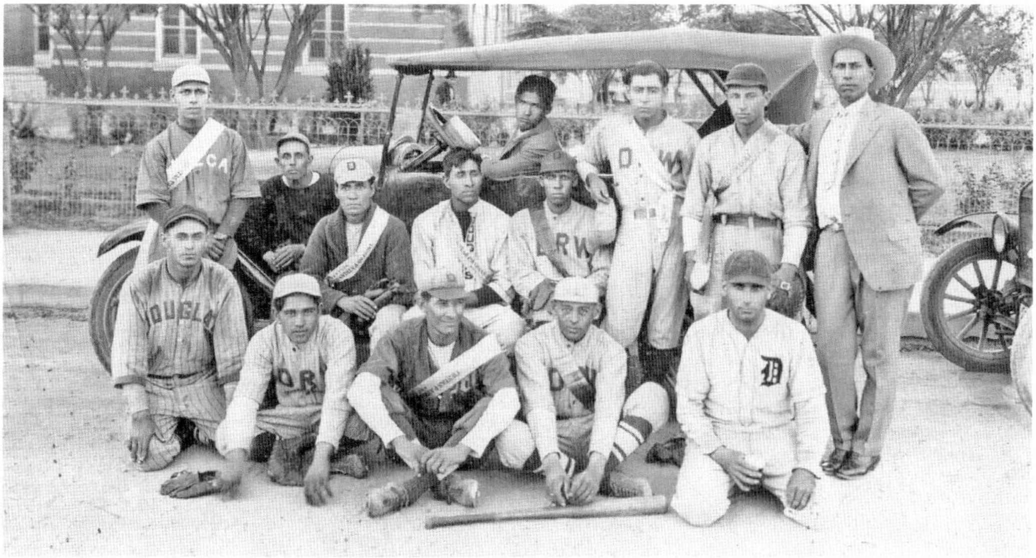

Amado Gutíerrez (second row, fourth from left) played for the semipro 1921 Douglas White Sox. They traveled nearly 100 miles on dirt roads to Nogales, home of their archrivals, the Cuervos (Crows). The teams sometimes drew 20,000 fans. The games were often played in 100-degree heat. Many players had served in World War I, while others had fought for or against Francisco "Pancho" Villa. Gutíerrez hit a three-run home run and pitched the ninth inning to preserve the victory. (Courtesy of Tom Danehy and the Amado Gutíerrez estate.)

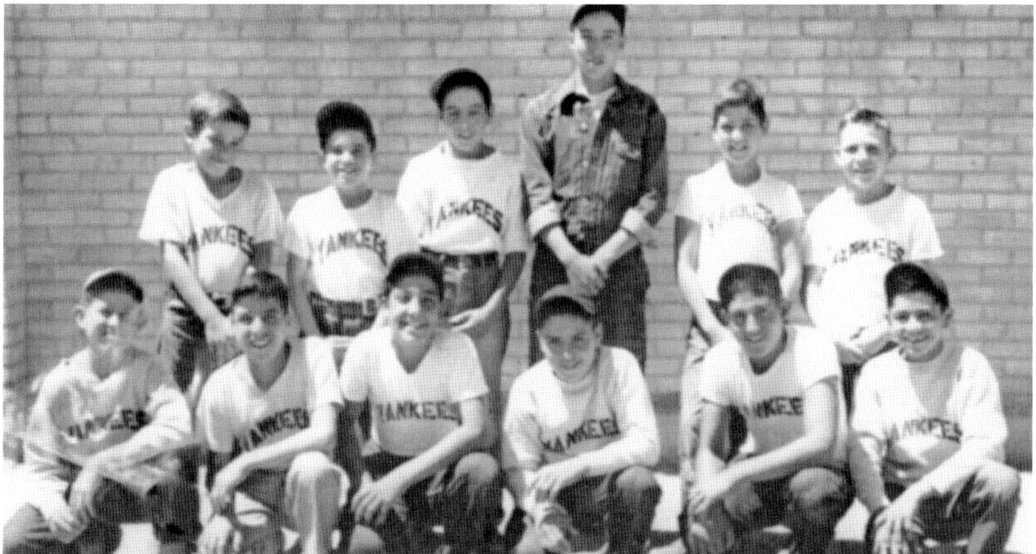

Art Velarde (first row, third from left) is seen in Gallup, New Mexico, playing for the Santa Fe Yankees in 1947. Shortly after, his family moved to Boyle Heights in East Los Angeles. Art was an outstanding player on the Roosevelt High School varsity team. He and two other teammates, Conrad Muñatones and Ernie Rodríquez, were recruited by UCLA to play ball. All three continue to be tireless supporters of East Los Angeles sports. (Courtesy of Art Velarde.)

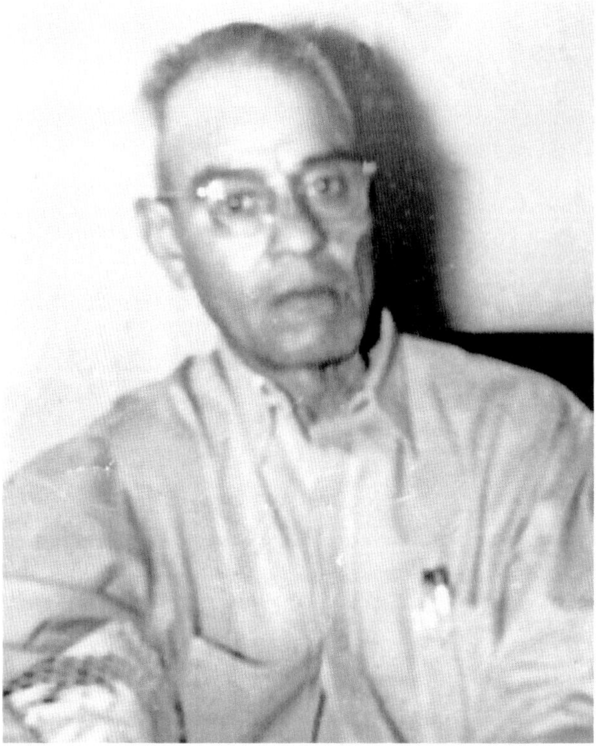

The Great Western Sugar Company recruited Mexican laborers in the Northern Colorado sugar beet fields beginning around 1920. The company realized it had to build housing to maintain a steady and experienced workforce. By 1924, there were 13 Spanish-speaking colonies in Weld County alone. The workers configured several baseball fields and formed the Sugar Beet League. They worked six long days weeding, hoeing, blocking, and thinning sugar beets. On Sunday, baseball was their passion. In the summer of 1925, Dimas Salazar (seen in 1940) organized the first team in Greeley. The teams played baseball and softball on Sundays after church. (Courtesy of Beatrice Salazar and Gabriel and Jody López.)

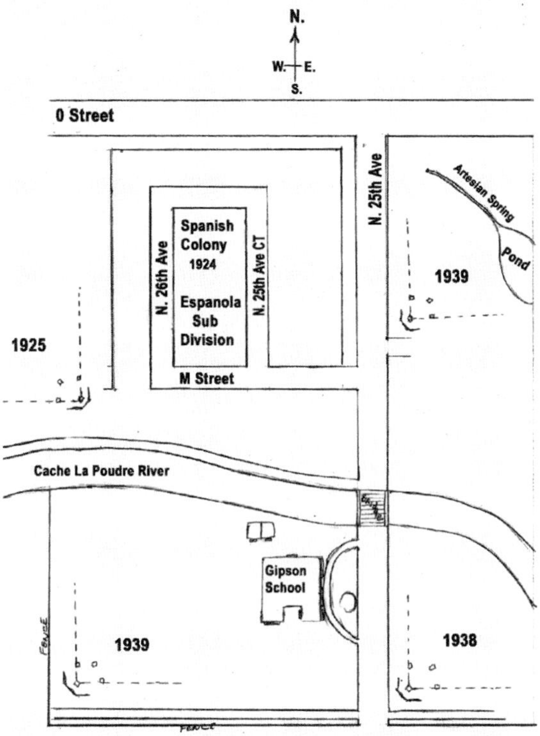

This 2008 sketch by Gabriel López, Alvin García, and Richard López pinpoints the diamonds in the Spanish colony in Greeley, Colorado. The Greeley Grays played on four of the fields. Alvin García received permission from local farmers to use fields not scheduled for cultivation that year. The fields were laid out and developed; children helped prepare the sandlot fields because they, too, would play. The residents removed rocks, pulled weeds, raked up cow manure, and harrowed the fields. During the games, spectators would sound their car horns when a home run was hit or if a player made an outstanding play, and sometimes to distract and irritate the other team. The women would yell things to the opposing team, and sometimes start arguments with the other team's wives, even if they were related. (Courtesy of Gabriel and Jody López.)

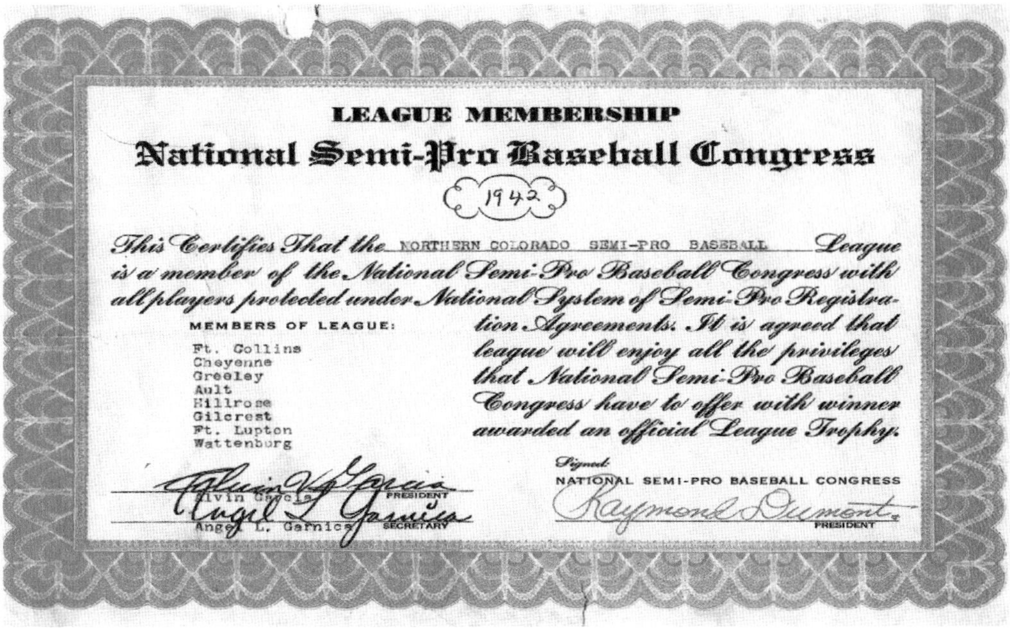

LEAGUE MEMBERSHIP

National Semi-Pro Baseball Congress

1942

This Certifies That the NORTHERN COLORADO SEMI-PRO BASEBALL League is a member of the National Semi-Pro Baseball Congress with all players protected under National System of Semi-Pro Registration Agreements. It is agreed that league will enjoy all the privileges that National Semi-Pro Baseball Congress have to offer with winner awarded an official League Trophy.

MEMBERS OF LEAGUE:
Ft. Collins
Cheyenne
Greeley
Ault
Hillrose
Gilcrest
Ft. Lupton
Wattenburg

Alvin García, PRESIDENT
Angel L. Garnica, SECRETARY

Signed:
NATIONAL SEMI-PRO BASEBALL CONGRESS
Raymond Dumont, PRESIDENT

This 1942 certificate bestows membership to the Northern Colorado Semi-Pro League by the National Semi-Pro Baseball Congress. The members of the league were Fort Collins, Cheyenne, Greeley, Ault, Hillrose, Gilcrest, Fort Lupton, and Wattenburg. These teams and their coaches were predominately Mexican Americans whose livelihood depended on the sugar beet industry. By 1920, a quarter of the nation's sugar originated in Colorado, and nearly 10,000 of the 12,000 workers were of Mexican origin. Companies spent thousands of dollars each year recruiting, transporting, and training their workforce. (Courtesy of Tito García and Gabriel and Jody López.)

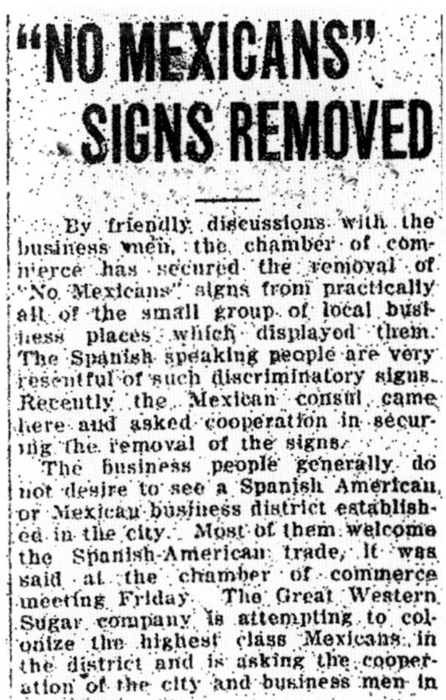

"NO MEXICANS" SIGNS REMOVED

By friendly discussions with the business men, the chamber of commerce has secured the removal of "No Mexicans" signs from practically all of the small group of local business places which displayed them. The Spanish speaking people are very resentful of such discriminatory signs. Recently the Mexican consul came here and asked cooperation in securing the removal of the signs.

The business people generally do not desire to see a Spanish American or Mexican business district established in the city. Most of them welcome the Spanish-American trade, it was said at the chamber of commerce meeting Friday. The Great Western Sugar company is attempting to colonize the highest class Mexicans in the district and is asking the cooperation of the city and business men in its efforts.

Overt discrimination was a tragic way of life for most Spanish-speaking people in Northern Colorado. Signs reading "No Mexicans" and "White Trade Only" were common. Mexican American teams earned a reputation for consistently higher-caliber players, drawing the attention of teams outside the colonias. Eventually, the Sugar Beet League became integrated as race became a non-factor and no color lines had to be crossed. Alvin García is the father of baseball for Mexican Americans in Northern Colorado. He made it fashionable for the Anglos to play on Mexican American teams. Moreover, he started the Grays and the Rocky Mountain League so that Mexicans could play outside their communities. By the 1930s and early 1940s, the league membership expanded throughout Northern Colorado, Southeast Wyoming, and Southwest Nebraska. (Courtesy of the *Greeley Tribute* and Gabriel and Jody López.)

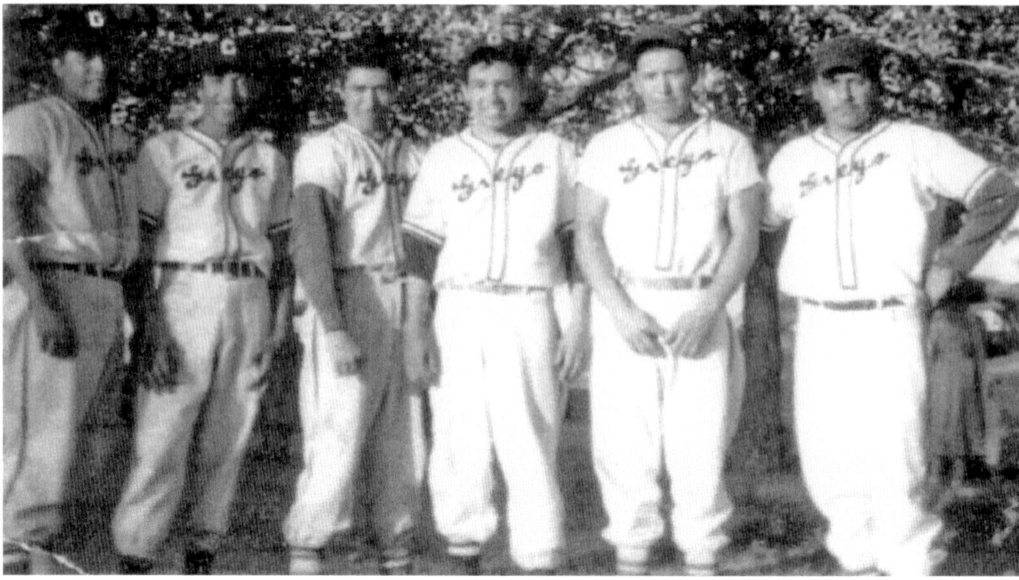

In 1952, the López brothers played on the Greeley Grays. From left to right are Arnulfo "Nudy," Frank, Mario, Rico, David, and Augustine "Gus." Gus López was considered the Babe Ruth of the league. When he came to the plate, there was always a hush in the crowd—not a person would leave for fear of missing something spectacular. Gus's son, Gabriel, has written books and articles about the history of baseball in Northern Colorado, including *From Sugar to Diamonds: Spanish/ Mexican Baseball 1925–1969.* (Courtesy of Bob, Gabriel, and Jody López.)

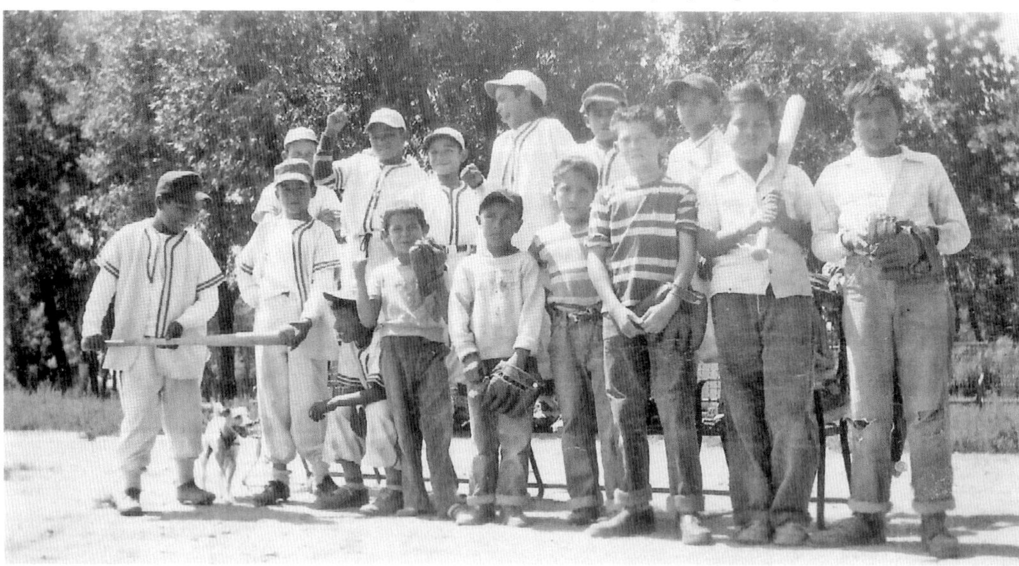

Sandlot games were training fields where young people emulated their elders and hoped to play someday on the adult teams. The players on this 1952 sandlot team are, from left to right, (first row) Frank Villa, Frank Carbajal, Leo Solís, Adolf Durán, Claudie García, Abe García, Sam López, and Johnny Martínez; (second row) Henry Martínez, Robert Nuañez, Jerry Pisano, Danny Tellez, Steve García, and Jerry Tellez. (Courtesy of Alvin García.)

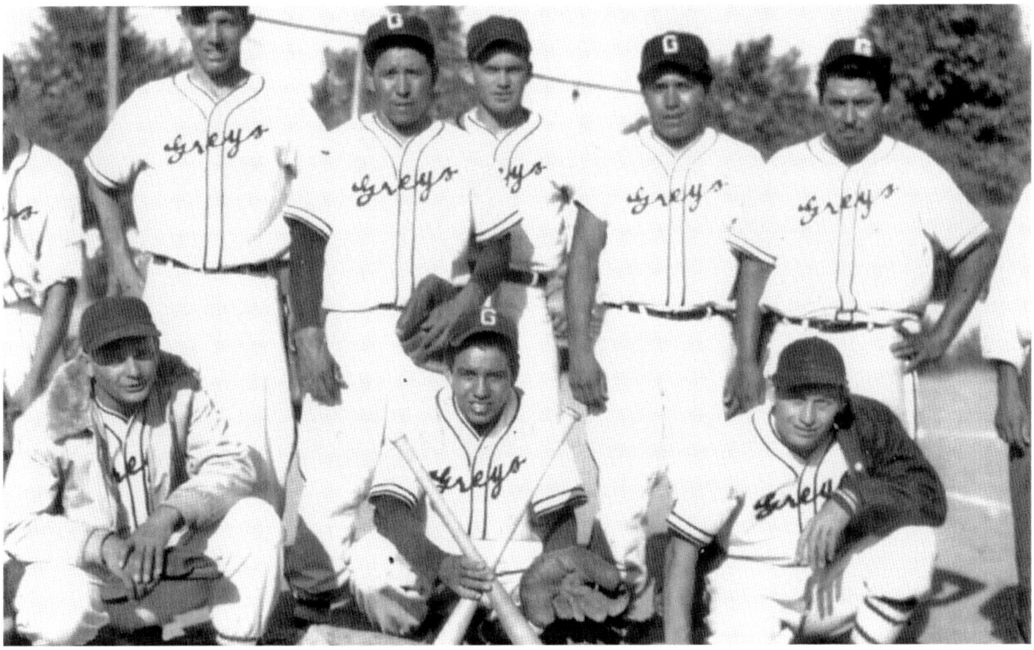

The Greeley Grays were often subjected to racial taunts. In Wheatland, Wyoming, one Gray team was called "beet pickers" and other demeaning ethnic names. After they beat Wheatland, they had to be escorted out of the city for their own safety. Some of the members of the 1952 Grays are Bob Fectch, Ricardo López, Charlie Smith, Frank López, Jimmy Mock, David López, Robert Lind, Arnulfo López, George Villa, Augustine "Gus" López, and Alvin García. (Courtesy of Robert Durán and Gabriel and Jody López.)

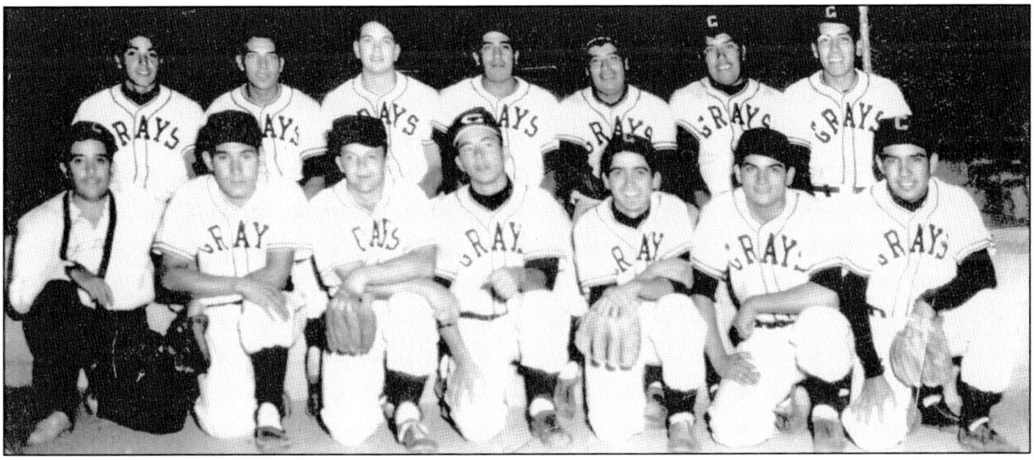

The 1959 Greeley Grays are, from left to right, (first row) manager Alvin García, Gil Carbajal, Doug Smith, Frank Carbajal, Vic Mondragón, Ernie Andrade, and Rick López; (second row) Robert Hernández, Joe García, Ron English, Paul and George Villa, Arnulfo López, and Sam López. Frank Carbajal noted that "baseball didn't care if you were big or small, fast or slow, or not so strong, and it didn't care if you were white, black, yellow, brown, or red, baseball just wanted you to play." (Courtesy of Tito García and Gabriel and Jody López.)

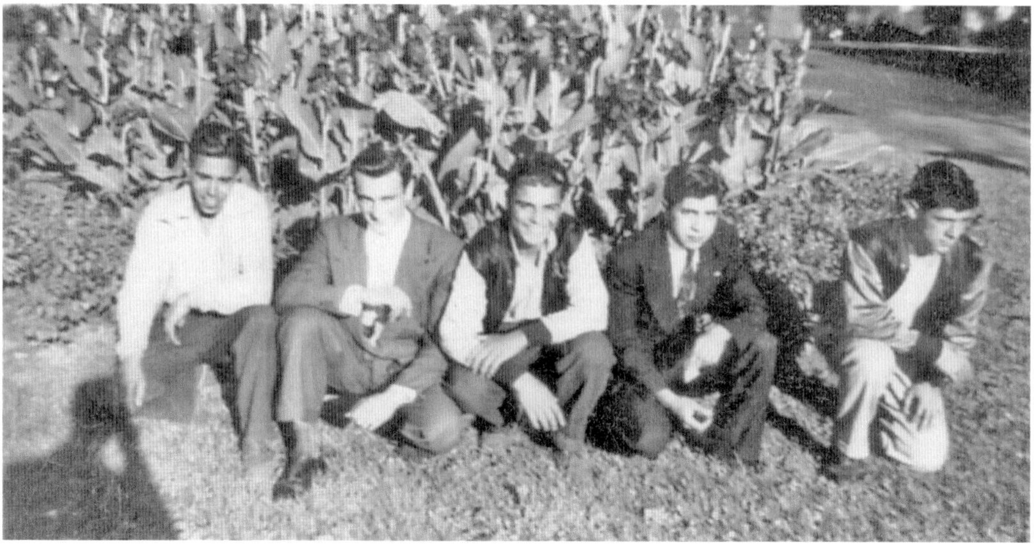

Lexington is in central Nebraska. Mexicans were recruited to work in the sugar beet fields and with the railroads. None of the players are identified in this September 1941 photograph, taken at a game against a Mexican American team from Omaha. Three months later, Pearl Harbor was attacked. Players on both teams likely served in World War II and later in Korea. Lexington had a population of 67 in 2016, one-third of whom speak Spanish at home. All of the non-native-born population came from Mexico. (Courtesy of Isabel Ramírez.)

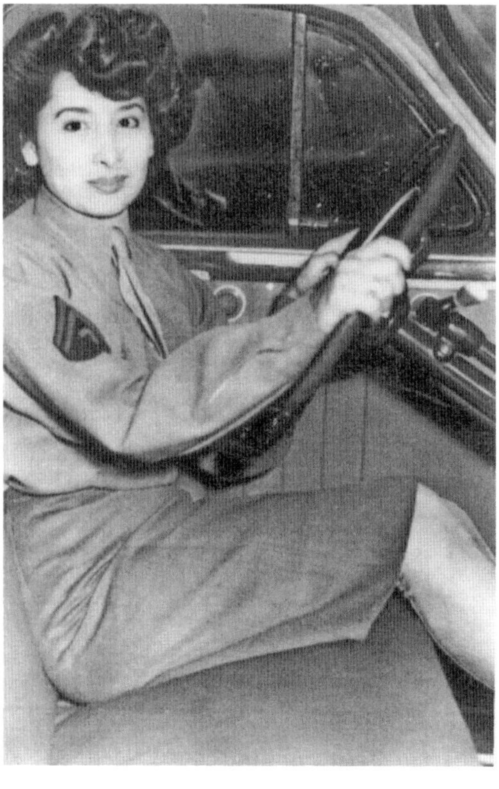

Margaret Villanueva Lambert was raised in Lincoln, Nebraska, and played softball on a Mexican American girls' team before World War II. She recalled playing against Mexican American girls' teams throughout eastern Nebraska. Margaret enlisted in the Women's Army Air Corps and was sent to San Antonio to organize sports activities for returning veterans adjusting to civilian life. Other Midwest Mexican American women served in the military during World War II. The tiny community of Depue, Illinois, had two young women serve, while the Harbor community of East Chicago, Indiana, had seven serve with distinction. The Torres family from Kansas City had two daughters who enlisted in the military. (Courtesy of Margaret Villanueva Lambert.)

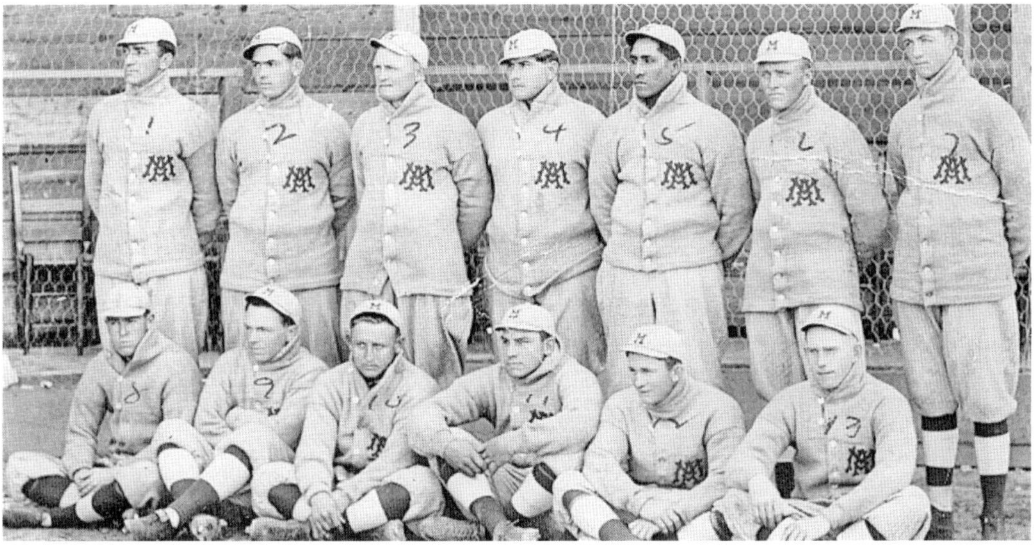

Amado Gutiérrez (second row, third from right), seen here with a Marshall, Texas, team in 1913, was born around 1889 and died in Douglas, Arizona, in 1974. He once hit a home run out of a Mexican stadium that landed on the US side of the border—the only man to ever hit an international home run. Gutiérrez, like the character Joe Louis Brown (who also hits an international home run in the movie *Long Gone*), had superior athletic abilities to be invited to pitch on all-white teams in the deep south of Texas. (Courtesy of Tom Danehy and the Amado Gutíerrez estate.)

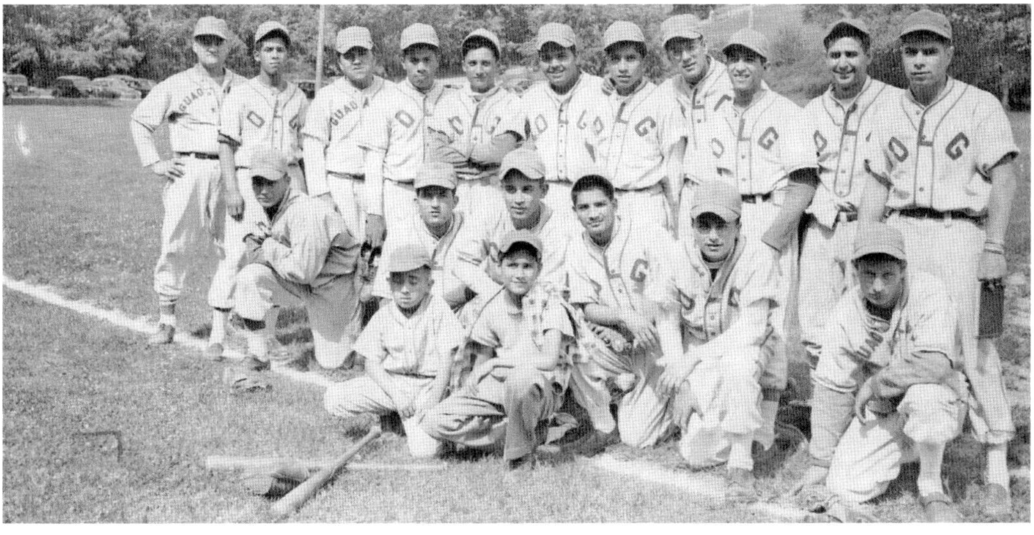

This 1942 Our Lady of Guadalupe Church team played in South Omaha. Players include Manuel García, Epifanio Alba, Leo Barajas, Atilano Oropeza, Joe Ramírez, Tomás Oropeza, Antonio Águilar, Abdias Alba, Ramón Vásquez, Paul Vásquez, Camilo Alba, Isaias Alba Jr., Símon Noriega, Joe Juárez, and Eddie Gómez. Atilano Oropeza, now 93, is considered an important leader for Mexican American civil rights, as is Joe Ramírez. Tomás Oropeza lost his life in World War II. Joe Juárez, who is still alive, is a founder of the American GI Forum. (Courtesy of the Mexican American Historical Society of the Midlands.)

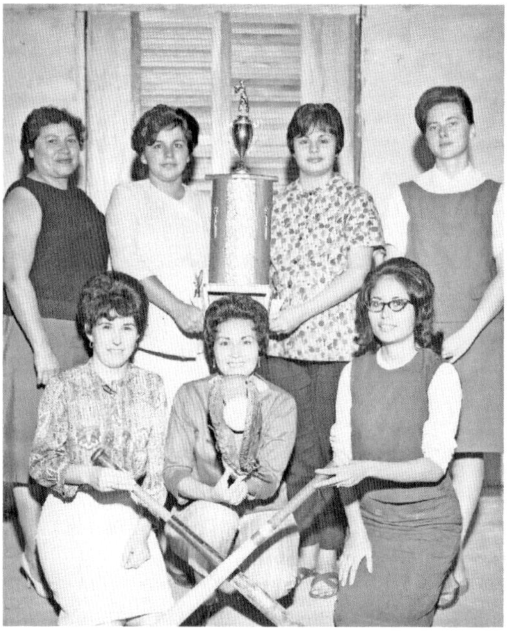

This 1960s women's softball team was comprised of the wives of ballplayers. Two of the women, Dolores "Dee Dee" Martínez (kneeling at left) and Marian García Martínez (kneeling at right) became prominent leaders in the Omaha Mexican American community. Dee Dee was involved at Our Lady of Guadalupe and raised a large family. Two of her sons became police officers, the oldest becoming the chief federal marshal for Nebraska. Marian become one of the first Mexican American women entrepreneurs and a remarkable leader for the American GI Forum, a civil rights organization dedicated to promoting the rights of Mexican American veterans and their families. (Courtesy of the Mexican American Historical Society of the Midlands.)

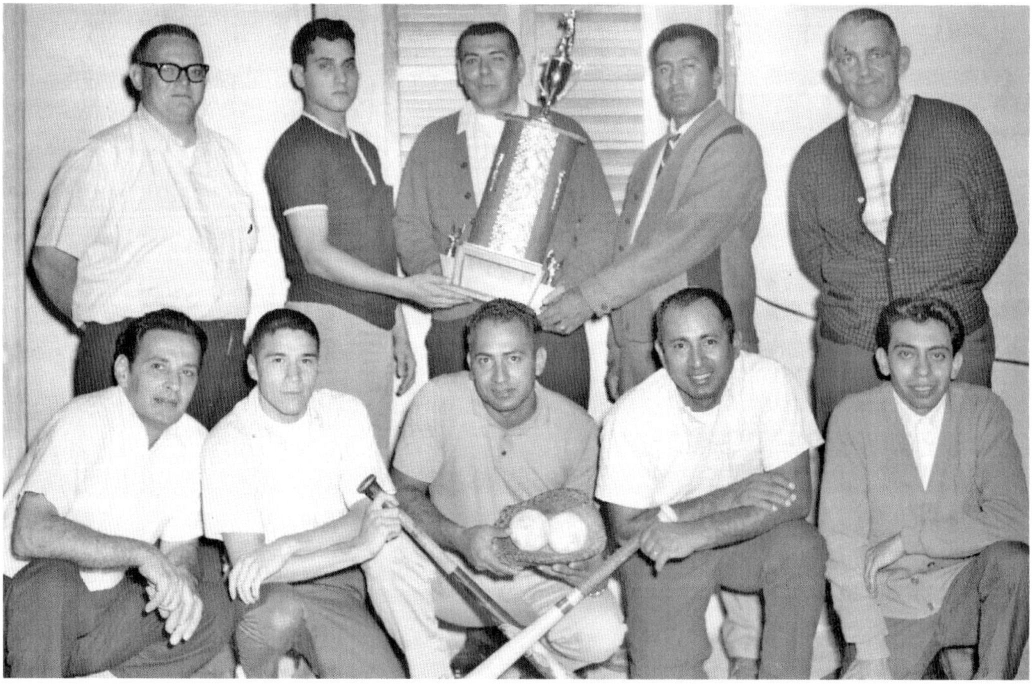

The Omaha Royals were one of numerous working-class teams in South Omaha during the late 1940s and early 1950s. The team won several championships. Standing at far left is George Dasovitch, who coached the team along with Atilano Oropeza (standing at far right). Dasovitch owned several taverns on Q Street. Also prominent on this team are the four Martínez brothers, Charlie, Al Sr., Angelo, and Robert, who all played several sports. Al and Charlie became career police officers. (Courtesy of the Mexican American Historical Society of the Midlands.)

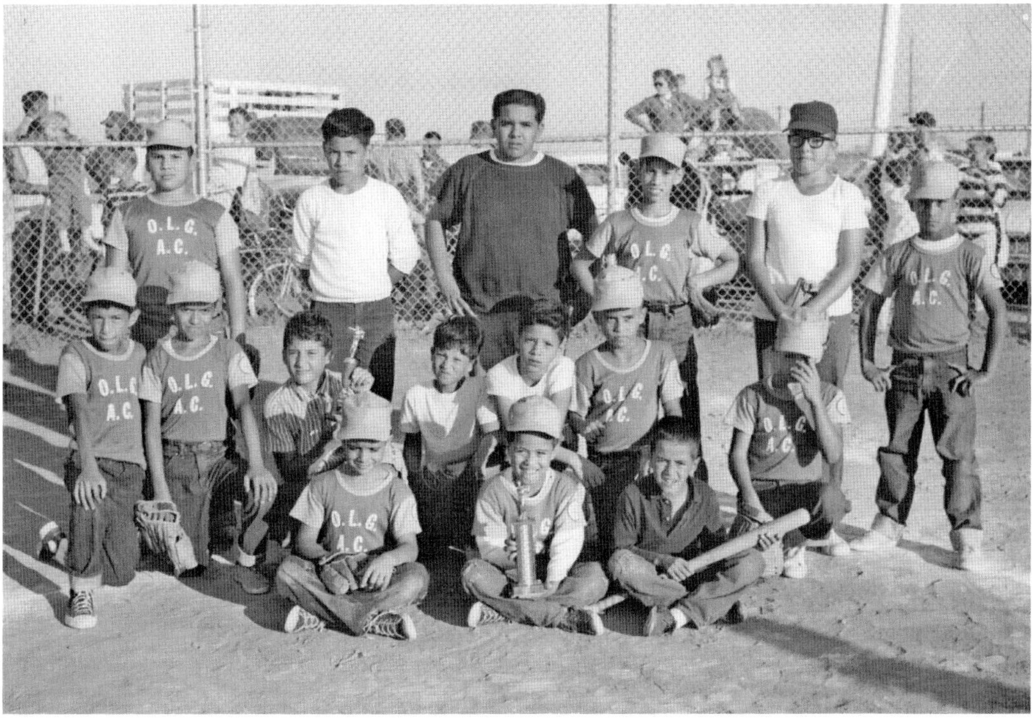

This Our Lady of Guadalupe Church team was comprised of the sons of the first generation of Omaha Mexicans. Standing in the third row, third from left, is coach Jack Martínez, one of the first Mexican American insurance agents, who also served as a deacon. Jim Ramírez (standing fifth from left) received his doctorate in education and served as an administrator at the University of Nebraska at Omaha and in the Omaha public school system. Luís Sauza (kneeling third from right) and Joe Cabral (kneeling second from right) had distinguished careers with the US Postal Service. (Courtesy of the Mexican American Historical Society of the Midlands.)

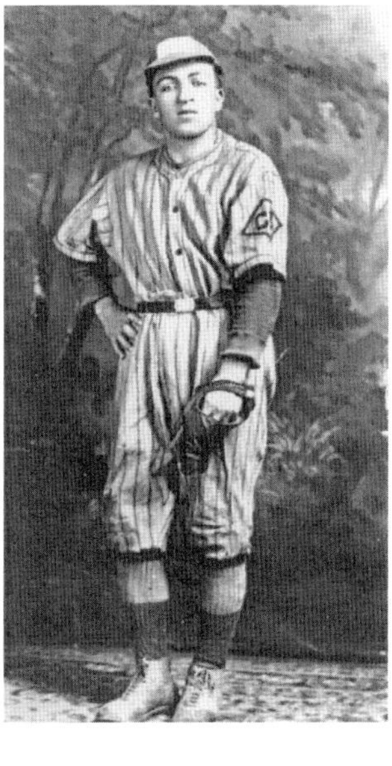

In 1922, the Pfister-Vogel tannery in Milwaukee recruited about 100 Mexican men to take jobs from striking Anglos. The Mexican men were from Tanganicuaro, Michoacan. Other Mexicans worked on the railroads and foundries. Federico Herrera, a 22-year-old Mexican immigrant, settled in Milwaukee in 1925 after playing baseball in Texas for the owners of Mexico's Dos Estrellas mines. With Miguel Sevilla Chávez and Jesús C. Pérez, he cofounded Circulo Social de Amigos "Emilio Carranza" in 1930, honoring the first Mexican to pilot a plane between Mexico City and Washington, DC. Herrera also founded Milwaukee's first Spanish-language newspapers, *Sancho Panza* and *Boletin Informativo.* Most early Mexicans settled in the Walker's Point area, where the housing was less than ideal but the rent was acceptable. Mexicans dealt with discrimination and poverty by turning inward and forming societies known as mutualistas. (Courtesy of Joséph A. Rodríguez and Walter Sava.)

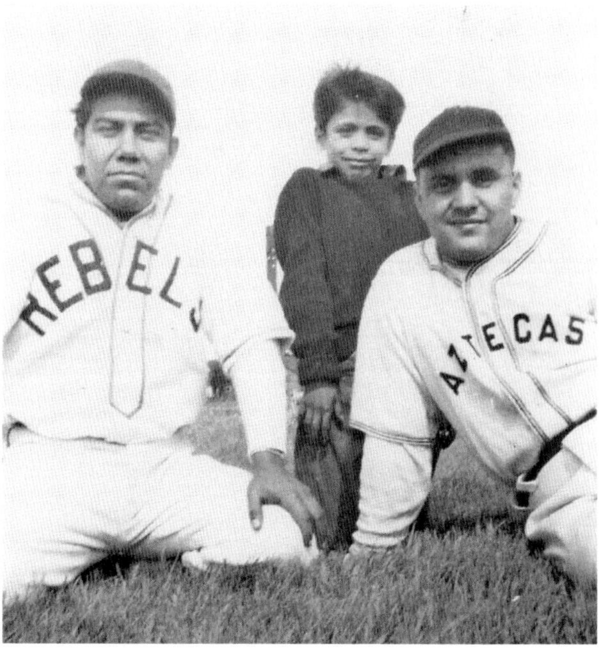

Mexicans settled early in the 20th century in the Quad Cities of Silvis and Moline, Illinois, and Davenport and Bettendorf, Iowa. The Rebels and the Aztecas were Mexican American teams from Silvis in the 1940s and 1950s. From left to right are Manuel Terronez, batboy Johnny Hernández, and Pete Hernández. With the implementation of the 1930s Repatriation Program, many Midwest Mexican Americans fled to Pennsylvania and New York to avoid deportation. There, they established mutual aid societies, fiestas, baseball teams, churches, and other organizations. (Courtesy of Tony Solíz.)

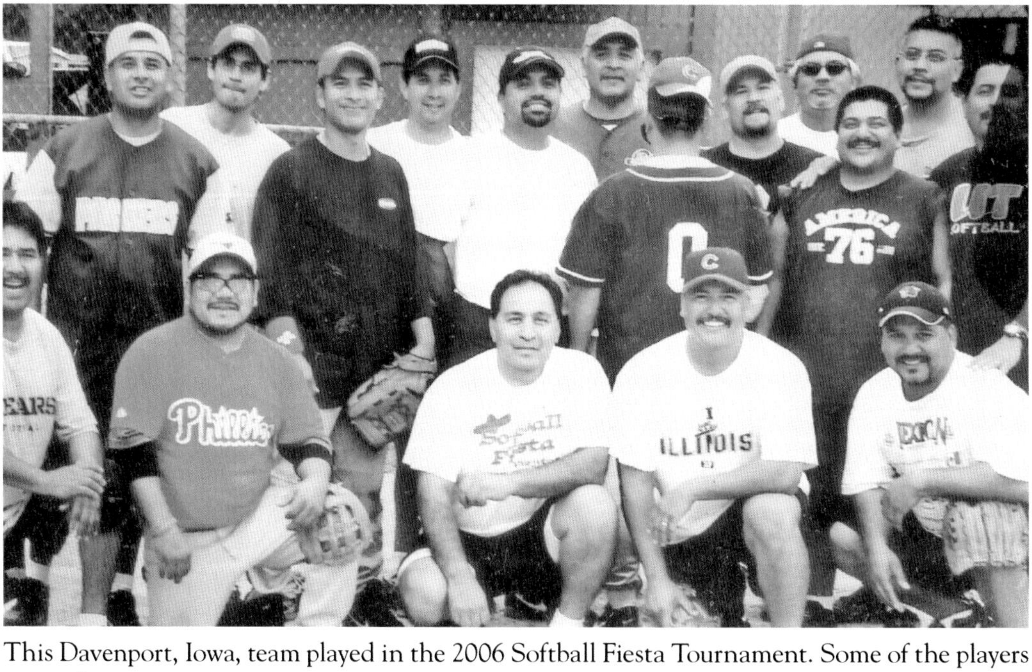

This Davenport, Iowa, team played in the 2006 Softball Fiesta Tournament. Some of the players are Gilbert Terronez, Dan Munos, Roland Rasso, Tony Rasso, Bob Escontrias, Tomás Solís, Richard Esparza, Al Savala, Fred Hernández, Dave Cortéz, Philipe González, Steve Ramírez, Chris Rivera, Joe Ramos, Alfred Terronez, and Pedro Vallejo. The Mexican community in Davenport was called Cook's Point. The residents confronted substandard and overcrowded housing, the odors of nearby city dumps, the lack of indoor plumbing and heat, and unpaved and unlit streets. (Courtesy of Hank Carrillo.)

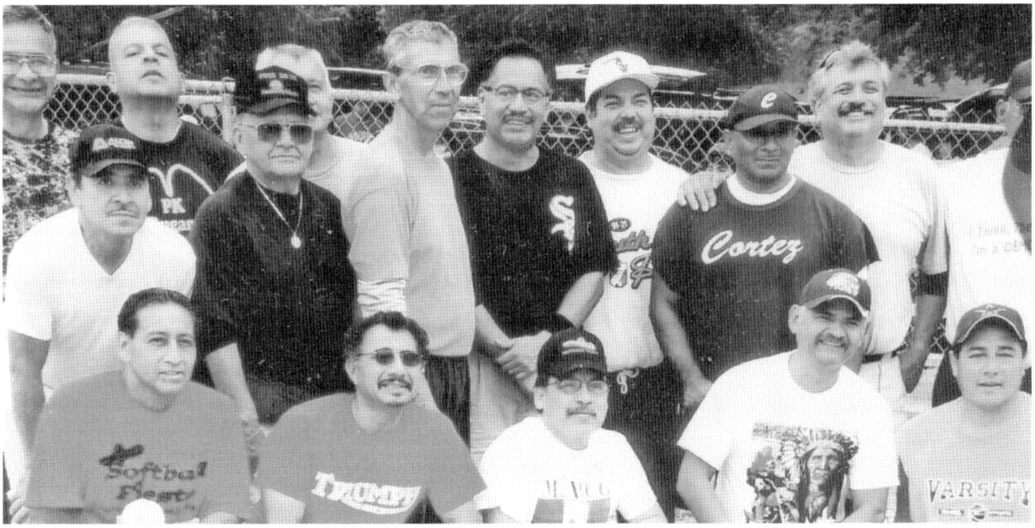

Mexican Americans settled in Davenport early in the 20th century, working in factories, railroads, agriculture, and munitions plants. Davenport has been historically linked to the Mexican communities throughout the Quad Cities, including Silvis, Illinois. This team represented Silvis in the 2006 Softball Fiesta Tournament. From left to right are (first row) Jerry Montez, Ed Tapia, Ray Terronez, Marty Sandoval, and Javier Riojas; (second row) Ponse Esparza, Mike Sandoval, Tim Alonzo, Mike Ortez-O, Carlos Tapia, and John Alonzo; (third row) Steve Campos, Paul Palos, Jaime Rodríguez, Marty Sandoval, Chris Rivera, and Reuben Rangel. (Courtesy of Hank Carrillo.)

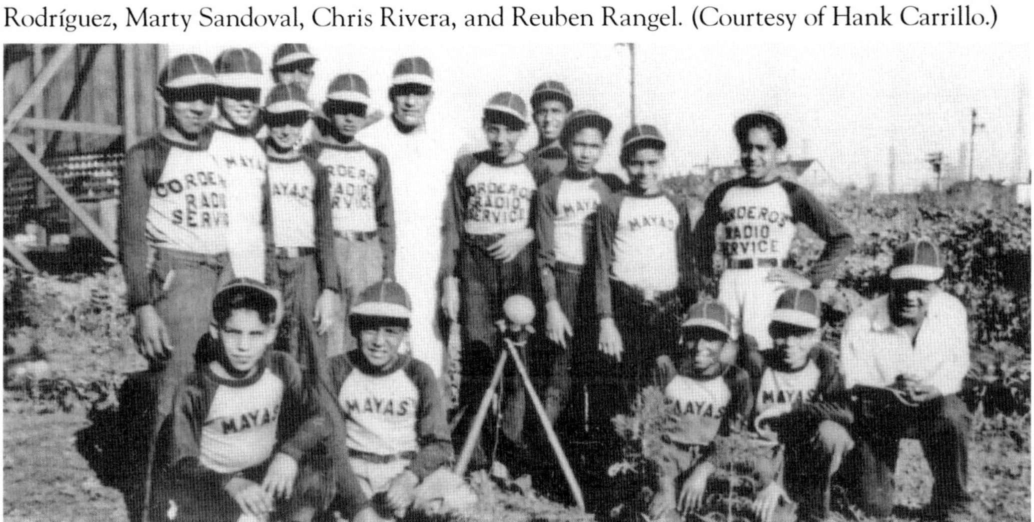

The Mexican American community of South Chicago has a long and rich history of sports, including baseball, basketball, boxing, and football. The Yaquis and Mayas were powerhouse baseball teams that produced outstanding players and coaches. During the Great Depression, Mexican baseball teams drew over 1,000 fans per game. Mexican boys also organized their own pick-up baseball games and softball leagues with teams named after the streets they lived on, such as the Baltimore Aces and the Buffalo Braves. A 1934 Mexican newspaper mentions Mexican girls' basketball teams. (Courtesy of the Southeast Historical Society and Michael D. Innis-Jiménez.)

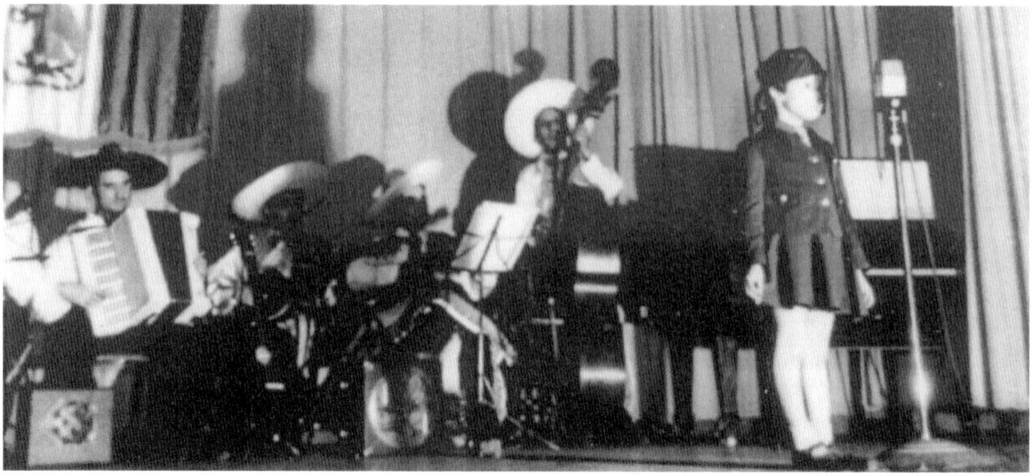

This Mexican American Shirley Temple lookalike sings at a war bond rally in St. Louis around 1943. This community event was sponsored by the Benito Juárez Mutual Aid Society at the St. Louis Auditorium and drew Mexican residents from East St. Louis, Granite City, and Fairmont City. Mexicans arrived in this region in the late 1800s and early 1900s to work in the steel mills, cement plants, oil refineries, textile mills, foundries, and railroads. Many of these communities formed baseball teams. (Courtesy of José Inez Santa Cruz.)

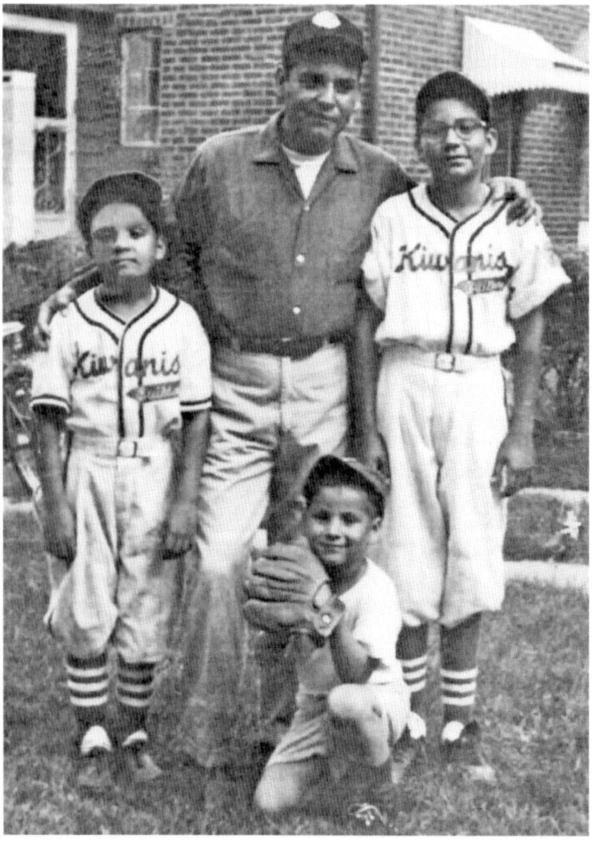

Indiana Harbor's Mexican American community lived in a small area near the shore of Lake Michigan, stretching west with the numerous railroad tracks that ran beside the Inland Steel plant to Block and Pennsylvania Avenues, or as the locals called it, "El Pennsy." They survived repatriation and intense discrimination, participated in unionization drives and steel strikes, served with distinction in World War II and Korea, endured Red Scare and "Americanization" drives initiated by the more racist segments of the region's residents, and spent their entire lives as steelworkers or in other hard jobs. They also played a variety of sports in nearby neighborhoods. Seen here in 1960 in Gary, Indiana, are brothers (from left to right) Rock, John, and Gabriel, with their father, Gabriel Fraire. (Courtesy of John Fraire.)

7

Field of Dreams

The last several years have witnessed the well-deserved recognition and indispensable documentation of the immense contributions of Mexican Americans to the history of baseball and softball in the United States. The Baseball Hall of Fame is expanding exhibits highlighting the historical weight of Spanish-speaking communities in the sport, while the Smithsonian Institution has undertaken a national initiative to collect, document, and display this rich and remarkable history, including an upcoming show in Washington, DC, in 2020. Since 2005, the Latino Baseball History Project has become the principal promoter of the nationwide Mexican American baseball community. The project is housed at California State University at San Bernardino and dedicates itself to publicly sharing to date over 5,000 amazing stories and vintage photographs of Mexican Americans playing youth ball, high school and college games, globally with the military, on semiprofessional and community teams, in Mexico, on church and women's teams, and in the major leagues in the United States and Mexico.

The project endorses these extraordinary tales and breathtaking photographs in special ways, including books, newsletters, forums, oral interviews, luncheons, academic courses, first-pitch ceremonies, exhibits, media outreach, and more. The project, originally a California-based operation, has published several Texas books, this book on Kansas and Missouri, and is currently working with baseball enthusiasts in Arizona and Indiana. Mexican American communities have sponsored baseball and softball tournaments for generations, especially in the Midwest. In Kansas and Missouri, many of these tournaments have included an old-timers game before the official tournament.

In Kansas City, the old-timers wear T-shirts with the words *los sabios* (the Wise Ones) during their game. In Newton, Kansas, an old-timers' game precedes the regular games. These old-school players are enthusiastically introduced to loud applause by the faithful in the stands, screaming their nicknames or those of the teams they played for in their early years. They generally play two or three innings, followed by a group photograph. During the game, there is much horseplay, bantering, teasing, laughter, and even some happy tears among these ancient rivals. There are a few who appear physically fit to play with the younger players, while others can barely reach first base. These heartfelt tributes are designed to let the players know how much they are still loved by families, friends, and fans who remember their extraordinary skills on the diamond.

This chapter includes some of these old-timers and the devoted individuals helping document their wonderful stories and remarkable photographs. Many of these players dedicated their later lives to coaching, mentoring, and establishing fields for subsequent generations.

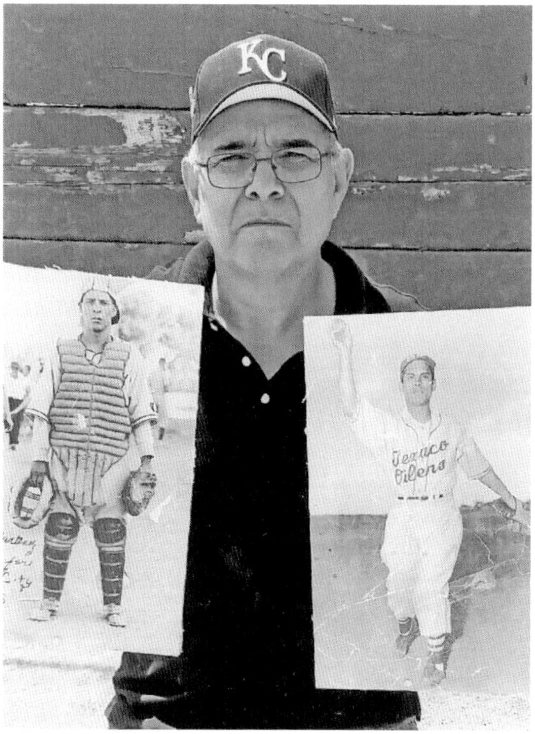

Rod Martínez, author and board member of the Latino Baseball History Project, holds photographs of his uncle Jesús Martínez (left) and his father, Ramón Martínez. They were raised in the small farming town of Copeland, Kansas. Their father, Nazario, a Santa Fe Railroad foreman, and their mother, Carmen, emigrated from Mexico in the early 1900s. Ramón and Jesús were outstanding high school athletes in Kansas known as the "two red hot chili peppers." Their ability to play went unnoticed by professional baseball scouts. (Courtesy of Rod Martínez.)

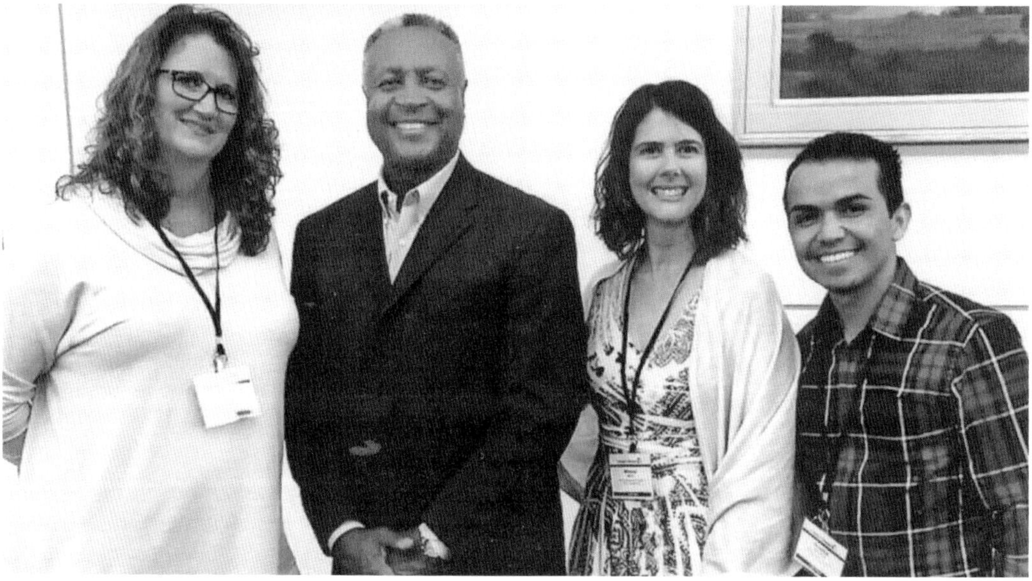

Dodge City was represented at the Kansas League of Municipalities Conference in Overland Park in 2016. The keynote speaker was Frank White, ex–Kansas City Royals coach and second baseman, seen here with members of the Dodge City government. In July 2016, the Dodge City administration also welcomed Rod Martínez of the Latino Baseball History Project. From left to right are Cherise Tieben, city manager; Frank White, Kansas City Royals; Melissa McCoy, assistant to city manager; and Ernesto De La Rosa, assistant to city manager. (Courtesy of Melissa McCoy.)

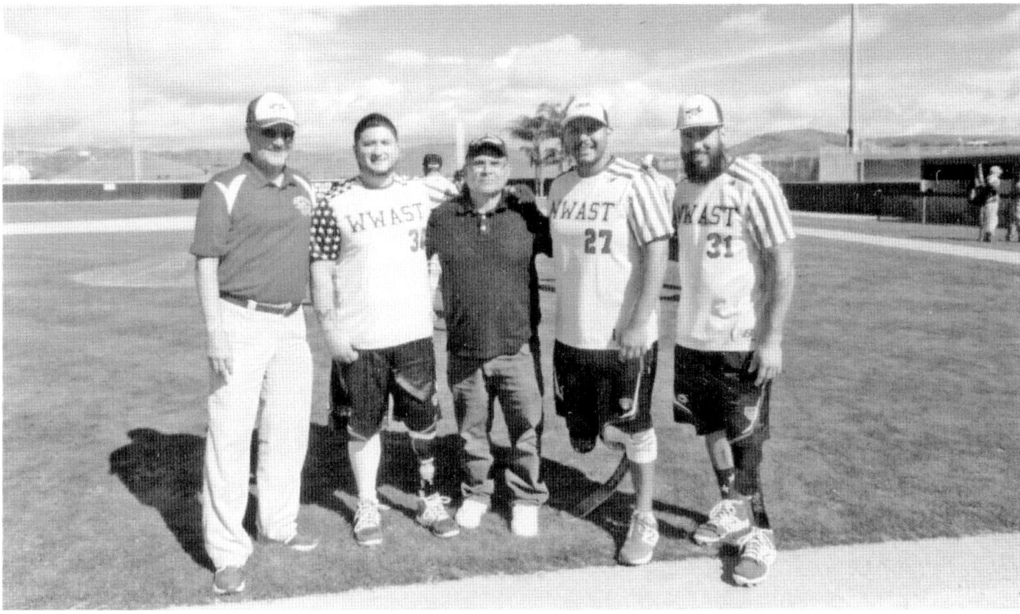

On March 25, 2017, Rod Martínez visited Saddleback College in Mission Viejo, California, to see the Wounded Warrior Amputee Softball Team (WWAST), consisting of Latino members of the armed forces who lost a limb or limbs in the defense of their country. Martínez met the executive director and three WWAST teammates. From left to right are Dennis Wince, executive director; Cpl. Saul Bosquez; Manny Del Rio from Van Nuys, California; and Sgt. Mike Gallardo from Los Angeles. (Courtesy of Rod Martínez.)

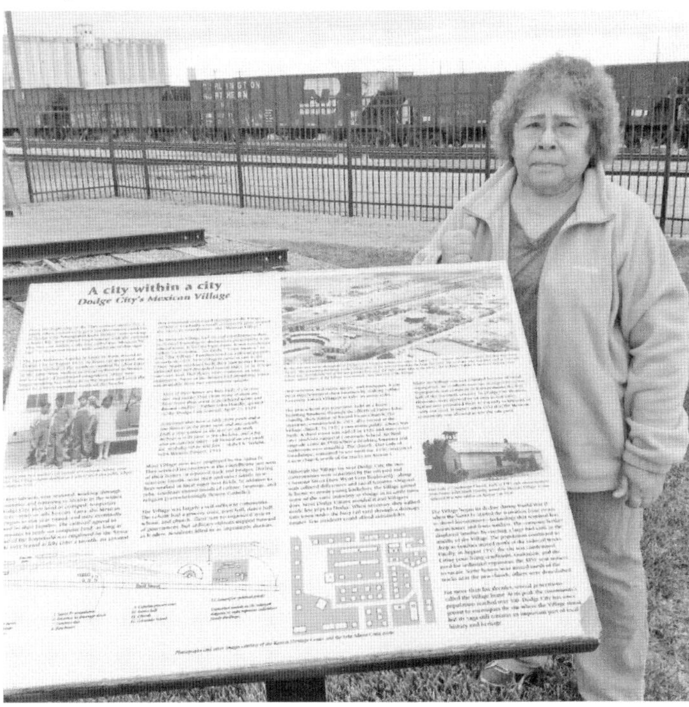

In November 2017, Ruth Ann Martínez Waldron of Dodge City, daughter of Jay and Ruth Martínez, visited the site of the Mexican Village in Dodge City. The village was home to Santa Fe Railroad employees and their families living on railroad property as early as 1903. Segregation was a fact of life for many Mexicans in Dodge City and throughout Kansas. For years, the village was a self-sufficient community, but it began to decline during World War II. (Courtesy of Ruth Ann Martínez Waldron.)

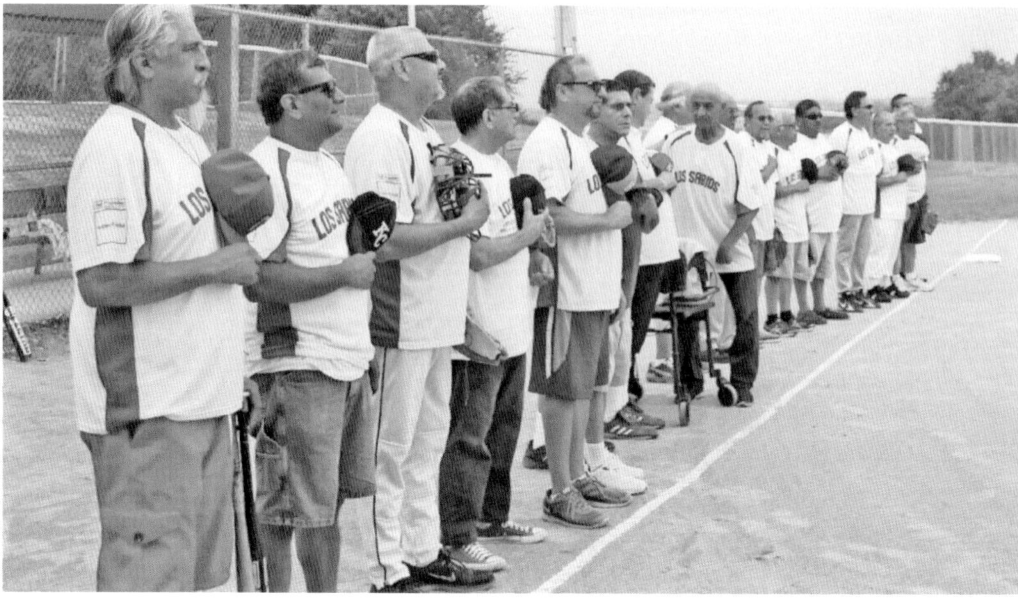

In 2014, the Kansas City Museum launched an annual commemorative men's fast pitch softball competition called Los Sabios Games. The games, open to players 40 years and older, attract former fast pitch players from around the region. In this 2014 photograph, players are, from left to right, Chris González, Martín Olvera, John Amayo, Rick Sauceda, George Vega, Brian Padilla, Anthony Scott Gómez, Paul Hernández Jr., Dan Salas, Chris Ramos, Richard Moreno, John Chacón, Danny Olvera, Joe Amayo, Jesse García, Tony Quiroga, and Mike Quiroga. (Courtesy of the Kansas City Museum.)

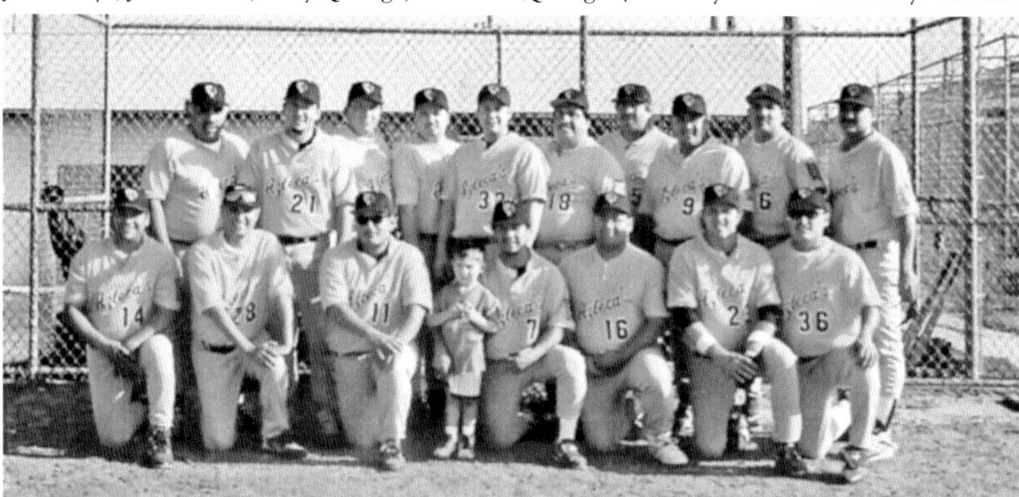

In this 1997 photograph, a younger iteration of the Kansas City Aztecas are poised to play in St. Charles, Missouri, at the ASA Four State Regional Tournament. From left to right are (first row) Harry Medellín, Anthony Villegas, Ed Díaz Jr., batboy Lucas Porras, Gilbert Tinoco, John Chacón, Dave Smith, and Mike Ceceña; (second row) Dan Salas, Anquilino Villegas, Ron Porras, José Páez, Steve Roach, Tom García, Chris González, Mike Amayo, John Ruano, and John Amayo. (Courtesy of Dan Salas.)

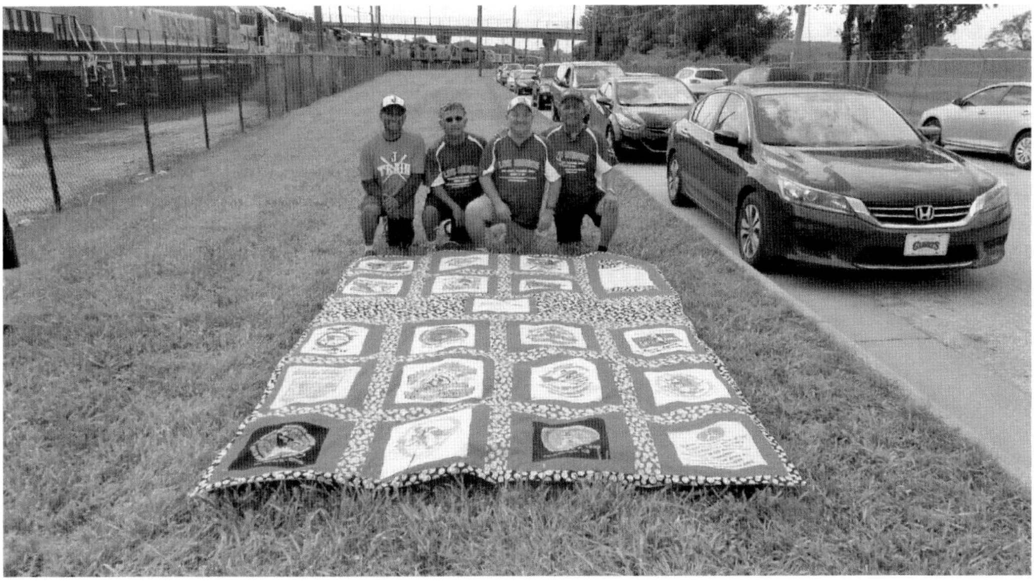

Pictured at the Eagles Nest in 2017 are the Jaso brothers (from left to right) Steve, Raymond, Manuel, and George, displaying a commemorative quilt that their sister, Anita Jaso Plummer, made. It features the logos of various Newton Mexican American fast pitch softball game T-shirts and is symbolic of the Jaso family's long history in Newton, Kansas, since the early 1900s. Raymond Olais, who has designed some of the T-shirts since the 1990s, recounts that the earliest T-shirt designs that he remembers were created for the Fourth of July tournaments of the late 1970s or early 1980s. Other Newton artists Alberto Martínez, Freddy González, and Carlos Fernández have designed T-shirts. (Courtesy of Manuel Jaso.)

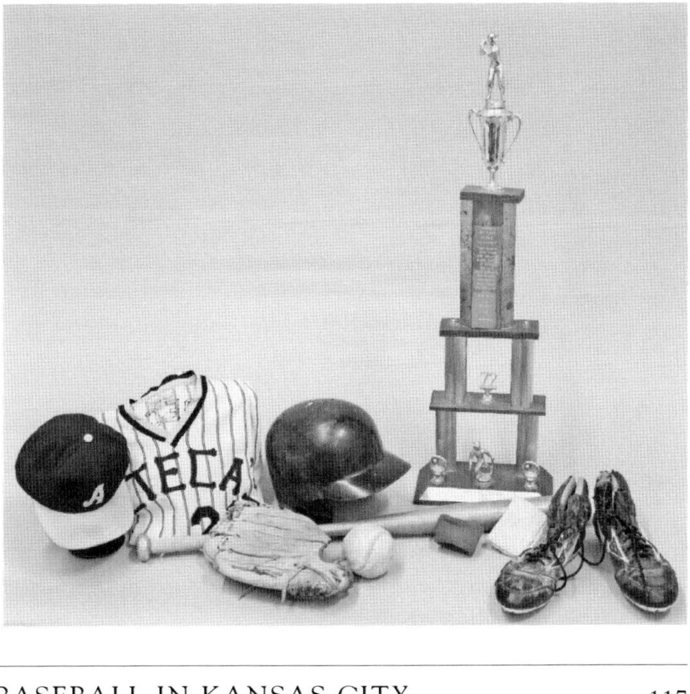

Chris González grew up playing softball at the Eagles Nest. His paraphernalia from various MASA teams includes an outfielder's softball mitt, a 1970s-era regulation fast pitch softball, wrist bands, cleats donated by the Kansas City Royals and worn by González throughout his playing career, a metal bat, a 1980s-era Azteca cap and jersey, a regulation batting helmet, and a 1972 Angels Tournament first place trophy. (Courtesy of Chris González.)

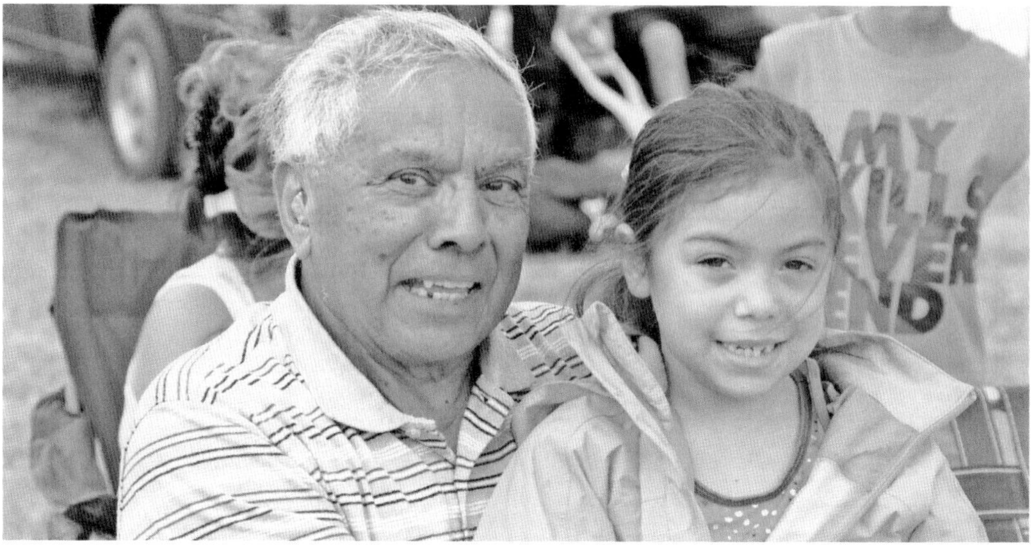

Baseball was a way of life for Reynaldo González, who played semipro ball early in his career. Later, he spearheaded the building of a ballpark behind Our Lady of Guadalupe. He organized fellow parishioners with the same passion for the sport, and it opened in 1963. Their enthusiasm persuaded local businesses to contribute materials and machinery. A founder of the Newton Mexican American Athletic Club (NMAAC) in 1995, Reynaldo's enormous impact upon the tournament and ballpark as a player, coach, umpire, and director is undeniable. He is pictured with his granddaughter Caroline Dunn. (Courtesy of Reynaldo González.)

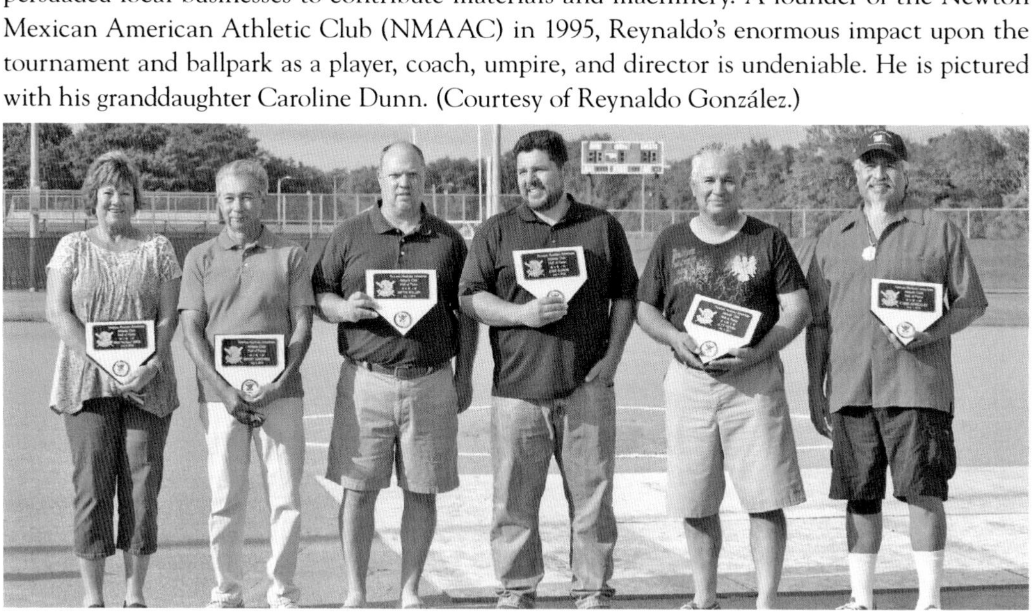

Opening ceremonies of the 68th annual tournament included the presentation of the 2016 NMAAC Hall of Fame class. From left to right are a woman representing Vince García, Benny Martínez, Newton's Bryce Buller, José Ramos, Alex Vieyra of Hutchinson, and Chris González of Kansas City. MVPs were first acknowledged in 1963, while 1978 saw the introduction of the all-star team. Hall of fame inductions began in 1994, with Raymond Arellano from Newton being the sole inductee. Since then, more than 130 players from teams that participated in the tournament throughout the years have been inducted. (Courtesy of Robert Sandoval.)

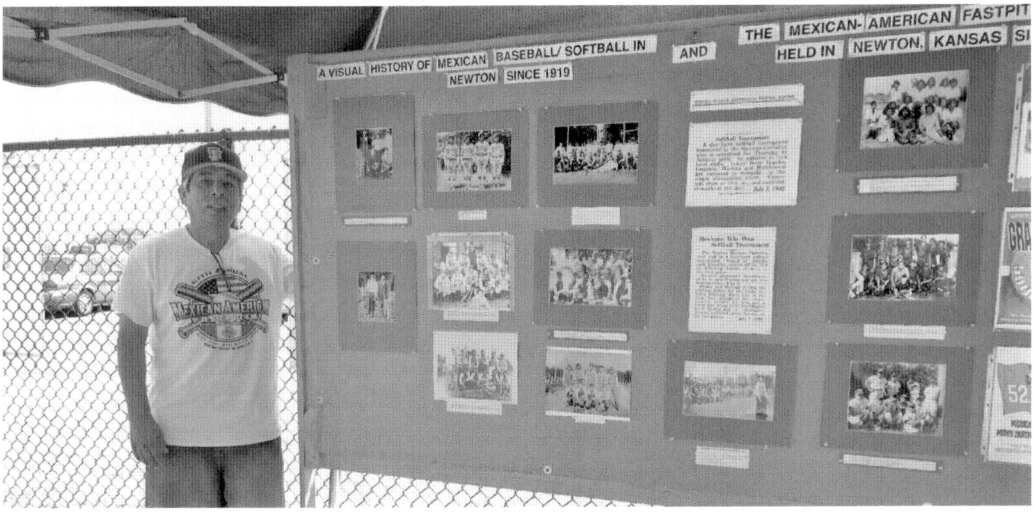

Community historian Raymond Olais stands beside a display of Newton's Mexican baseball history illustrating the founding of the tournament. The display is sheltered behind the bleachers at Athletic Park to be closer to the action and the appreciative fans at Newton's 69th annual tournament. The photographs are part of Newton's September 16 Fiestas historical collection of the 1990s. The first year documented Newton's Mexican bands from the 1920s to the 1970s, and succeeding years included the early Ranchito and Our Lady of Guadalupe Chapel, Working on the Railroad, A League of Our Own, Veterans Who Served, and First Families. (Courtesy of Patrice Olais.)

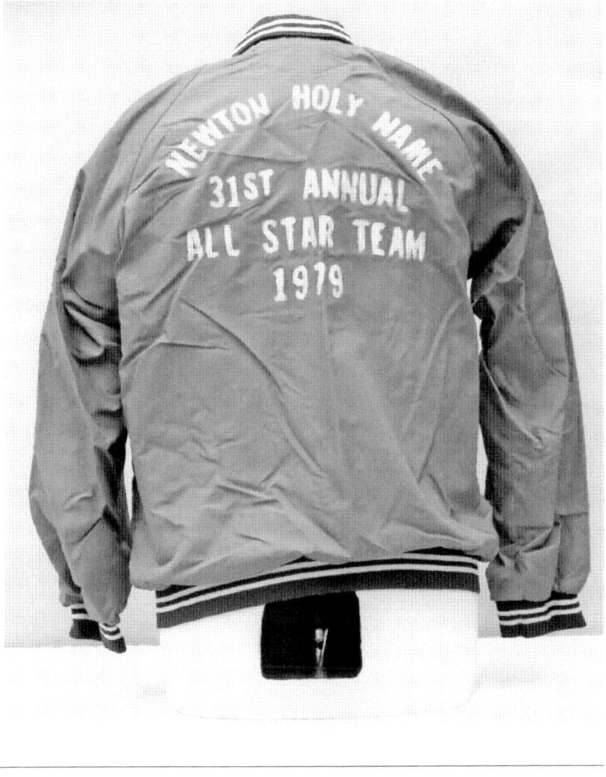

In 1979, the 31st annual tournament awarded Newton Holy Name jackets to the all-tourney team instead of trophies. Topeka GI Forum won the championship, going undefeated, with Blanco Gómez selected as most valuable pitcher. Though Blanco earned most valuable pitcher at Newton's 1963 tournament, this win was especially memorable since his three sons, Scott, Steve, and Mark Gómez, played with him and were named to the all-tourney team. Pictured is Anthony Scott Gómez's jacket, worn proudly for many years to other tournaments throughout the Midwest until he retired it from use. (Courtesy of Anthony Scott Gómez.)

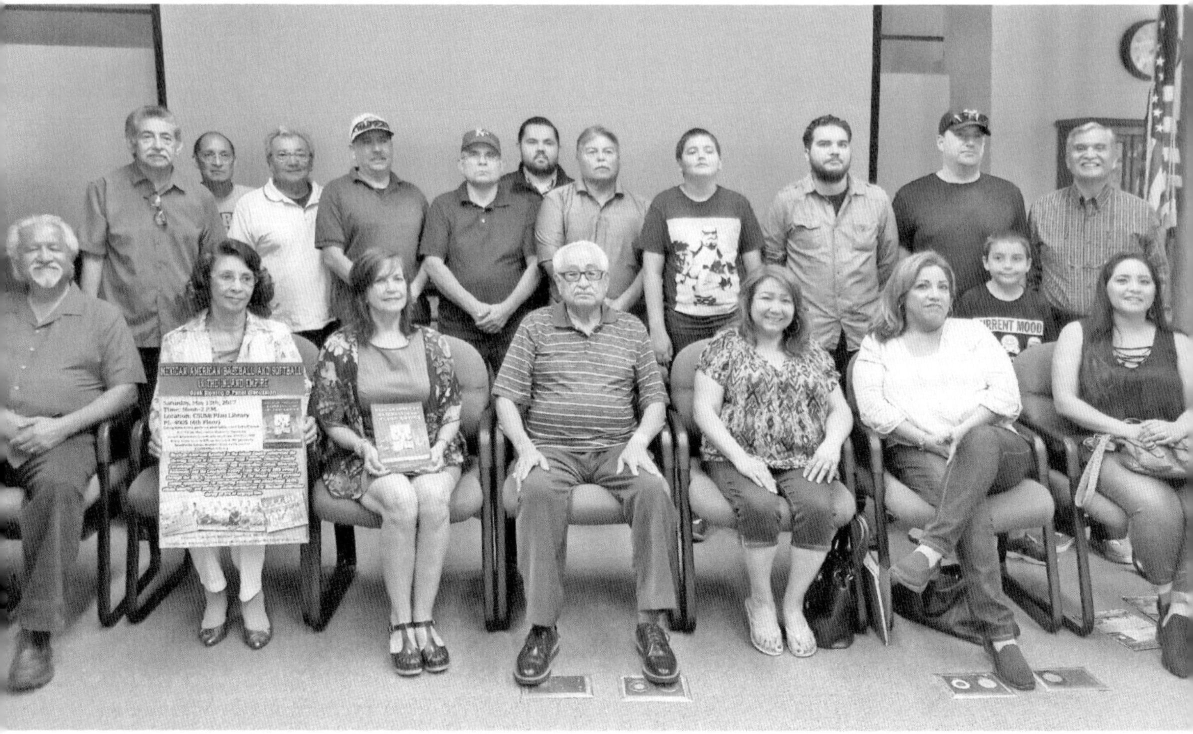

On May 13, 2017, a symposium on Mexican American baseball and softball in the Inland Empire was held at California State University at San Bernardino. Several former players and family members shared wonderful stories and pictures. Participants included César Caballero, Dorothy Serrano Avance, Liz Serrano González, Tom Pérez, Dale Suchill, Rey León, Mark García, Rod Martínez, Ray Rodríguez, Mark Ocegueda, and Richard A. Santillán. (Courtesy of Richard A. Santillán.)

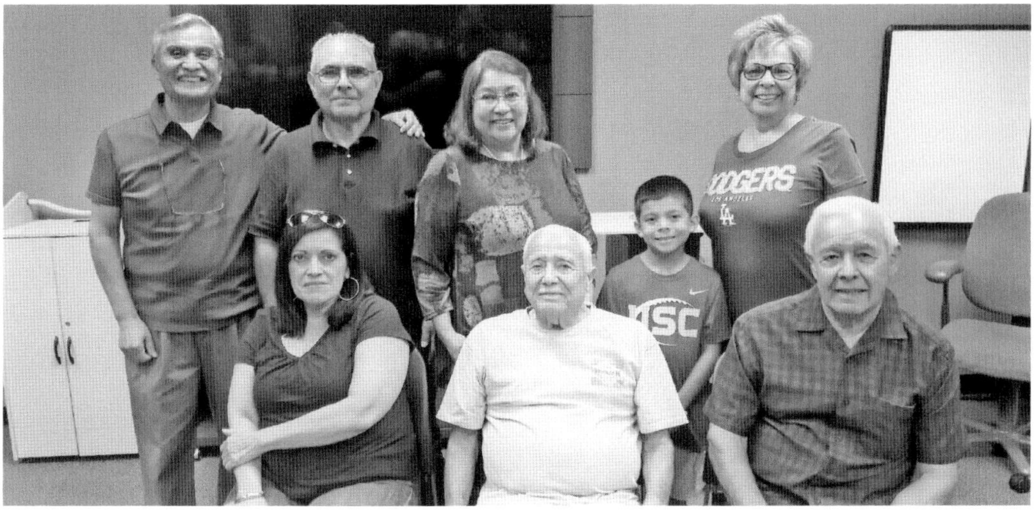

On October 25, 2017, the Upland, California, public library hosted a forum on Mexican American baseball and softball in the Greater Pomona Valley. The turnout was small, because the Los Angeles Dodgers were playing in the World Series against the Houston Astros at Dodger Stadium. Needless to say, everyone was anxiously checking the score. From left to right are (first row) Irene C. González, Joe Romero, and Manuel Martínez; (second row) Richard A. Santillán, Rod Martínez, Luana Y. Hernández, Noah Sinay, and Patti E. García (Noah's grandmother). (Courtesy of Richard A. Santillán.)

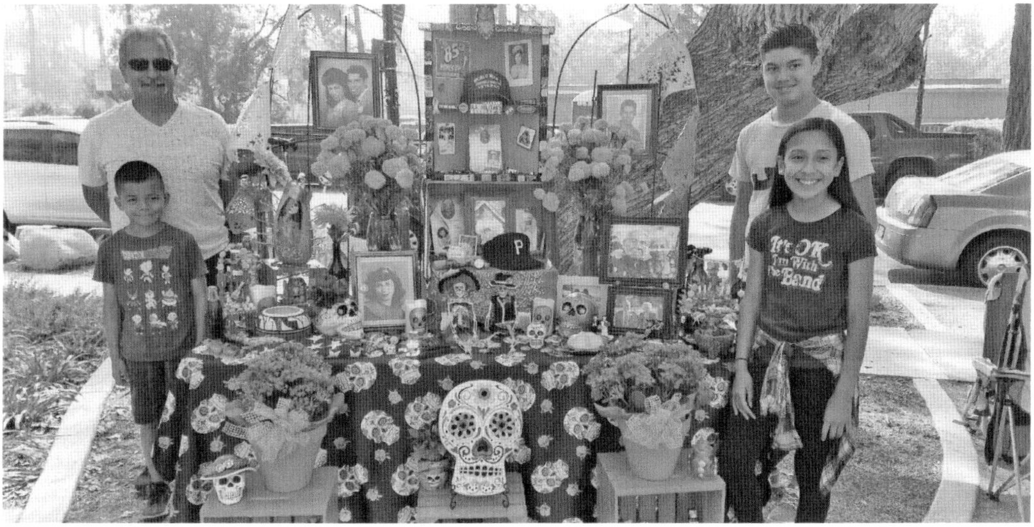

El Día de los Muertos is a time to savor the memory of dear ones. Altars are made to commemorate their remarkable lives. Tommie and Barbara Encinas's family members display an altar with special objects that remind them of their loved ones. It is a time to tell the story of who they were and what they liked. Tommie enjoyed playing baseball and served in the military. Barbara loved her garden. At left are Mike García, Tommy and Barbara's son-in-law, and Noah Sinay, their great-grandson. At right are Jacob Sinay, their great-grandson, and Alana Eudave, their great-granddaughter. (Courtesy of the García family.)

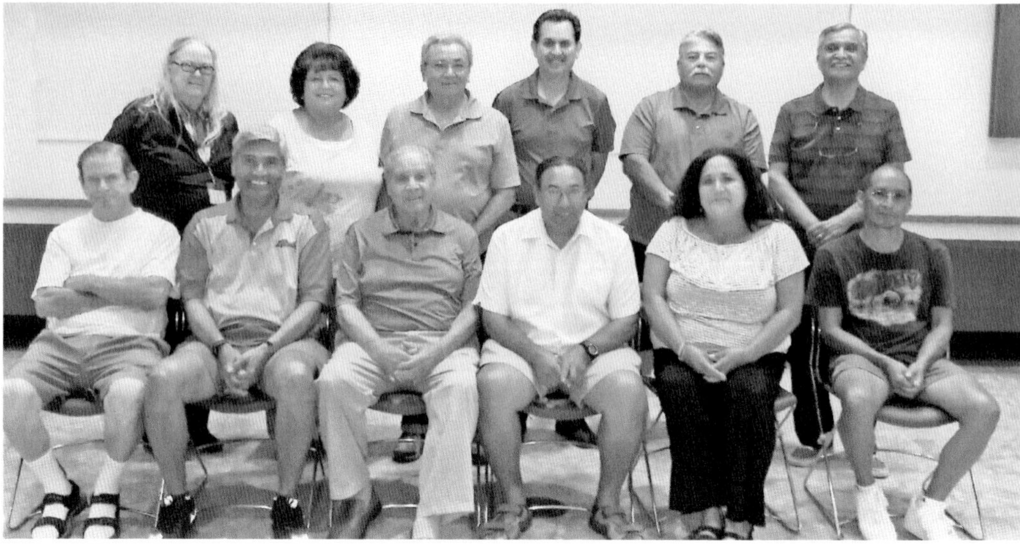

On August 19, 2017, the Ovitt Family Community Library in Ontario, California, sponsored a forum on Mexican American baseball and softball in the Inland and Pomona Valleys. Several players and family members shared photographs and stories. From left to right are (first row) Al Ledesma, Anthony Vásquez, Al Vásquez, Richard Vásquez, Paula ?, and Dale Suchill; (second row) Janis Young, Margie and Rey León, Rudy Félix, Ray Rodríguez, and Richard A. Santillán. Suchill, Rodríguez, and Santillán are coauthors of a forthcoming book on Mexican American baseball and softball in the San Bernardino Valley. (Courtesy of Richard A. Santillán.)

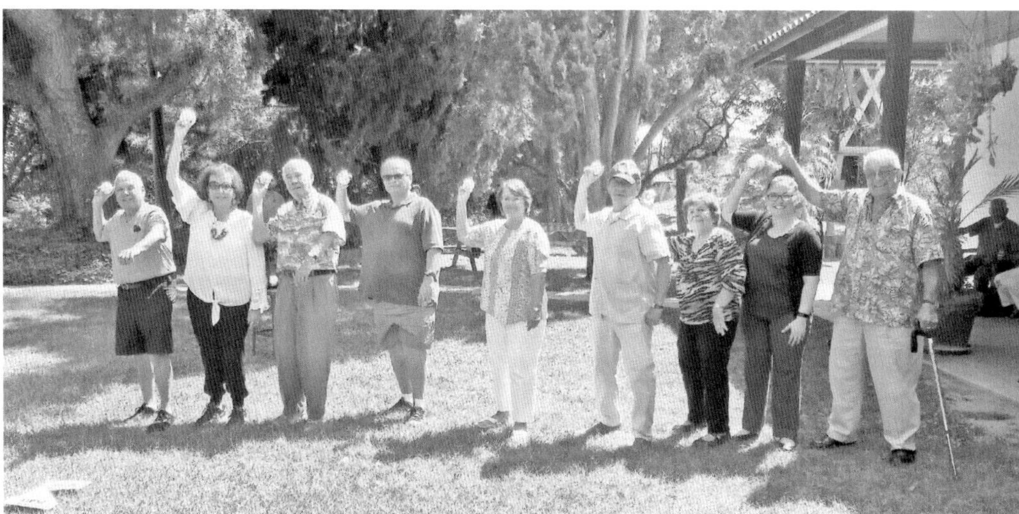

On August 5, 2017, the Dominguez Rancho Adobe Museum in Compton, California, held a symposium entitled Mexican American Baseball and Softball in the South Bay. Nearly 75 community members attended, including players and their families. One of the highlights of these events is the first-pitch ceremony. From left to right are Fred Padilla, Maria García, Marcelino Saucedo, Ron Gonzáles, Alicia S. Stevens, Alex Arayan, Alice Solís, Sandra Uribe, and Art Almeida. (Courtesy of Richard A. Santillán.)

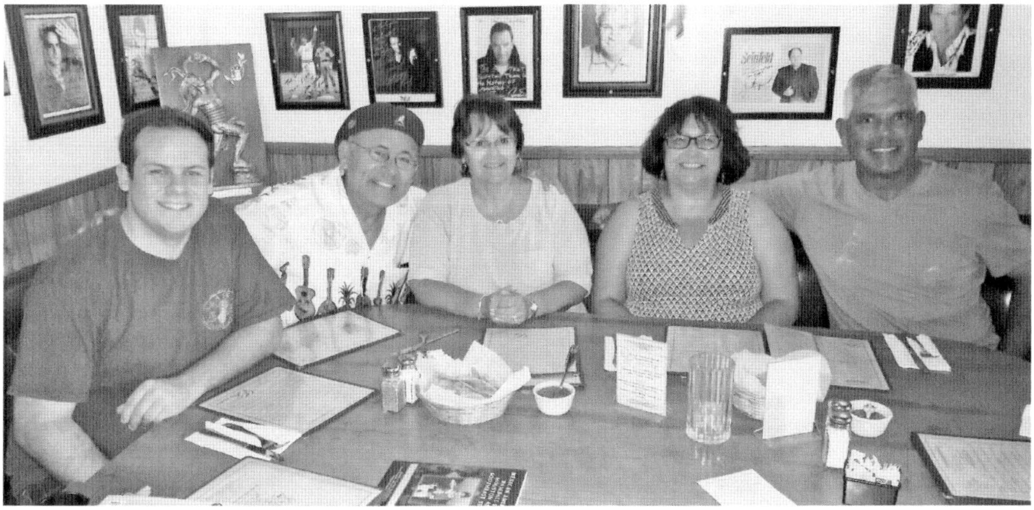

West Los Angeles has a rich history of Mexican Americans playing baseball and softball in Santa Monica, Culver City, Mid-City, Mar Vista, Venice, Pico-Robinson, and Ladera Heights. Seen on July 8, 2017, are the coauthors of *Mexican American Baseball in West Los Angeles.* From left to right are Chris Docter, Ray Serra, Alicia S. Stevens, and Margaret and Rick Prieto. Docter is a national scholar on Mexican American baseball and softball in the San Fernando Valley and coauthored a handful of books. Ray and Alicia published a chapter on Mexican American baseball and softball in Santa Monica. (Courtesy of Richard A. Santillán.)

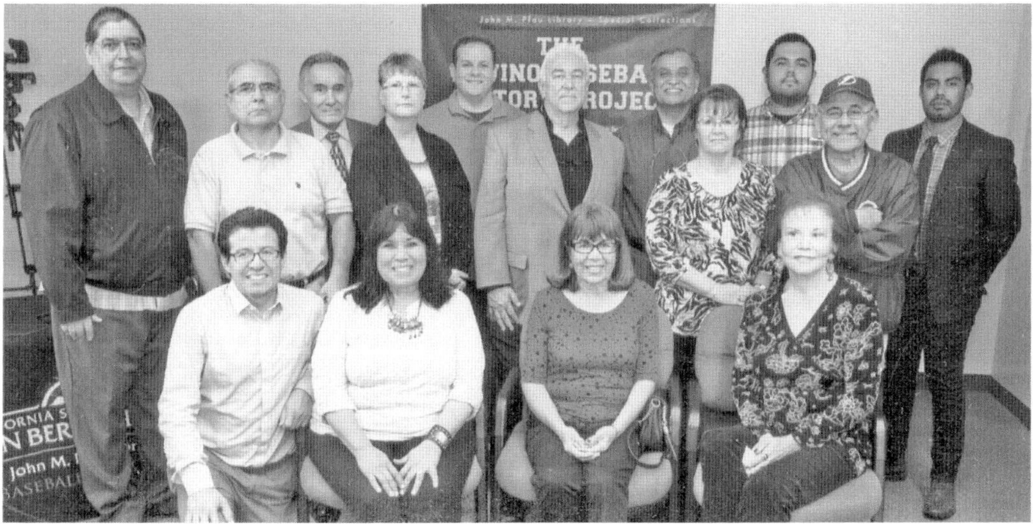

On February 18 and 19, 2016, the Latino Baseball History Project, with the Smithsonian Institution, hosted a two-day event at California State University at San Bernardino. The main purpose was to collect artifacts for a national exhibit on Latino baseball and softball in Washington, DC, and for a traveling exhibit throughout the United States. From left to right are (first row) José Alamillo, Anna Bermúdez, Teresa M. Santillán, and Maria García; (second row) Gabriel López, Rod Martínez, Gil Cabajal, Jody López, Chris Docter, Gene T. Chávez, Richard A. Santillán, Alicia S. Stevens, Mark Ocegueda, Ray Serra, and Juan Canchola. (Courtesy of Richard A. Santillán.)

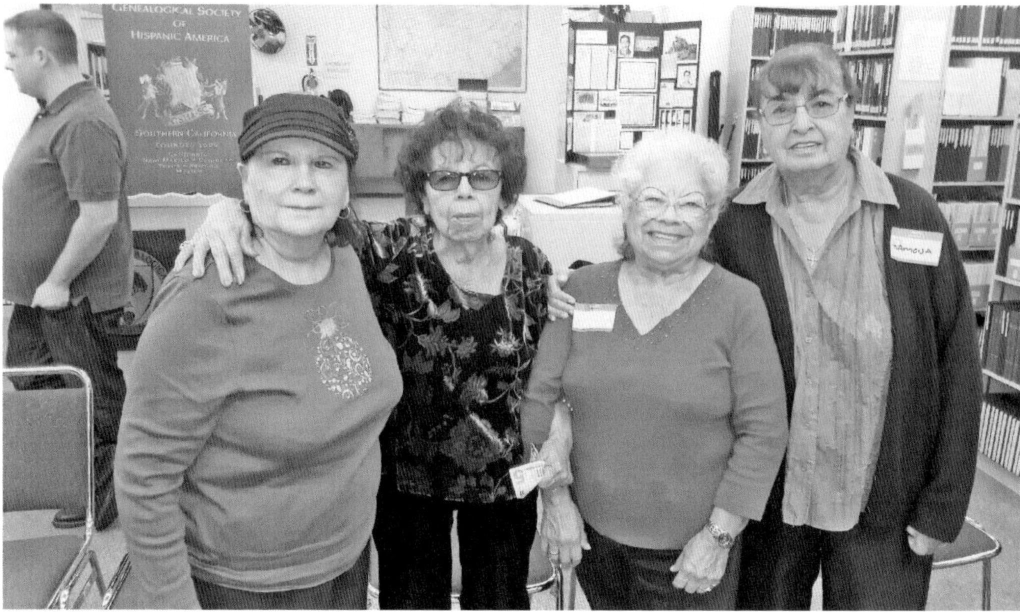

On December 2, 2017, the Genealogical Society of Hispanic America of Southern California hosted a presentation in Burbank on Mexican American baseball in the San Fernando Valley. Among the honored guests were four women whose teams played in the late 1940s. From left to right are Stella Quijada, Ramóna Cervantes, Rosie Díaz, and Ramóna Sarmiento. Quijada and Cervantes played for the North Hollywood Vixies, while Díaz and Sarmiento played for the Burbank B Bops. Other Mexican American women's teams included the North Hollywood Huskies, San Fernando Blue Jays, and Pacoima Honeydrippers. (Courtesy of Richard A. Santillán.)

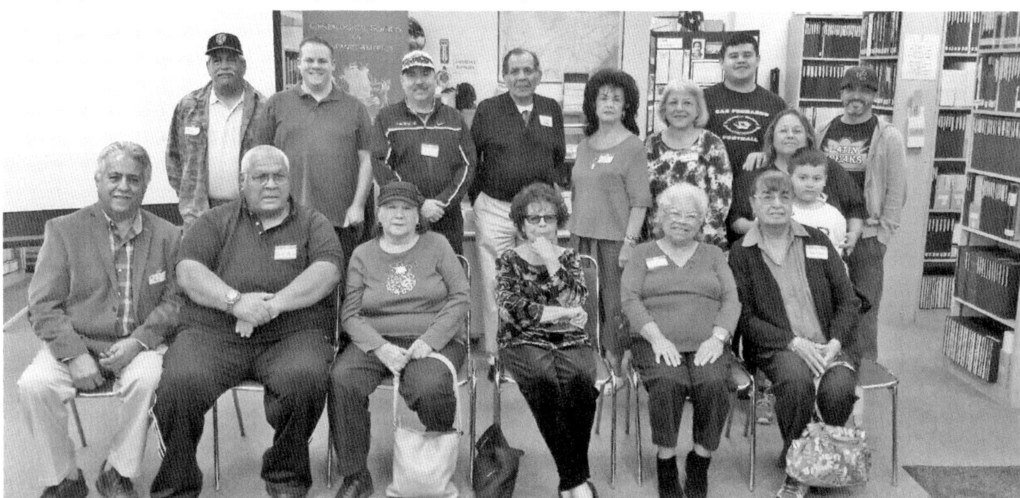

Several former and current players, families, and fans were in attendance at the December 2, 2017, event. Among those present were Everto Ruíz, Victoria C. Norton, Christopher Docter, Mark García, Stella Quijada, Ramóna Cervantes, Rosie Díaz, Ramóna Sarmiento, Lorrie Carrillo, Arnold Murillo, and Frank Baez. (Courtesy of Richard A. Santillán.)

A reception and book signing were held at the home of Richard A. and Teresa M. Santillán on June 26, 2017, for Eduardo Almada, who wrote a book about his father, Baldomero "Melo" Almada, a centerfielder from 1933 through 1939 for the Boston Red Sox, Washington Senators, St. Louis Browns, and Brooklyn Dodgers. From left to right are (first row) Al Padilla, Conrad Muñatones, Tom Pérez, and Martha Laird; (second row) Teresa M. Santillán, Pete López, Bob Lagunas, Tomás Benítez, Gaston Rodríguez, Eduardo Almada, Richard Seanez, and Jess Badillo. (Courtesy of Richard A. Santillán.)

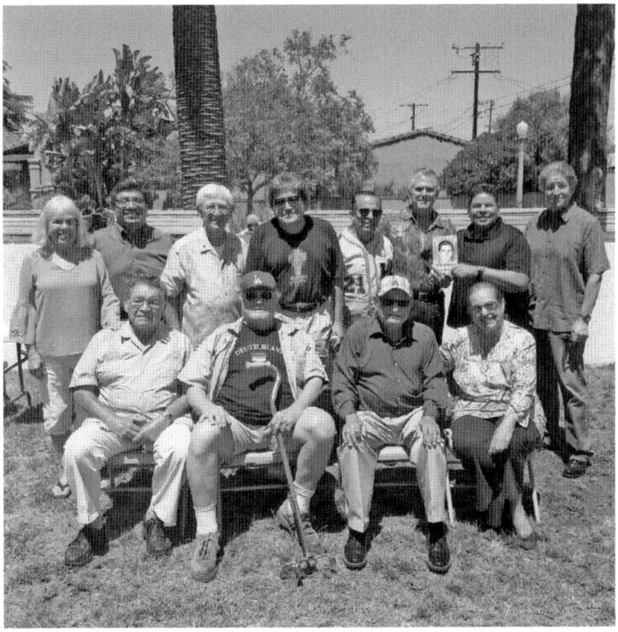

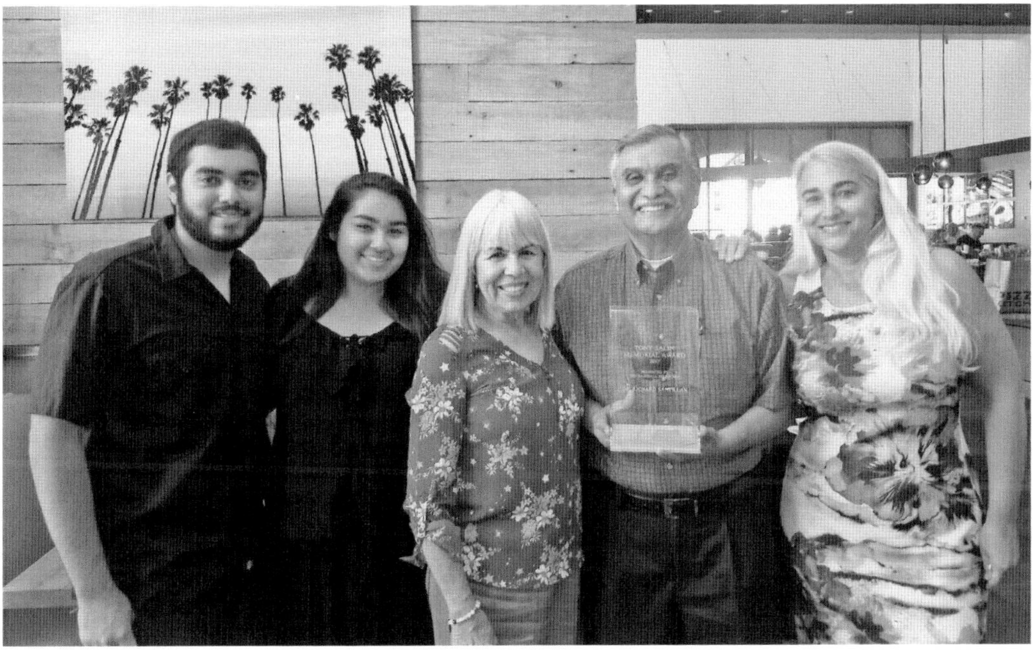

On July 16, 2017, Richard A. Santillán received the prestigious Tony Salin Memorial Award at the Shrine of the Eternals 2017 induction ceremony sponsored by the Baseball Reliquary. The event was held at the Donald R. Wright Auditorium at the Pasadena Central Library. Santillán was the 16th honoree to receive the award. The late Tony Salin was a baseball researcher who wrote *Baseball's Forgotten Heroes*. From left to right are Román and Rhiannon Mejía (Richard's grandchildren), Teresa (his wife), Richard, and Dianne Sánchez (his daughter). The three inductees were Vin Scully, Bob Uecker, and Charlie Brown. (Courtesy of Richard A. Santillán.)

BIBLIOGRAPHY

Alamillo, José. "Peloteros in Paradise: Mexican American Baseball and Oppositional Politics in Southern California, 1930–1950." *Western Historical Quarterly* 34 (2003): 191–211.

A Tribute to the Newton Holy Name Softball Ball Tournament Program, 1988.

Burgos, Adrian. *Playing America's Game: Baseball, Latinos, and the Color Line*. Berkeley, CA: University of California Press, 2007.

Chávez, Gene. *Mexican American Fast-Pitch Softball Leagues: Connecting Communities Across State Lines*. Documentary video, 2016.

———. "Latino Baseball and Fast-Pitch Softball in Kansas City." *Kansas City: Our Collective Memories*, edited by Bruce Mathews and Steve Noll, vol. 1, 119–125. Prairie Village, KS: DGHFKC Books, 2016.

———. "Pitch 'em Fast Pauly: The Mexican-American Fast-Pitch Softball Leagues." *Historical Journal of Wyandotte County* 3 (2015): 412–414.

Evening Kansan-Republic collection, Newton Public Library.

Fraire, John. "Mexicans Playing Baseball in Indiana Harbor, 1925–1942." *Indiana Magazine of History* 110 (June 2014).

———. *Mexicans Playing Baseball: Ethnic Identity Development in an Indiana Steel Town, 1920–1942*. Unpublished manuscript, 2017.

Garcilazo, Jeffrey M. *Traqueros: Mexican Railroad Workers in the United States, 1870–1930*. Denton, TX: University of North Texas Press, 2012.

Iber, Jorge. *Mike Tórrez: A Baseball Biography*. Jefferson, NC: McFarland Books, 2016.

Iber, Jorge, Samuel Regalado, José M. Alamillo, and Arnoldo de León. *Latinos in U.S. Sport: A History of Isolation, Cultural Identity, and Acceptance*. Champaign, IL: Human Kinetics, 2011.

Innis-Jiménez, Michael. *Steel Barrio: The Great Mexican Migration to South Chicago, 1915–1940*. New York, NY: New York University Press, 2013.

Laird, Judith Findher. *Argentine, KS: The Evolution of a Mexican-American Community, 1905–1950*. PhD dissertation, University of Kansas, 1975.

Platt, Kamala. *A Cultural History of Mexican Americans in Newton, Kansas*. MA thesis, University of Texas at Austin, 1992.

Lewandowski, Zack. "How Mexican-Americans in Kansas Built a Community around Softball." http://kcur.org/post/how-mexican-americans-kansas-built-community-around-softball, 2013.

Lujano, John D. *A Social History of the Mexican-American Community of Hutchinson, Kansas*. MA thesis, Emporia State University, 1996.

Mexican American fastpitch tournament booklets, 1998 and 2000. Newton, KS.

Santillán, Richard A. "Mexican Baseball Teams in the Midwest, 1916–1965: The Politics of Cultural Survival and Civil Rights." *Perspectives in Mexican American Studies and Research Center* VII. Tucson, AZ: University of Arizona Press, 2001.

Smith, Michael M. "Mexicans in Kansas City: The First Generation, 1900–1920." *Perspectives in Mexican American Studies and Research Center* II. Tucson, AZ: University of Arizona Press, 1989.

LATINO BASEBALL HISTORY PROJECT ADVISORY BOARD

José M. Alamillo
Eduardo B. Almada T.
Richard Arroyo
Gabriel "Tito" Ávila Jr.
Francisco E. Balderrama
Tomás Benítez
Anna Bermúdez
Juan J. Canchola
Terry A. Cannon
Ben Chappell
Gene T. Chávez
David Contreras Jr.
Juan D. Coronado
Raúl J. Córdova
Christopher Docter
Peter Drier
Robert Elias
Luís F. Fernández
Maria García
Gregory Garrett
Jorge Iber
Rumado Z. Juárez
William Lange
Alfonso Ledesma
Enrique M. López
Jody L. and Gabriel A. López
Susan C. Luévano
Amanda Magdalena
Rod Martínez
Douglas Monroy
Carlos Muñoz Jr.
Eddie Navarro
Victoria C. Norton
Mark A. Ocegueda
Alan O'Connor
Ray Olais
Monica Ortez
Al Padilla
Richard Peña
Al Ramos
Samuel O. Regalado
Vicki L. Ruíz
Anthony Salazar
Richard A. Santillán
Teresa M. Santillán
Marcelino Saucedo
Mikaela Selley
Ray P. Serra
Monserrath Segura
Alicia S. Stevens
Joe Talaugon
Joséph Thompson
Carlos Tortolero
Sandra L. Uribe
Elisa Urmston
David Vargas
Alejo L. Vásquez
Angelina F. Veyna
Alfonso Villanueva Jr.
Robert Zamora